T0214251

Lecture Notes in Computer Science　　12055

More information about this series at http://www.springer.com/series/7408

Jean-Michel Bruel · Manuel Mazzara ·
Bertrand Meyer (Eds.)

Software Engineering Aspects of Continuous Development and New Paradigms of Software Production and Deployment

Second International Workshop, DEVOPS 2019
Château de Villebrumier, France, May 6–8, 2019
Revised Selected Papers

Editors
Jean-Michel Bruel 🆔
Université de Toulouse
Toulouse, France

Manuel Mazzara 🆔
Innopolis University
Innopolis, Russia

Bertrand Meyer 🆔
Schaffhausen Institute of Technology
Schaffhausen, Switzerland

ISSN 0302-9743 ISSN 1611-3349 (electronic)
Lecture Notes in Computer Science
ISBN 978-3-030-39305-2 ISBN 978-3-030-39306-9 (eBook)
https://doi.org/10.1007/978-3-030-39306-9

LNCS Sublibrary: SL2 – Programming and Software Engineering

This Springer imprint is published by the registered company Springer Nature Switzerland AG
The registered company address is: Gewerbestrasse 11, 6330 Cham, Switzerland

Preface

The study of software development processes has a long and respectable history as a subdiscipline of software engineering, so long and venerable indeed that the field became a bit sleepy and complacent when the jolt of agile methods caught it by surprise in the 2000s. Another incentive to question long-established wisdom was the spectacular rise of technologies made possible by the World-Wide-Web, notably cloud computing and software-as-a-service. No longer could we content ourselves with the well-honed scheme in which a software system is analyzed, then designed, then programmed and tested, then released unto the world, then updated at a leisurely pace as problem reports and requests for new features get filed, weeded out, and patiently implemented. The pace frantically increases: for idea-development-deployment cycles that we used to think of as spreading over months, the timeline now is days, hours, even minutes.

In 2009 Patrick Debois coined the term DevOps to cover this new framework of software development. He and his colleague Andrew Shafer understood the need to combine the skills of software development and system administration, long considered disjoint. They also realized the critical role of deployment, often considered a secondary matter as compared to development. DevOps poses endless challenges to experts in software engineering: which of the traditional lessons gained over five decades of the discipline's development stand, and which ones need to be replaced in the dizzying world of immediate deployment? An example of a question that takes on a full new life is quality assurance: the stakes are quite different if you have a V&V (validation & verification) phase of a few weeks to prepare for the next release, as in the old world ("old" in IT means, like, 15 years ago), and in the brave new world of deploying this morning's change in the afternoon for the millions of users of your Web-based offering.

DEVOPS 2019 (https://www.laser-foundation.org/devops/devops-2019/), held during May 6–8, 2019, at the Château de Villebrumier, France, builds on top of the success of the first edition (DEVOPS 2018) also published by LNCS. The venue is one of the first scientific events devoted to the software engineering issues raised by the new development models and aims at building a community around this topic of interest. The event was kicked off by an outstanding introduction to the field by Professor Gail Murphy, Vice-President of Research & Innovation at the University of British Columbia. The participants came from diverse organizations, with a representation of both industry and academia. This volume gathers their papers, considerably enhanced thanks to the feedback received during the conference and during two different peer review phases.

The contributions cover a wide range of problems arising from DevOps and related approaches: current tools, rapid development-deployment processes, modeling frameworks, anomaly detection in software releases, DevDataOps, microservices, and other related topics, reflecting the thriving state of the discipline and, as is to be expected in such a fledgling field, raising new questions when addressing known ones. The topic of education and training is also covered, as a number of increasing specialists have to teach the new development paradigms to both university students and developers in companies. This contribution provides a fascinating insight into the state of the art in this new discipline.

DEVOPS 2019 is the second of a series of scientific events held at the new LASER center in Villebrumier near Montauban and Toulouse, France. Inspired by the prestigious precedent of the Dagstuhl center in Germany (the model for all such ventures), but adding its own sunny touch of accent *du sud-ouest* (the songful tones of Southwest France), the LASER center (http://laser-foundation.org, site of the foundation which also organizes the LASER summer school in Elba, Italy) provides a venue for high-tech events of a few days to a week in a beautiful setup in the midst of a region rich with historical, cultural, and culinary attractions. The proceedings enjoy publication in a subseries of the Springer *Lecture Notes in Computer Science*.

We hope that you will benefit from the results of DEVOPS 2019 as presented in the following pages and you may join one of the future events in Villebrumier.

November 2019

Jean-Michel Bruel
Manuel Mazzara
Bertrand Meyer

Organization

Program Committee

Muhammad Ahmad	University of Messina, Italy
Xavier Blanc	University of Bordeaux, France
Francis Bordeleau	École de Technologie Supérieure (ETS) and Université du Québec, Canada
Jean-Michel Bruel	Irit, France
Antonio Bucchiarone	FBK-irst, Germany
Alfredo Capozucca	University of Luxembourg, Luxembourg
Benoit Combemale	University of Toulouse and Inria, France
Rustem Dautov	South-East European Research Centre, Greece
Martina De Sanctis	Gran Sasso Science Institute, Italy
Salvatore Distefano	University of Messina, Italy
Nicola Dragoni	Technical University of Denmark, Denmark
Mohamed Elwakil	Innopolis University, Russia
Nicolas Guelfi	University of Luxembourg, Luxembourg
Manuel Mazzara	Innopolis University, Russia
Bertrand Meyer	ETH Zurich, Switzerland
Samim Mirhosseini	North Carolina State University, USA
Fabrizio Montesi	University of Southern Denmark, Denmark
Alberto Sillitti	Innopolis University, Russia

Additional Reviewers

Jahic, Benjamin
Katsikouli, Panagiota
Khan, Asad
Konchenko, Stanislav
Kuzminykh, Ievgeniia
Ries, Benoît

Contents

Teaching DevOps in Academia and Industry: Reflections and Vision

Evgeny Bobrov[1], Antonio Bucchiarone[3(✉)], Alfredo Capozucca[2],
Nicolas Guelfi[2], Manuel Mazzara[1], and Sergey Masyagin[1]

[1] Innopolis University, Innopolis, Russian Federation
{e.bobrov,m.mazzara,s.masiagin}@innopolis.ru
[2] University of Luxembourg, Luxembourg, Luxembourg
{alfredo.capozucca,nicolas.guelfi}@uni.lu
[3] Fondazione Bruno Kessler, Trento, Italy
bucchiarone@fbk.eu

Abstract. The new century brought us a kind of renaissance in software development methods. The advent of the Agile manifesto has led to greater appreciation of methodologies aimed at producing valuable software through continuous incremental cycles. More recently, a new set of practices enclosed under the term DevOps has appeared to attain manifesto's objectives in more efficient manner. The software development community has already noticed the benefits brought by DevOps. Thus, the necessity of education in the field becomes more and more important, both from the technical and organisational point of view. This paper describes parallel experiences of teaching both undergraduate and graduate students at the university, and junior professional developers in industry, compares the two approaches and sums up the lessons learnt. A vision driven by the DevOps practices aimed at implementing a shift in the Software Engineering Higher Education curricula to takeover its current limitations is also reported at the end of the paper.

1 Introduction

DevOps is a natural evolution of the Agile approaches [1,2] from the software itself to the overall infrastructure and operations. This evolution was made possible by the spread of cloud-based technologies and the everything-as-a-service approaches. Adopting DevOps is however more complex than adopting Agile [3] since changes at organisation level are required. Furthermore, a complete new skill set has to be developed in the teams [4]. The educational process is therefore of major importance for students, developers and managers.

DevOps way of working has introduced a set of software engineering activities and corresponding supporting tools that has disrupted the way individual developers and teams produce software. This has led both the world of research and industry to review software engineering life-cycle and all the supporting techniques to develop software in continuous operation and evolution. If we want to enclose DevOps in one word, it is *continuous*. Modelling, integration, testing,

J.-M. Bruel et al. (Eds.): DEVOPS 2019, LNCS 12055, pp. 1–14, 2020.
https://doi.org/10.1007/978-3-030-39306-9_1

and delivery are significant part of DevOps life-cycle that, respect to enterprise or monolithic applications developed some years ago, must be revised continuously to permit the continuous evolution of the software and especially an easy adaptability at context changes and new requirements. Adopting the DevOps paradigm helps software teams to release applications faster and with more quality. In this paper, we consider two sides of the same coin that are the usage of DevOps in academia and in industry.

Research in traditional software engineering settings has mainly focused on providing batch automation, as in the case of translation and re-engineering of legacy code [5], or on helping developers keep track of their changes, as in the case of version control [6]. The radically new development processes, introducing with the DevOps, have required major changes to traditional software practices [7]. New versions of software components are developed, released, and deployed continuously to meet new requirements and fix problems. A study performed by Puppet Labs in 2015[1] testifies that using DevOps practices and automated deployment led organisations to ship code 30 times faster, complete deployments 8,000 times faster, have 50% fewer failed deployments, and restore service 12 times faster than their peers. Due to the dramatically growing of the DevOps supporting tools[2], has seen a big change in the role played by the *software engineers* of a team. The latter today have the complication of covering both management and development aspects of a software product. They are part of a team and have the following responsibilities: (1) to be aligned with the new technologies to ensure that the high-performance software is released using smart tools to specify, develop, deploy and execute scalable software systems, (2) to define procedures to guarantee the high security level of the running code, (3) to monitor the software in operation and guarantee the right level of adaptability.

As long as DevOps became a widespread philosophy, the necessity of education in the field become more and more important, both from the technical and organisational point of view [4]. This paper describes parallel experiences of teaching both undergraduate and graduate students at the university, and junior professional developers in industry. There are similarities and differences in these two activities, and each side can learn from the other. We will discuss here some common issues and some common solutions. We also propose a vision to implement a shift in the Software Engineering Higher Education curricula.

The paper is organised as follows: after this introduction of the context in Sect. 1, we first discuss the experience gained in teaching DevOps at the university (Sect. 2). We then present the key elements of training and consultancies delivered in industry on the same subject (Sect. 3) and we analyse similarities and differences in Sect. 4. Section 5 proposes a vision to implement a shift in the Software Engineering Higher Education curricula. Finally, in Sect. 6 we present our conclusion.

---

[1] https://puppet.com/resources/whitepaper/2015-state-devops-report.

[2] https://raygun.com/blog/best-devops-tools/.

2   Teaching in Academia

DevOps experienced significant success in the industrial sector, but still received minor attention in higher education. One of the few and very first courses in Europe focusing on DevOps was delivered at the university of Luxembourg [8].

This course is part of a graduate programme aimed at students pursuing a degree in computer science. Students following this programme either continue their development either in the private sector or doing a PhD at the same university (most of the cases). Therefore, most of the courses in such a programme are designed as a sequence of theoretical lectures and assessed by a mid-term and final exam. Our course is the exception in the programme as it is designed according to the Problem-based learning (PBL) method.

Organisation and Delivery

Following a problem-based approach, the learning of the students is centred on a complex problem which does not have a single correct answer. The complex problem addressed by the course corresponds to the implementation of a Deployment Pipeline, which needs to satisfy certain functional and non-functional requirements. These requirements are:

– Functional Requirements (FR)
  - Create separated environments (Integration, Test, and Production).
  - Make use of a version control system.
  - Make use of a continuous integration (CI) server.
  - Automate the build of the selected product.
  - Automate the execution of the test cases.
  - Automate the deploy and release of the selected product.
– Non-Functional Requirements (NFR)
  - Rely on technologies open-source and available for Unix-based OS.
  - The Product to test the functioning of the pipeline should be a Web App (SaaS) done in Java, if possible with an already available set of test cases.

This means that students work in groups all along the course duration to produce a solution to the given problem. By working in groups students are immerse in a context where interactions problems may arise, and so allowing them to learn soft-skills to deal with such as problems. Therefore, the success to achieve a solution to the problem depends on not only the technical abilities, but also the soft-skills capacities each group member either has already had or is able to acquire during the course. Notice that DevOps is not only about tools, but also people and processes. Thus, soft-skills capabilities are a must for future software engineers working expected to work in a DevOps-oriented organisations.

Structure

The course is organised as a mix of lectures, project follow-up sessions (aimed at having a close monitoring of the work done for each group member and helping solve any encountered impediments), and checkpoints (sessions where each group presents the advances regarding the project's objectives). Lectures are aimed at presenting the fundamental DevOps-related concepts required to implement a Deployment Pipeline (Configuration Management, Build Management, Test Management, and Deployment Management). Obviously, the course opens with a general introduction to DevOps and a (both procedural and architectural) description of what a Deployment Pipeline is. In the first project follow-up session each group presents the chosen product they will use to demonstrate the functioning of the pipeline. The remaining of the course is an interleaving between lectures and follow-up sessions. The first check-point takes place at the fifth week, and the second one at the tenth week. The final checkpoint, where each group has to make a demo of the Deployment pipeline, takes place at the last session of the course.

Execution

Most of the work done by the students to develop the Deployment Pipeline was done outside of the course hours due to the limited in-class time assigned to the course. However, examples (e.g. virtual environments creation, initial setup and provisioning) and references to well-documented tools (e.g. Vagrant, Ansible, GitLab, Jenkins, Maven, Katalon) provided during the sessions helped students on moving the project ahead. Moreover, students had the possibility to request support either upon appointment or simply signalling the faced issues with enough time in advance to be handled during a follow-up session, the teaching. Nevertheless, the staff was closely supervising the deployment pipeline development by both monitoring the activity on the groups' working repositories and either asking technical questions or requesting live demos during the in-class sessions.

Assessment

As described in [8], each kind of activity is precisely specified, so it lets students know exactly what they have to do. This also applies to the course assessment: while the project counts for 50% of the final grade, the other half is composed of a report (12.5%) and the average of the checkpoints (12.5%). The aim at requesting to each group submit a report is to let students face with the challenge of doing collaborative writing in the same way most researchers do nowadays. Moreover, this activity makes the course to remain aligned with programme's objectives: prepare the student to continue a research career. It is also in this direction the we have introduced peer-reviewing: each student is requested to review (at least one) no-authored report (this activity also contributes to the individual grading of the student). Despite of these writing and reviewing activities may seem specific to the programme where the course fits, we do believe that they also contribute to the development of the required skills software engineers need to have.

Latest Experience and Feedback

Based on our latest experience the relevant points to highlight are: (1) the positive feedback obtained from students, (2) the absence of drops out, and (3) the quality of the achieved project deliverables. Regarding the first point, the evidence was found through a survey filled out by students once the course was over: 100% strongly agreed that the course was well organised and ran smoothly, 75% (25%) agreed (strongly agreed) the technologies used in the course were interesting, and 75% was satisfied with the quality of this course. We are very happy about the second point as it was one of the objectives (i.e. reduced the number of drops out - it used to reach up to 70%) when we decided to redesign the course to its current format. Moreover, the absence of drops out can also be confirmed by the fact that (based on the survey) 75% of the students would advise other students to take the course, if it were optional. Last, but not least, the survey also helped to confirm that PBL is the right pedagogical approach to tackle subjects like DevOps (and any others related to software engineering): 100% of the students agreed that they would like to have more project-oriented courses like this one. The third relevant point was about the quality of the project deliverables: considering the limited time to present and work out the subjects related to a Deployment Pipeline, each group succeed to provide deliverables able to meet the given functional and non-functional requirements.

3   Teaching in Industry

Our team is specialised in delivering corporate training for management and developers and has long experience of research in the service-oriented area [9–11]. In recent years we have provided courses, training and consultancies to a number of companies with particular focus on east Europe [12]. For example, only in 2018 more than 400 h of training were conducted involving more than 500 employees in 4 international companies. Although we cannot share the details of the companies involved, they are mid to large size and employ more than 10k people.

The trainings are typically focusing on:

- Agile methods and their application [3].
- DevOps philosophy, approach and tools [13].
- Microservices [14,15].

Organisation and Delivery

In order for the companies to absorb the DevOps philosophy and practice, our action has to focus on people and processes as much as on tools. The target group is generally a team (or multiple teams) of developers, testers and often mid-management. We also suggest companies to include representatives from businesses and technical analysts, marketing and security departments. These participants could also benefit from participation and from the DevOps culture. The nature of the delivery depends on the target group: sessions for management focus more on effective team building and establishment of processes. When the audience is a technical team, the focus goes more on tools and effective collaboration within and across the teams.

Structure

The events are typically organised in several sessions run over a one-day to three-day format made or frontal presentations and practical sessions. The sessions are generally conducted at the office of the customer in a space suitably arranged after the previous discussion with the local management. Whenever possible the agenda and schedule of the activities have to be shared in advance. In this way, the participants know what to expect, and sometime a preparatory work is required.

Limitations of the Set-Up

One of the limitations we had to cope with, often but not always, is the fact that bilateral previous communication with teams is not always possible or facilitated, and the information goes through some local contact and line manager. At times this demands for an on-the-fly on-site adaptation of the agenda. In order to collect as much information as possible on the participants and the environment, we typically send a survey to be completed a few days in advance, and we analyse question by question to give specific advice depending on the answers.

Lessons Learnt and Optimisation

In retrospective, the most effective training for DevOps and Agile were those in which the audience consisted of both management and developers. Indeed the biggest challenge our customer encountered was not how to automatise existing processes, but in fact how to set up the DevOps approach itself from scratch. Generally, technical people know how to set up automatisation, but they may have partial understanding about the importance and the benefits for the company, for other departments, the customer and ultimately for themselves. It is important therefore to show the bigger picture and help them understanding how their work affects other groups, and how this in turn affects themselves in a feedback loop. The presence of management is very useful in this process. The technical perspective is often left for self-study or for additional sessions.

Latest Experience and Feedback

The feedback from participants surpassed our expectation. In synthesis, this are the major achievements of the past sessions:

- Marketers now understand how they may use A/B testing and check the hypothesis.
- Security engineers find positive to approve small pieces of new features, not the major releases.
- Developers developed ways to communicate with other departments and fulfil their needs step by step based on the collaboration.
- Testers shifted their focus on product testing (integration-, regression-, soak-, mutation-, penetration- testing) rather than unit testing, and usually set future goals for continuing self-education on the subject.

Often multiple session can be useful. The primary objective is to educate DevOps ambassadors, but it is also important to create an environment that can support the establishment of DevOps processes and the realisation of a solid DevOps culture, when every department welcome these changes. This does not typically happen in a few days.

4   Discussion

The experience of teaching in both an academic and industrial context emphasised some similarities and some differences that we would like to discuss here. Understanding these two realities may help in offering better pedagogical programme from the future since each domain can be cross-fertilised by the ideas taken by the other.

What we have seen in terms of similarities:

- **Pragmatism**: Both students and developers appreciate hands-on sessions.
- **Hype**: Interest and curiosity in the topic has been seen both in academia and industry, demonstrating the relevance of the topic.
- **Asymmetry**: Classic education and developers training put more important on Development than Operations and presenting the two sides as interrelated strengthen the knowledge and increase efficacy.

What we have seen in terms of differences:

- **Learners initial state**: based on the academic curriculum where the course is included, it is possible to know (or at least to presume) the already acquired knowledge for the participant students. This may not be the case in a corporate environment, where the audience is generally composed by people with different profiles and backgrounds.

- **Learners attitude**: different motivations move different kind of audience. Students too often are grade-focused and put effort depending on how they will be assessed, they tend to find shortcuts to reach their objectives. Developers may not have a bigger picture of the company and a long-term vision, they are interested in the approach as long as it can improve their working conditions, so it is important to focus on this aspect in the delivery. Manager see things in terms of cost savings and care less about technical details.
- **Pace of education**: short and intense in a corporate environment, can be long and diluted in academia.
- **Assessment/measure of success**: classic exam-based at the university, a corporate environment often does not require a direct assessment at the end of the sessions and the success should be observed in the long run.
- **Expectation:** corporate audience is more demanding. This may nor be a surprise given the costs and what is a stake. Students are also subject to a cost, but it is more moderate and spread over a number of course attended in one year.

5   Vision

After reporting experiences in teaching DevOps-based courses in both academic and industrial environments (reflection), in this section we will look at the future and we will describe our vision for the modernisation of university curricula in Computer Science, in particular for the Software Engineering tracks. While our vision and conclusions can be effectively applied in every Higher Education institution, we are here considering a specific case study: Innopolis University, a new IT educational institution in the Russian Federation. This is the reality we have more direct experience of. In [16] the first five years of Innopolis University and the development of the internationalisation strategy is discussed, while [17] presents some teaching innovations and peculiarities of the university. At Innopolis University students have a 4-year bachelor, the first two years are fundamental, and a specific track is chosen at the third year (Software Engineering, Data Science, Security and Network Engineering or Artificial Intelligence and Robotics). There are also 2-year Master Programs, following exactly the same four tracks. The last two years of the bachelors are characterised by a fewer number of courses. Moreover, some of these courses are elective, and delivered either by academic or industrial lecturers. These elective courses are aimed at covering specific topics required by industry.

While working with industry we realised that the obstacles for the full adoption of DevOps are not only of technical nature, but also of mindset. This issue is difficult to solve since companies need to establish a radically new culture and transfer it to the new employees who join the company with a legacy mindset. The same situation may occur for fresh graduates. Classic curricula are very often based on the idea of *system as a monolith and process as a waterfall*. Of course, in the last twenty years, innovations have been added to the plan of study worldwide. However, when focusing on the first two years of Bachelor education, it can be seen that the backbone of the curricula is still outdated (due to legacy reasons, and sometimes, ideological ones). It is therefore necessary to explain students the DevOps values from scratch, establishing clear connections of every course with DevOps, and describing how fundamental knowledge works within the frame of this philosophy. Furthermore, Computer Science curricula have a strong emphasis on the "Dev" part, but cover the "Ops" part only marginally, for example as little modules inside courses such as Operating Systems and Databases.

To cover the "Ops" part we need to teach how to engineer innovative software systems that can react to changes and new needs properly, without compromising the effectiveness of the system and without imposing cumbersome a priori analyses. To this end, we need to introduce courses on *learning and adaptation* theories, algorithms and tools, since they are becoming the key enablers for conceiving and operating quality software systems that can automatically evolve to cope with errors, changes in the environment, and new functionalities. At the same time, to continuously assess the evolved system, we need also to think to teach *validation* and *verification* techniques pushing more them at runtime.

The DevOps philosophy is broad, inclusive, and at the same time, flexible enough to work as a skeleton for Software Engineering education. This is what drives our vision and we described in the next parts of this section.

5.1 Phases of Software Engineering Education

The DevOps philosophy presents recurring and neat phases. It has been shown that companies willing to establish a strong DevOps culture have to pay attention to every single phase [18]. Missing a phase, or even a simple aspect of it, might lead to poor overall results. This attention to every single phase should also be applied also to university education.

In this interpretation (or proposal), every phase corresponds to a series of concepts and a skill-set that the student has to acquire along the process. It is therefore possible to organise the educational process and define a curriculum for software engineering using the DevOps phases as a backbone (Fig. 1 summarises these phases). This path would allow students to realise the connection between different courses and apply the knowledge in their future career. The plan described here is what we are considering to experiment at Innopolis University, expanding the experience acquired on the delivery of specialised DevOps courses to the entire plan of study. We will use the idea described in [19] as a backbone for curriculum innovation.

We consider ideal an incremental and iterative approach for bachelors to fully understand and implement the DevOps philosophy. We utilise the following taxonomy:

1. How to code.
2. How to create software.
3. How to create software in a team.
4. How to create software in a team that someone needs.
5. How to create software in a team that business needs.

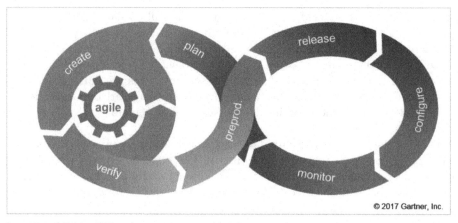

Fig. 1. DevOps phases

In details, this is the path we propose for the bachelor[3] programme, based on Agile and DevOps according to the taxonomy:

1. The first three semesters are devoted to fundamental knowledge of hard and soft skills, which are essential to create software, especially following Agile and DevOps. We want to educate the next generations of students providing them not only with knowledge of programming languages and algorithms, but also with software architectures, design patterns and testing. This way students know how to create quality software fulfilling the essential non-functional requirements (such as reliability, maintainability, and scalability).
2. The fourth semester has a software project course (to be considered as an introduction to the software engineering track) based on the trial and error approach without any initial constraints and thorough analysis of identified problems in the second part of the semester.
3. The fifth semester has a new iteration of the software project course with a deep understanding of the Agile philosophy and the most popular Agile frameworks.
4. The sixth semester is based on the same project that has been created earlier and adds automaton, optimisation of the Development, and it introduces the Operational part and the feedback concept.
5. During the last two semesters (i.e. seventh and eighth), students start to work with real customers from industry and try to establish all processes and tools learnt in the previous three years.
6. During the third and fourth years, we propose additional core and elective courses in order to explore deeper modern technologies, best practices, patterns and frameworks.

---

[3] 4-year.

5.2   Transition Towards the New Curriculum

In this section we will address the transition from the current curriculum to the new one identifying the iterations and steps year by year until the full implementation, and we will emphasise the role of industry in this process. For the last years since foundation (2012), the curriculum for Software Engineers at Innopolis University was mostly waterfall-based with a clear focus on hard skills. Each course was delivering methods and tools specific of a certain phase, but not always the *"fil rouge"* between courses was emphasised. Courses connecting the dots and providing the basis for an iterative and incremental approach are now under development. The first four semesters of the bachelor provide the prerequisites for Software Engineering (and for Computer Science in general), whereas the last four semesters are track-based (see Figs. 2 and 3).

The transition is planned to happen in 5-year time:

- **Year 1.** Make minor changes to the curriculum, targeting in particular two courses: *Software Project* for second-year spring semester, and *Project for Software Engineers* at the third year, fall semester. The first one has to be adapted to teach students how to establish processes and develop software according to Agile. The second one will be increased by adding the possibility to collaborate with industry and develop actual projects. The students interact with industry representatives and define project objectives with industry under the control of the university.
- **Year 2.** Work more closely with industry and add more elective courses covering skills required by companies. A course on DevOps will be added to the spring semester of the third year of the bachelor to be intended as a continuation of *Software Project*. The content of some courses will be adjusted to contain DevOps philosophy.
- **Year 3.** Update fundamental courses at the first and second year according to the Software Engineering Body of Knowledge (SWEBOK) standard [20] (chapters "Mathematical Foundations", "Computing Foundations" and "Engineering Foundations"). Furthermore, soft skills courses such as *"personal software process"*, *"critical writing"* and *"effective presentations"* will be added to the first three semesters.
- **Year 4.** Follow the SWEBOK and deliver the most essential knowledge areas.
- **Year 5.** Analyse the results of the changes introduced, and then tune the fundamental courses with more notions of DevOps and Agile philosophies along with incremental-iterative approaches. By year 5 we are planning to establish a framework helping to update the curriculum to give more focus on industry demands and IT evolution.

Fundamental knowledge			
Semester	Focus	Hard skills	Soft skills
1st semester	How to code	Programing language (low level)	Personal software process
		Data structure	
		Algorithms	
2nd semester	How to add architecture to the code	Data Modeling and Databases	Critical writing
		Design Patterns	
		Frameworks	
3rd semester	How to add tests to the code	Unit tests	Effective presentations
		User Experience/User Interface tests	
		Project tests	
4th semester	Preparation to future career	Software project (Trial & Error perspective) [intro to Software Engineering track]	
		Networks [intro to Security and Network Engineering track]	
		Probability and Statistics [intro to Data Science track]	
		Introduction to Artificial inelegance [intro to Artificial Intelligence and Robotics track]	

Fig. 2. Curriculum of year 1 and year 2

Software engineering track			
Semester	Focus	Soft and hard skills blending	Extra material
5th semester	How to create software in a team	Software project (Agile perspective)	Distributed systems and cloud computing
			Experience/User Interface design
			Requirements elicitation
6th semester	How to create software in a team that someone needs	Software project (DevOps perspective)	Software Quality and Reliability
			Security systems
7th semester	How to create software in a team that business needs	Software project (Industry perspective) part I	Data Science and Machine Learning for software engineers
			Big data analysis for software engineers
8th semester		Software project (Industry perspective) part I	Project thesis (reflection)

Fig. 3. Curriculum for software engineering track

6   Conclusions

Ultimately, DevOps [2,13] and the microservices architectural style [14] with its domains of interests [21–23] may have the potential of changing how companies run their systems in the same way Agile has changed the way of developing software. The critical importance of such cultural change should not be undervalued. It is in this regard that higher education institutions should put a major effort to fine tune their curricula and cooperative programme in order to meet this challenge.

In terms of pedagogical innovation, the authors of this paper have experimented for long with novel approaches under different forms [17]. However, DevOps represents a newer and significant challenge. Despite of the fact current educational approaches in academia and industry show some similarities, they are indeed significantly different in terms of attitude of the learners, their expectation, delivery pace and measure of success. Similarities lay more on the perceived hype of the topic, its typical pragmatic and applicative nature, and the minor relevance that education classically reserves to "Operations". While similarities can help in defining a common content for the courses, the differences clearly suggest a completely different nature of the modalities of delivery.

From the current experience we plan to adjust educational programs asbreak follows:

- **University teaching**: trying to move the focus out of final grade, emphasising more the learning aspect and give less importance to the final exam, maybe increasing the relevance of practical assignments. It may be also useful to intensify the theoretical delivery to keep the attention higher and have more time for hand-on sessions. Ultimately, our vision is to build a Software Engineering curricula on the backbone derived from the DevOps philosophy.
- **Corporate training**: it is important not to focus all the training activity as a frontal session university-like. Often the customers themselves require this classical format, maybe due to the influence of their university education. We believe that this makes things less effective and we advocate for a change of paradigm.

References

1. Kim, G., Debois, P., Willis, J., Humble, J.: The DevOps Handbook: How to Create World-Class Agility, Reliability, and Security in Technology Organizations. IT Revolution Press, Portland (2016)
2. Bass, L., Weber, I., Zhu, L.: DevOps: A Software Architect's Perspective, 1st edn. Addison-Wesley Professional, Boston (2015)
3. Agile and DevOps: Friends or Foes? https://www.atlassian.com/agile/devops. Accessed 01 July 2018
4. Bucena, I., Kirikova, M.: Simplifying the DevOps adoption process. In: Joint Proceedings of the BIR 2017 Pre-BIR Forum, Workshops and Doctoral Consortium Co-Located with 16th International Conference on Perspectives in Business Informatics Research (BIR 2017), Copenhagen, Denmark, 28–30 August 2017
5. Trudel, M., Furia, C.A., Nordio, M., Meyer, B.: Really automatic scalable object-oriented reengineering. In: Castagna, G. (ed.) ECOOP 2013. LNCS, vol. 7920, pp. 477–501. Springer, Heidelberg (2013). https://doi.org/10.1007/978-3-642-39038-8_20
6. Estler, H.-C., Nordio, M., Furia, C.A., Meyer, B.: Unifying configuration management with merge conflict detection and awareness systems. In: Australian Software Engineering Conference, pp. 201–210. IEEE Computer Society (2013)
7. Bass, L.J., Weber, I.M., Zhu, L.: DevOps - A Software Architect's Perspective. SEI Series in Software Engineering. Addison-Wesley, Boston (2015)
8. Capozucca, A., Guelfi, N., Ries, B.: Design of a (yet another?) DevOps course. In: Bruel, J.-M., Mazzara, M., Meyer, B. (eds.) DEVOPS 2018. LNCS, vol. 11350, pp. 1–18. Springer, Cham (2019). https://doi.org/10.1007/978-3-030-06019-0_1
9. Mazzara, M.: Towards abstractions for web services composition. Ph.D. thesis. University of Bologna (2006)

10. Yan, Z., Mazzara, M., Cimpian, E., Urbanec, A.: Business process modeling: classifications and perspectives. In: Business Process and Services Computing: 1st International Working Conference on Business Process and Services Computing, BPSC 2007, Leipzig, Germany, 25–26 September 2007, p. 222 (2007)
11. Yan, Z., Cimpian, E., Zaremba, M., Mazzara, M.: BPMO: semantic business process modeling and WSMO extension. In: 2007 IEEE International Conference on Web Services (ICWS 2007), Salt Lake City, Utah, USA, 9–13 July 2007, pp. 1185–1186 (2007)
12. Mazzara, M., Naumchev, A., Safina, L., Sillitti, A., Urysov, K.: Teaching DevOps in corporate environments: an experience report. In: Bruel, J.-M., Mazzara, M., Meyer, B. (eds.) DEVOPS 2018. LNCS, vol. 11350, pp. 100–111. Springer, Cham (2019). https://doi.org/10.1007/978-3-030-06019-0_8
13. Jabbari, R., bin Ali, N., Petersen, K., Tanveer, B.: What is DevOps?: a systematic mapping study on definitions and practices. In: Proceedings of the Scientific Workshop Proceedings of XP 2016, XP 2016 Workshops, pp. 12:1–12:11. ACM, New York (2016)
14. Dragoni, N., et al.: Microservices: yesterday, today, and tomorrow. In: Mazzara, M., Meyer, B. (eds.) Present and Ulterior Software Engineering, pp. 195–216. Springer, Cham (2017). https://doi.org/10.1007/978-3-319-67425-4_12
15. Dragoni, N., Lanese, I., Larsen, S.T., Mazzara, M., Mustafin, R., Safina, L.: Microservices: how to make your application scale. In: Petrenko, A.K., Voronkov, A. (eds.) PSI 2017. LNCS, vol. 10742, pp. 95–104. Springer, Cham (2018). https://doi.org/10.1007/978-3-319-74313-4_8
16. Karapetyan, S., Dolgoborodov, A., Masyagin, S., Mazzara, M., Messina, A., Protsko, E.: Innopolis going global: internationalization of a Young IT University. In: Ciancarini, P., Mazzara, M., Messina, A., Sillitti, A., Succi, G. (eds.) SEDA 2018. AISC, vol. 925, pp. 138–145. Springer, Cham (2020). https://doi.org/10.1007/978-3-030-14687-0_12
17. de Carvalho, D., et al.: Teaching programming and design-by-contract. In: Auer, M.E., Tsiatsos, T. (eds.) ICL 2018. AISC, vol. 916, pp. 68–76. Springer, Cham (2020). https://doi.org/10.1007/978-3-030-11932-4_7
18. Building a healthy DevOps culture. https://www.wired.com/insights/2013/06/building-a-healthy-devops-culture/. Accessed 08 Feb 2019
19. Avoid failure by developing a toolchain that enables DevOps, October 2017. https://www.gartner.com/doc/3810934/avoid-failure-developing-toolchain-enables
20. IEEE Computer Society, Bourque, P., Fairley, R.E.: Guide to the Software Engineering Body of Knowledge (SWEBOK(R)): Version 3.0, 3rd edn. IEEE Computer Society Press, Los Alamitos (2014)
21. Salikhov, D., Khanda, K., Gusmanov, K., Mazzara, M., Mavridis, N.: Microservice-based IoT for smart buildings. In: Proceedings of the 31st International Conference on Advanced Information Networking and Applications Workshops (WAINA) (2017)
22. Nalin, M., Baroni, I., Mazzara, M.: A holistic infrastructure to support elderlies' independent living. In: Cruz-Cunha, M.M., Miranda, I.M., Martinho, R., Rijo, R. (eds.) Encyclopedia of E-Health and Telemedicine. IGI Global, Hershey (2016)
23. Bucchiarone, A., Dragoni, N., Dustdar, S., Larsen, S.T., Mazzara, M.: From monolithic to microservices: an experience report from the banking domain. IEEE Softw. **35**(3), 50–55 (2018)

A Model-Driven Approach Towards Automatic Migration to Microservices

Antonio Bucchiarone[1(✉)], Kemal Soysal[2], and Claudio Guidi[3]

[1] Fondazione Bruno Kessler, Trento, Italy
bucchiarone@fbk.eu
[2] LS IT-Solutions GmbH, Berlin, Germany
kemal.Soysal@ls-it-solutions.de
[3] italianaSoftware s.r.l., Imola, Italy
cguidi@italianasoftware.com

Abstract. Microservices have received and are still receiving an increasing attention, both from academia and the industrial world. To guarantee scalability and availability while developing modern software systems, microservices allow developers to realize complex systems as a set of small services that operate independently and that are easy to maintain and evolve. Migration from monolithic applications to microservices-based application is a challenging task that very often it is done manually by the developers taking into account the main business functionalities of the input application and without a supporting tool. In this paper, we present a model-driven approach for the automatic migration to microservices. The approach is implemented by means of JetBrains MPS, a text-based metamodelling framework, and validated using a first migration example from a Java-based application to Jolie - a programming language for defining microservices.

1 Introduction

The life cycle of an application is bound to changes of domain and technical requirements. Non functional requirements as scalability and availability may lead to a rewrite of the application as is for a new architecture or programming language. DevOps [1] and Microservices-based Applications (MSA) [2,3] appear to be an indivisible pair for organizations aiming at delivering applications and services at high velocity. The philosophy may be introduced in the company with adequate training, but only if certain technological, organizational and cultural prerequisites are present [4–6]. If not, the prerequisites should be developed to guarantee adequate instruments to model and verify software systems and support developers all along the development process in order to deploy correct software.

Microservices allow developers to break up monolithic applications (MA) in a set of small and independent services where each of them represents a single business capability and can be delivered and updated autonomously without any impact on other services and on their releases. In common practice, it is

J.-M. Bruel et al. (Eds.): DEVOPS 2019, LNCS 12055, pp. 15–36, 2020.
https://doi.org/10.1007/978-3-030-39306-9_2

also expected that a single service can be developed and managed by a single team [7,8]. Microservices [8] recently demonstrated to be an effective architectural paradigm to cope with scalability in a number of domains [9], however, the paradigm still misses a conceptual model able to support engineers starting from the early phases of development. Several companies are evaluating pros and cons of a migrating to microservices [6].

Model-driven software development [10,11] supports expressing domain requirements regarding contained data, function points, workflows, configurations, requirement tracking, test cases, etc. by appropriate domain specific languages [12]. In this respect, this work discusses the provision of an model-driven approach for the automatic migration of monolithic applications to microservices. In particular, domain-specific languages (DSLs) [13] allow the definition and deployment of microservices, while model transformations are exploited to automatize the migration and the containerization phases.

The implementation of the migration framework is realised by means of JetBrains MPS (briefly, MPS)[1]. MPS is a meta-programming framework that can be exploited as modelling languages workbench, it is text-based, and provides projectional editors [14]. The choice of MPS is due to the inherent characteristics of MSAs, which are by nature collections of small services that must interacts to satisfy the overall business goal. In this respect, graphical languages do not scale with the complexity of the MSAs. Moreover, MPS smoothly supports languages embedding, such that our definition of microservice mining, specification, and deployment phases for the migration that are easily implemented.

As a validation of our approach, we have migrated a simple Java application in the corresponding Jolie[2] [15] microservices deployed inside the Docker[3] container.

1.1 Structure of the Paper

The remainder of the paper is organized as follows: Sect. 2 presents the basics about microservices, the metamodelling framework used in the proposed approach and the Jolie language for defining and deploying microservices. Starting from this preliminary information, Sect. 3 surveys related works, Sect. 4 presents the migration framework proposed, and Sect. 5 shows its implementation. We conclude the paper with final remarks in Sect. 6.

2   Background

2.1 Microservices

Microservices [8] is an architectural style originating from Service-Oriented Architectures (SOAs) [16]. The main idea is to structure systems by composing small independent building blocks communicating exclusively via message

---

[1] http://www.jetbrains.com/mps/.

[2] http://www.jolie-lang.org/.

[3] https://www.docker.com.

passing. These components are called *microservices*. The characteristic differentiating the new style from monolithic architectures and classic Service-Oriented is the emphasis on *scalability*, *independence*, and *semantic cohesiveness* of each unit constituting the system.

Each microservice it is expected to implement a single *business capability*, bringing benefits in terms of service maintainability and extendability. Since each microservice represents a single business capability, which is delivered and updated independently, discovering bugs or adding a minor improvements do not have any impact on other services and on their releases.

Microservices have seen their popularity blossoming with an explosion of concrete applications seen in real-life software [17]. Several companies are involved in a major refactoring of their backend systems in order to improve scalability [9].

Such a notable success gave rise to academic and commercial interest, and ad-hoc programming languages arose to address the new architectural style [18]. In principle, any general-purpose language could be used to program microservices. However, some of them are more oriented towards scalable applications and concurrency [19]. The Jolie programming language (see Sect. 2.4), crystalizes the basic mechanisms of service oriented computing within a unique linguistic domain in order to simplify the design and the development phases of microservices. As another advantage, Jolie has already a community of users and developers [20] and it has been validated in production environments. Finally, Jolie is available on Docker and is possible to develop and run a microservice inside a container[4].

2.2 Model-Driven Engineering and Domain Specific Languages

Model-Driven Engineering (MDE) [12] is a software engineering methodology that proposes to shift the focus of the development from coding to modelling. The goal is to reduce the complexity of software development by raising the level of abstraction, analyzing application properties earlier, and introducing automation in the process. In fact, models are expected to allow domain experts to reason about a certain solution by means of concerns closer to their area of expertise than to implementation details. Moreover, automated mechanisms, i.e. model transformations, can manipulate those models to evaluate attributes of the application and/or to generate implementation code.

Domain Specific Languages (DSLs) have been introduced with the aim of meeting the needs of particular software applications, industry or business challenges that would be less effectively addressed by using mainstream general-purpose languages. In fact, DSLs are languages introduced for expressing problems by using terms closer to a particular domain of application [21].

The definition of DSLs can be challenging due to a number of reasons, notably the nature of the specific domain, how the concepts should be interconnected to ease the modelling activity without sacrificing the quality of the produced

---

[4] https://jolielang.gitbook.io/docs/containerization/docker.

models, what kind of concrete syntaxes the users desire to exploit, and so forth. To support the development of DSLs, it is common practice to use a language workbench, that is a toolkit supporting the definition of various aspects of the DSL under development (syntax, semantics, validation constraints, generators) as well as user interaction features (code completion, syntax coloring, find usages, refactorings, etc.).

2.3 JetBrains MPS: A Text-Based Metamodelling Framework

MPS by JetBrains[5] is a text-based meta-programming system that enables language oriented programming [22]. MPS is open source and is used to implement interesting languages with different notations [14]. In particular, based on MPS *BaseLanguage* it is possible to define new custom languages through extension and composition of *concepts* [23]. A new language is composed by different *aspects* making its specification modular and therefore easy to maintain [13,24]. Notably, the *Structure Definition* aspect is used to define the Abstract Syntax Tree (AST) of a language as a collection of *concepts*. Each concept is composed of properties, children, and relationships, and can possibly extend other concepts. The *Editor Definition* aspect deals with the definition of the concrete syntax for a DSL: it specifies both the notation (i.e., tabular, diagram, tree, etc.) and the interaction behavior of the editor. The *Generators Definition* aspect is used to define the denotational semantics for the language concepts. In particular, two kinds of transformation are supported: (1) AST to text (model-to-text), and (2) AST to AST (model-to-model). Other aspects like the *Type System Definition*, the *Constraints Definition*, etc. are provided. For the sake of brevity, we refer the reader to [25] and [26].

2.4 Jolie Language for Microservices

Jolie [15] is a programming language which offers a native linguistic tool for defining microservices following a structured service oriented paradigm. In Jolie some basic concepts of service oriented computing have a direct representation within the primitives of the language. In particular:

- it provides an integrated syntax for defining API interfaces and types;
- it provides specific communication primitives for dealing with communication both synchronous and asynchronous;
- it allows for defining the service behaviour in a workflow manner thus allowing for an easy definition of orchestrators and coordinators of services.

Thanks to these features, we considered Jolie as a good candidate for demonstrating how our approach works because it allows us to directly map the microservice meta-model into a unique linguistic technology instead of exploiting a mix of technologies. Such a characteristic permits us to avoid specific technicalities related to the chosen technology selection and focusing just on the core

---

[5] https://www.jetbrains.com/mps/.

concepts of microservices. Starting from a jolie representation, the microservice generation can be easily extended to other technologies. A detailed discussion about Jolie is out of the scope of this paper, the reader may consult the technical documentation of Jolie for a deeper investigation [15]. In order to show how the basic primitives of Jolie work, in the following we present a simple example where a calculator is implemented in Jolie.

A Calculator in Jolie. The design of a Jolie service always starts from the design of its interface which permits to define the *operations* exposed by the service and its related message types.

Listing 1: Microservice Interface in Jolie

```
type CalculatorRequest: void {
    .operand[1,*]: double
}
type DivisionRequest: void {
    .dividend: double
    .divisor: double
}
interfaces CalculatorInterface {
RequestResponse:
    sum( CalculatorRequest )( double ),
    sub( CalculatorRequest )( double ),
    mul( CalculatorRequest )( double ),
    div( DivisionRequest )( double )
        throws DivisionByZeroError
}
```

In the example above we defined an interface for a calculator service which exposes four operations: *sum, sub, mul* and *div*. Their definitions are scoped within the language keyword *interfaces* followed by the name of the interface *CalculatorInterface*. Note that each operation comes with a request message and a response message, thus we are defining synchronous operations which receive a request message and will reply with a response one. In Jolie request-response operations are defined below the keyword *RequestResponse* within the interface definition. In the example three operations (*sum, sub* and *mul*) have the same signature whereas operation *div* has a different one. In particular, the first operations receive a message with type *CalculatorRequest* and reply with a native type *double*. On the contrary, the last operation receive a message with type *DivisionRequest* and reply with a double. Moreover, operation *div* could also raise a fault called *DivisionByZeroError*. The type *CalculatorRequest* defines an array of double operands which will be elaborated by the related operation, whereas the type *DivisionRequest* define a couple of field, one for the dividend and the other for the divisor. It is worth noting that in Jolie all the messages and the internal variables are structured as trees where each node is potentially a vector of elements. Moreover, in Jolie it is possible to express the cardinality for each node of tree structure as it happens for the node *operand* where it must contain at least one element (minimum cardinality is 1) and it can have as many elements as preferred (maximum cardinality is *). Such a structure recalls those of XML trees and JSON trees, indeed a Jolie value can be easily converted in one of them.

Once a Jolie interface has been defined, it is possible to implement its operations within a service. In the following we report a possible implementation of the *CalculatorInterface*:

Listing 2: Microservice implementation in Jolie

```
include "CalcultorInterface.iol"

execution{ concurrent }

inputPort Calculator {
Location: "socket://localhost:8000"
Protocol: sodep
Interfaces: CalculatorInterface
}

main {
    [ sum( request )( response ) {
        response = request.operand[ 0 ]
        for( i = 0, i < #request.operand, i++ ) {
            response = response + request.operand[ i ]
        }
    }]

    [ sub( request )( response ) {
        response = request.operand[ 0 ]
        for( i = 1, i < #request.operand, i++ ) {
            response = response - request.operand[ i ]
        }
    }]

    [ mul( request )( response ) {
        response = request.operand[ 0 ]
        for( i = 0, i < #request.operand, i++ ) {
            response = response * request.operand[ i ]
        }
    }]

    [ div( request )( response ) {
        if ( request.divisor == 0 ) {
            throw( DivisionByZeroError )
        } else {
            response = request.dividend/request.divisor
        }
    }]
}
```

The definition of a service in Jolie is mainly divided in two parts: a declarative part where all the interfaces and ports are defined, a behavioral part, represented by the scope *main*, where the implementation of the operations is provided. Note that in the definition of the service above we use the primitive *include* for automatically import the code written in file *CalculatorInterface.iol* where we suppose we saved the definition of interface *CalculatorInterface*. In this case the Jolie engine reads the content of the file and put it instead of the include declaration. The primitive *execution* defines the execution modality of the service which can assume three possible values:

- *concurrent*: the engine will serve all the received request concurrently;
- *sequential*: the engine will serve all the received request sequentially;
- *single*: the engine will execute the behaviour once then the service will stop.

Finally, the definition of the *inputPort* permits to define the listener where the messages will be received by the service. The *inputPort* is also in charge to dispatch the message to the right operation. The *inputPort* requires three elements in order to be correctly defined:

- Location: it defines where the service is listening for messages. Briefly, a location defines the medium (*socket*, the IP (in the example is *localhost*) and the port (in the example is 8000)).
- Protocol: it defines the protocol used for performing the communication. It could be HTTP, HTTPS, SOAP, etc. In the example we use *sodep* that is binary protocol released with the Jolie engine which does not require any particular header like it happens for other protocols.
- Interfaces: it lists all the interfaces joined with that port, thus it defines all the operations enabled to receive messages on that listener.

Note that more than one input port could be defined in the same Jolie service.

Finally, let us analyze the implementation of the operations. Note that each of them is defined to store the received message in a variable called *request* and take the response message from a variable called *response*. The response is automatically sent to the invoker once the body of the request response is successfully finished. This means that inside the body of each operations, the developer must fill the variable response with a proper message which matches with the related type defined in the interface. Indeed, if we analyze the code of the first three operations, we see that the service ranges over the array of operands calculating the related operation $(+, -$ or $*)$. in the case of operation *div*, the service checks if the divisor is equal to zero and, if it is the case, it raises a fault *DivisionByZeroError* which is automatically sent to the invoker instead of a usual response.

The calculator service can be run by simply typing the following command on a shell:

```
jolie calculator.ol
```

where *calculator.ol* is the name of the file which contains the definition of service depicted above.

Before continuing, here we also show how to create and run a Jolie client which uses the operation of the service calculator.

```
Listing 3: Jolie Client implementation

include "CalcultorInterface.iol"
include "console.iol"

execution{ single }

outputPort Calculator {
Location: "socket://localhost:8000"
Protocol: sodep
Interfaces: CalculatorInterface
}

main {
    with( request ) {
        .operand[ 0 ] = 1;
        .operand[ 1 ] = 2;
        .operand[ 2 ] = 3;
        .operand[ 3 ] = 4
    }
    sum@Calculator( request )( result )
    println@Console( result )()
}
```

This Jolie client calls the calculator service on its operation *sum* passing an array of four elements and receiving as a reply their sum (*10*). The result is then printed out on the shell exploiting the operation *println@Console(result)()* which comes with the built-in Jolie service imported at the beginning (*include "console.iol"*). Note that the invocation of the calculator is performed with the line

```
sum@Calculator( request )( result )
```

where we specify the name of the operation (*sum*) and the output port to be used (*Calculator*). The output port *Calculator* is defined before the scope main and it identifies the endpoint to which sending the message. It is not a case indeed, that the elements *Location, Protocol* and *Interfaces* of the outputPort correspond to those of the inputPort of the calculator service. The client can be easily run in a shell typing the following command:

```
jolie client.ol
```

where *client.ol* is the name of the file which contains the definition of the client.

The Calculator Example in Java. In the following we report how the Jolie example of the calculator described in the previous section can be implemented as a Java class.

Listing 1: Java implementation of the Calculator

```java
import java.util.ArrayList;

public class JavaCalculator {

  public Double sum( ArrayList<Double> operand ) throws Exception {
    if ( operand.size() > 0 ) {
      throw new Exception("At_least_one_operand_must_be_specified");
    }
    Double response = operand.get( 0 );
    for( int i = 1; i < operand.size(); i++ ) {
      response = response + operand.get( i );
    }
    return response;
  }

  public Double sub( ArrayList<Double> operand ) throws Exception {
    if ( operand.size() > 0 ) {
      throw new Exception("At_least_one_operand_must_be_specified");
    }
    Double response = operand.get( 0 );
    for( int i = 1; i < operand.size(); i++ ) {
      response = response - operand.get( i );
    }

    return response;
  }

  public Double mul( ArrayList<Double> operand ) throws Exception {
    if ( operand.size() > 0 ) {
      throw new Exception("At_least_one_operand_must_be_specified");
    }
    Double response = operand.get( 0 );
    for( int i = 1; i < operand.size(); i++ ) {
      response = response * operand.get( i );
    }
    return response;
  }
  public Double div( Double dividend, Double divisor )
                          throws Exception {
    Double response = new Double(0);
    if ( divisor == 0 ) {
      throw new Exception("Division_by_Zero_Error");
    }
    response = dividend / divisor;
    return response;
  }
}
```

Note that in the case of Java we need to check at the beginning of methods *sum*, *sub* and *mul* that the received array contains at least one element. In Jolie the type checking is automatically performed by the engine.

Deploying a Jolie Service in a Docker Container. Deploying a jolie microservice within a Docker container is very simple. The first thing to do is preparing the image of the container starting from the public and available image *jolielang/jolie* which provides a core layer where both Java and Jolie are installed. In the following we show the *Dockerfile* which allows for the creation of the docker image of the service *calculator* described in the previous section.

Listing 4: Docker file for a microservice

```
FROM jolielang/jolie
EXPOSE 8000
COPY calculator.ol
CMD jolie calculator.ol
```

Such a Dockerfile can be used as an input for the command *docker build* for actually creating the image of the container. Note that the file *calculator.ol* must be located in the same directory from which the command *docker build* is executed. The file *calculator.ol* indeed, will be directly copied within the image. Once the image is created, a container which derives from it can be easily run following the standard procedure of Docker.

3   Related Work

Since the 2014, as shown by Balalaie et al. [27], microservices steadily grown as a concept, and plenty of businesses decided to migrate their monolithic and service-oriented architectures to microservices ones. Taibi et al. [6] conducted an empirical investigation and interviewed experienced practitioners in order to identify the common motivations that led to the migration of monoliths to microservices, as well as the issues they ran into. According to the interviewees, the main reasons for migrating from a monolithic architecture to a microservices one were both maintainability and scalability. Unsurprisingly, the main issue related to migration was the monetary expenditure that such operation entails. Finally, from such interviews, the authors outlined three different migration processes adopted by practitioners.

In another study, Knoche and Hasselbring [28] report that discussions with practitioners highlighted how industry looks at microservices as a promising architecture to solve maintainability issues, even in those cases where scalability is not a critical priority. First, this work shows that incremental approaches that gradually decompose a monolith in separated microservices are the most adopted, even though cases of full-scale code rewriting exist as well. Then, based on their industrial experience, the authors provide a decomposition process to achieve an incremental migration. Besides, authors argue that when dealing with critical migrations, it makes sense to first migrate clients applications, while implementing new functionalities in the existing monolith, and then incrementally migrate all the services to the microservices architecture. On the contrary, when dealing with less critical instances, authors acknowledge that these efforts are not justified, and suggest to directly implement all the new services as microservices.

Di Francesco et al. [5] conducted another empirical study, similar to the one conducted by Taibi et al. [6] but with two main differences. First, in this study the authors put greater focus on the details of each migration phase; second, they investigated not only migrations of monolithic architecture to microservices architectures, but also of service-oriented architectures to microservice architectures. Again, authors highlight that there is no unified strategy into approaching the migration, as some businesses choose to proceed by means of increments, whereas others tackle down the problem as a single big project. They also report a surprising result, where more than half of the participants reported that the existing data is not migrated together with the architecture, arguing that this does not align well with the two microservices typical principles: hiding internal implementations details, and managing data in a decentralized fashion.

In a 2015 manuscript, Levcovitz et al. [29] proposed a technique to identify, within monoliths, service candidates for migrating to microservices based on mapping the dependencies between databases, business functions, and facades. The authors evaluated their technique on a real case study (a 750 KLOC monolith programmed in C) in the banking domain, and show that they identified successfully candidate subsystems. To the best of our knowledge, apart from our work, this is the only alternative publication that discusses migration techniques applied to a specific banking case study. Moreover, it is useful to notice that while their approach aims to automatize the identification based on the legacy monolithic deployment, our case study was primarily business-driven. Therefore, our approach had to be necessarily manual and iterative.

Again, Balalaie et al. [27,30] reported their experience of performing an incremental migration of a mobile back-end as a service (MBaaS) to microservices, coupling with DevOps methodologies. Citing the on-demand capability as the main driver of migration, they caution *a posteriori* about two important lessons learned. In first instance, the authors warn that the service contracts are critical and that changing a lot of services that only interact with each other could expose to a number of errors, as small errors in the contracts can break down substantial part of the architecture. Second, they caution against considering microservices a silver bullet, as it can be beneficial to bring scalability to services, but it can introduce higher complexity as well.

Following the previous works, the authors collected and reported some empirical migration patterns derived from medium to large-scale industrial projects, aiming to help others to perform a smooth migration [31]. They evaluate such patterns through qualitative empirical research, and cite as future work the development of a pattern language that would allow to automatically compose the patterns.

In a recent work, Furda et al. [32] agree on defining the migration to microservices a promising way to modernize monolithic architectures and to enable full-scale utilization of cloud computing. At the same time, they identify three major challenges in migrating monolithic architectures to microservices ones, namely: multitenancy, statefulness, and data consistency.

Finally, Bucchiarone et al. [33] report an experience from of a real-world case study in the banking domain, of how scalability is positively affected by re-implementing a monolithic architecture into microservices. Even if it presents a real and complex application migration, the approach proposed was not supported by an automatic migration tool but was only business-driven and

outside-in, i.e., the system has been designed and implemented one business
functionality at a time.

Analyzing all the lessons learned by the previous works we can conclude
saying that despite the fact that there is an extreme and increasingly emerging need to migrate applications from monolithic to microservices, rare are the
approaches that try to make this process automatic and tool supported. Most
of the migration approaches proposed are guided by the developers experience
and are not supported by a specific tool or language. They consider case by case
whether a functionality should result in a new service or not. If the business
functionality seemed isolated and big enough, or it was shared among numerous
other business functionalities, then it resulted in a new service.

At the same time, to the best of our knowledge, there is no Model-Driven
Engineering approach addressing the support of migration in the sense addressed
in this paper. The migration approach introduced in the next section shows
our solution in this direction with the aim towards the realization of a general
framework for automatic migration to microservices.

4   Model-Driven Migration Approach

In this Section we introduce the migration process, showing how a MA can be
converted into a MSA and deployed in a Docker container. In this respect, our
contribution is visualized in Fig. 1, which depicts the different artifacts realized and their relations. Technically, the solution is composed by two fundamental components: (a) the `Microservices Miner` and (b) the `Microservices
Generator`, by two Domain Specific Languages (DSLs) (i.e., for the `Microservice`
specification and for their `Deployment`), by a set of `generators` used to support
the overall migration from MA (developed in Java) to MSA (developed using
Jolie) and the corresponding deployment in a `Docker Container`. The following
sections provide detailed descriptions of each of the previous artifacts.

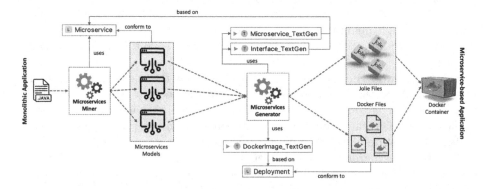

Fig. 1. The model-driven migration approach.

4.1   The Microservice Language

The Microservice language relies on how microservices can be defined in Jolie (see Sect. 2.4) and allows the developers to design concrete microservices. An excerpt on the concepts defined to realize this DSL are depicted in Fig. 2. In particular at this level of abstraction the developer can specify a microservice including its interface, inputPort, outputPort and the respective behavior. Moreover it comprises a property called directive that is used to set the execution modality. For example setting it to concurrent will allow the service to process all the incoming requests concurrently. The behaviour children of the Microservice concept is used to define the implementation of the functionalities offered by a microservice.

Fig. 2. Concepts of the microservice language.

The Interface concept is used to specify the type of each exchanged message (i.e., requestResponseMessage) in a microservice. To enable a communication between microservices, we need to specify the input and the output endpoints. In Jolie this is done by using primitives input ports and output ports. In our DSL we have introduced two concepts. InputPort is used for defining a listener endpoint whereas the OutputPort concept is used for sending messages to an inputPort.

Figure 3 shows how the `calculator` microservice can be specified using the `Microservice` language. The `calculator` microservice provides an `inputPort` which is listening on port 8999 where the `CalculatorInterface` is defined.

Fig. 3. Calculator microservice model.

In this interface the request also contains the subnode `.op:string`, which permits to specify the operation type (i.e., SUM or SUBT). Moreover, it includes also a fault sent as a response (i.e., `OperationNotSupported`).

The interface called `OperationServiceInterface` provides a `RequestResponse` operation called `execute`. A RequestResponse operation is an operation which receives a request message and replies with a response message. In this case, the request message type is defined by `ExecuteRequest`, which contains two subnodes: x and y. Both of them are integers. On the other hand, the response is just an integer.

The `outputPort` of the `calculator` microservice requires the same parameters of the `inputPort` (i.e., `Location`, `Protocol`, `Interfaces`) but in our example the `Location` is omitted because it is dynamically bound at runtime depending on the value of request node op. Indeed, we bind the port Operation to a different location depending on if we call the service SUM or the service SUBT in the microservice behavior (i.e., `main` part of the `calculator` microservice).

4.2   The Deployment Language

In this Section we show how a microservice modelled using our approach can be deployed inside a Docker container. Basically, the only thing to do is to create a Dockerfile which allows for creating a Docker image that can be used for generating containers. For this purpose we have defined a specific language called Deployment (see Fig. 4) devoted to the specification of the microservices Dockerfiles. At the same time is important to know that there is a Docker image which provides a container where Jolie is installed. Such an image can be found on dockerhub[6] and is used as base layer for deploying jolie services modelled or automatically generated by our approach.

Fig. 4. DockerImage concept of the deployment language.

To create a docker image of a microservice (as the one in Fig. 3), it is necessary to specify down a Dockerfile exploiting the DockerImage concept of the Deployment language. To do this we have created an MPS editor (as shown in Fig. 5 left side) that helps developers to specify Dockerfile models as depicted in the right side of Fig. 5.

The FROM child of the DockerImage concept us used to load the image *jolielang/jolie*, while the MAINTAINER is used to specify the name and the email address of the file maintainer. EXPOSE is used to expose the port 8000 to be used by external invokers of the microservice. This means that the jolie microservice always listens on this port within the container. COPY is used to copy the file calculatore.ol within the image renaming it into main.ol. Finally CMD specifies the command to be executed by Docker when a container will be start from the image described by this Dockerfile.

4.3   Microservices Miner

To analyze the monolithic application written in Java and to retrieve from it the set of needed microservices, we have implemented the Microservices Miner component. Its main task is to search in the abstract syntax tree of the imported Java

---

[6] https://hub.docker.com/r/jolielang/jolie.

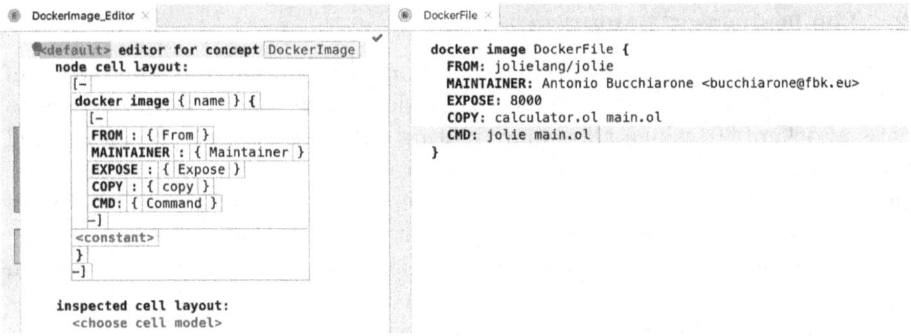

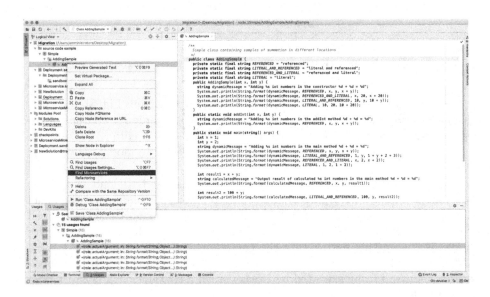

Fig. 5. Dockerfile editor and model.

code for patterns of interest and suggest to the developer the set of microservices for the migration. This is done thanks the realization of two subcomponents, the *orchestrator* and a set of *searchers*. The orchestrator is a generic implemented action in the miner language and can be invoked on the MPS *logical view* or on the specific imported Java code *editor*.

Fig. 6. Microservice finder in action.

The MPS logical view shows a tree presenting the project structure. When the implemented finder is selected (the `Find microservices` action in Fig. 6), MPS, using the *searchers* available in the project executes the searchers. The result of this search is usually visualized in the *Usage View*, as depicted at the bottom of Fig. 6, and contains the occurrences of the *pattern* specified in the specific searcher. Each searcher is realized by implementing the interface or the abstract implementation and finds nodes in the AST that comply to the semantic understanding of the searcher. As a simple example, Fig. 7 presents the `PlusExpressionFinder` definition and its usage in the more general `MicroServiceSearcher`. When it is invoked in the project *logical view* it searches for all the occurrences of the *plus expression* in the Java source code and returns all the occurrences retrieved in the *Usage View*. This outcome is exploited by the developer to identify the set of microservices that must be specified using the `Microservice` language introduced in Sect. 4.1 and that can be directly deployed in a Docker container using the `Microservice Generator` illustrated in the next Section.

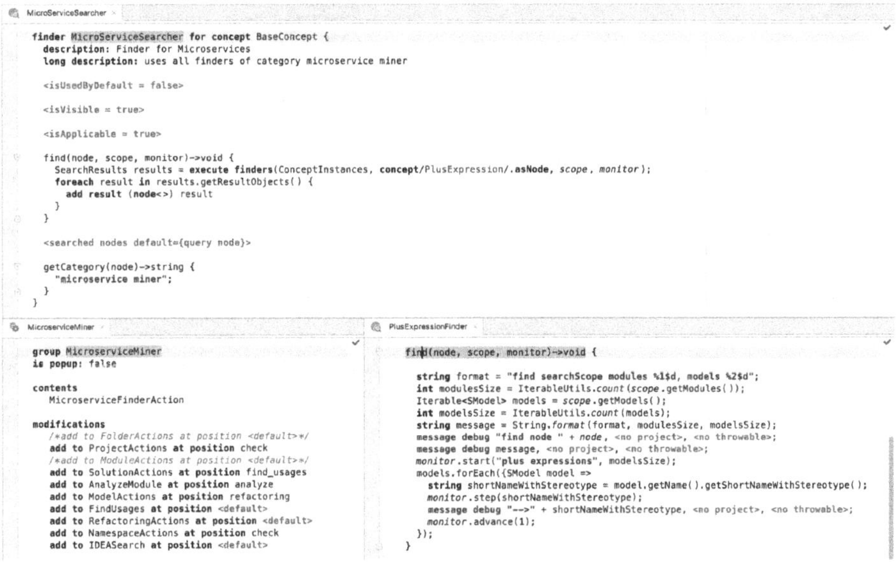

Fig. 7. Microservice miner.

4.4 Microservices Generator

To generate all the needed files to deploy a microservice in a Docker container we have used one of the transformation feature provided by MPS, it is the AST to text (model-to-text) transformation. As we have already introduced in Sect. 2, to run a microservice we need to provide one file for the service specification (with extension .ol), one file for each interface the microservice uses (with extension .iol), and the Dockerfile used to deploy the microservice in a Docker container. To do this we have implemented three generators (depicted in Fig. 1) called:

Microservice_TextGen, Interface_TextGen, and DockerImage_TextGen. As illustrated in Figs. 8 and 9, generators specifications are given by means of template mechanisms. Templates are written by using the output language (i.e., Jolie and Dockerfile in our case), and are parametric with respect to the elements retrievable from the input model through Macros, denoted by the $ symbol. In our case, the Microservice and the Interface generators are used to generate the corresponding Jolie .ol and .iol files. The Dockerfile generator instead is used to generate the corresponding Dockerfile document needed to deploy the microservice in a Docker container.

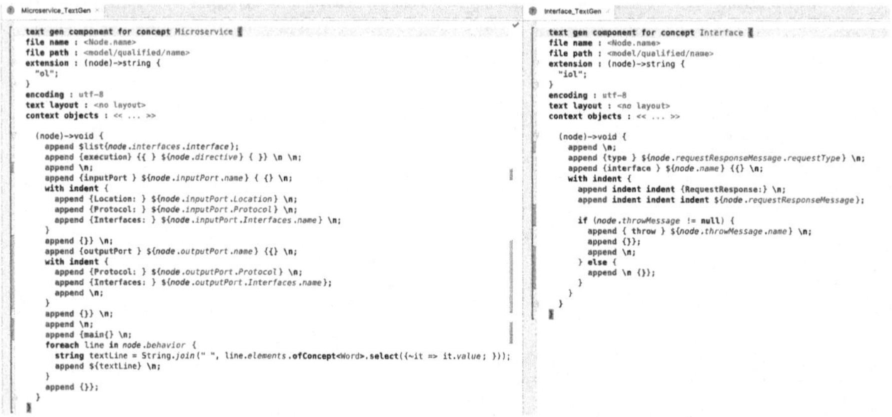

Fig. 8. Microservice and Interface generators.

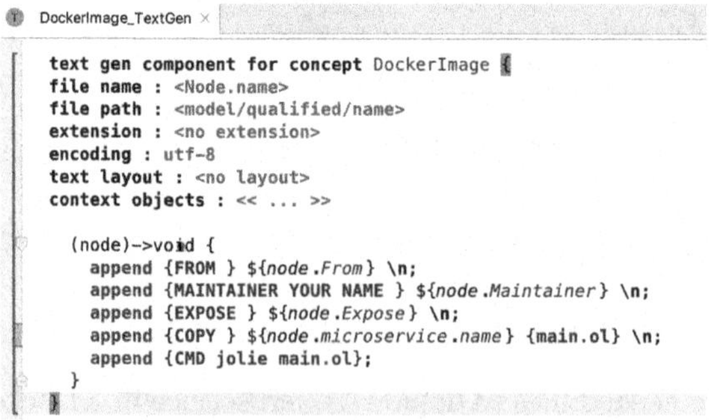

Fig. 9. Dockerfile generator.

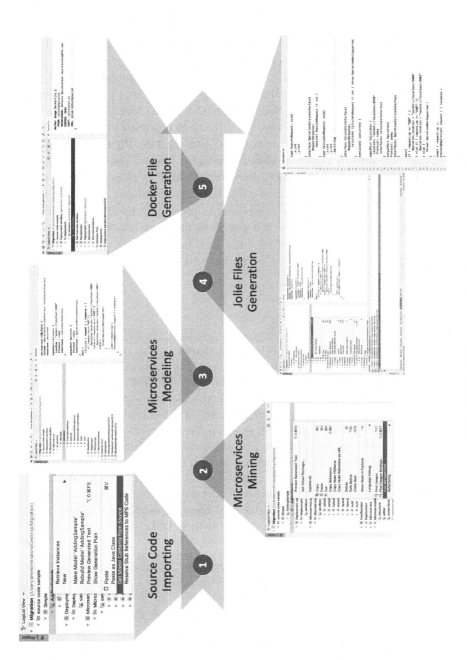

Fig. 10. Prototype execution steps.

5   Prototype Implementation

As a first iteration towards realizing the framework proposed in this paper, we developed the model-driven approach described in Sect. 4[7]. The implementation includes all the phases depicted in Fig. 10 and has been experimented using the motivating scenario presented in Sect. 2.4.

Using our solution, a developer can start the migration process importing the Java source code of the monolithic application in phase ①. This is done using the native MPS action `Get Models Content from Source` that can be invoked by the main menu. In this way the Java code is parsed into MPS' base language and imported in the editor as input Java models. Phase ② is used to interrogate the imported Java models for patterns of used packages, classes, methods and members to identify microservice candidates. In phase ③, with the `Microservice` domain specific language in the hand the developer can create the different models of the identified microservices. In phase ④, using the provided generators described in Sect. 4.4, the microservices models with their respective interfaces are transformed in the target Jolie files. In the end, in phase ⑤, for each Jolie microservice a `Dockerfile` is created and used to deploy the overall application in a Docker container.

6   Conclusion

In this paper we presented the experiences matured in the development of a Model-Driven approach for the migration of monolithic applications to microservice applications. The proposed solution is based on the definition of two domain specific languages, one for the microservices specification and one for their deployment in a Docker container, and on a set of generators that make the migration approach automatic and with less manual intervention by developers. The framework have been implemented by means of the MPS text-based language workbench and evaluated with an initial with the aim to demonstrate the feasibility of the approach, and calls for future research. To make is scalable and usable in real contexts we are interested to test it using different industrial case studies to further investigate the soundness of the proposed methodology and eventually to extend the specification of the provided DSLs in MPS to make it more general.

References

1. Bass, L., Weber, I., Zhu, L.: DevOps: A Software Architect's Perspective. Addison-Wesley Professional, Reading (2015)
2. Fowler, M., Lewis, J.: Microservices, ThoughtWorks (2014)

---

[7] A prototype implementation of the approach and the related artefacts are available at the GitHub repository: https://github.com/antbucc/Migration.git.

3. Jamshidi, P., Pahl, C., Mendonça, N.C., Lewis, J., Tilkov, S.: Microservices: the journey so far and challenges ahead. IEEE Softw. **35**(3), 24–35 (2018)
4. Mazzara, M., Naumchev, A., Safina, L., Sillitti, A., Urysov, K.: Teaching DevOps in corporate environments: an experience report, CoRR, vol. abs/1807.01632 (2018)
5. Francesco, P.D., Lago, P., Malavolta, I.: Migrating towards microservice architectures: an industrial survey. In: 2018 IEEE International Conference on Software Architecture (ICSA), pp. 29–2909, April 2018
6. Taibi, D., Lenarduzzi, V., Pahl, C.: Processes, motivations, and issues for migrating to microservices architectures: an empirical investigation. IEEE Cloud Comput. **4**, 22–32 (2017)
7. Parnas, D.L.: On the criteria to be used in decomposing systems into modules. Commun. ACM **15**, 1053–1058 (1972)
8. Dragoni, N., et al.: Microservices: yesterday, today, and tomorrow. In: Mazzara, M., Meyer, B., et al. (eds.) Present and Ulterior Software Engineering, pp. 195–216. Springer, Cham (2017). https://doi.org/10.1007/978-3-319-67425-4_12
9. Dragoni, N., Lanese, I., Larsen, S.T., Mazzara, M., Mustafin, R., Safina, L.: Microservices: how to make your application scale. In: Petrenko, A.K., Voronkov, A. (eds.) PSI 2017. LNCS, vol. 10742, pp. 95–104. Springer, Cham (2018). https://doi.org/10.1007/978-3-319-74313-4_8
10. France, R., Rumpe, B.: Model-based development. Softw. Syst. Model. **7**(1), 1–2 (2008)
11. Atkinson, C., Kühne, T.: Model-driven development: a metamodeling foundation. IEEE Softw. **20**, 36–41 (2003)
12. Schmidt, D.C.: Guest editor's introduction: model-driven engineering. Computer **39**, 25–31 (2006)
13. Voelter, M., et al.: DSL Engineering - Designing, Implementing and Using Domain-Specific Languages (2013). dslbook.org
14. Voelter, M., Lisson, S.: Supporting diverse notations in MPS' projectional editor. In: Proceedings of the 2nd International Workshop on the Globalization of Modeling Languages Co-located with ACM/IEEE 17th International Conference on Model Driven Engineering Languages and Systems, GEMOC@Models 2014, pp. 7–16 (2014)
15. The Jolie language website. http://www.jolie-lang.org/
16. MacKenzie, M.C., Laskey, K., McCabe, F., Brown, P.F., Metz, R., Hamilton, B.A.: Reference model for service oriented architecture 1.0, vol. 12. OASIS Standard (2006)
17. Newman, S.: Building Microservices. O'Reilly Media Inc, Sebastopol (2015)
18. Montesi, F., Guidi, C., Zavattaro, G.: Service-Oriented Programming with Jolie. In: Bouguettaya, A., Sheng, Q., Daniel, F. (eds.) Web Services Foundations, pp. 81–107. Springer, New York (2014). https://doi.org/10.1007/978-1-4614-7518-7_4
19. Guidi, C., Lanese, I., Mazzara, M., Montesi, F.: Microservices: a language-based approach. Present and Ulterior Software Engineering, pp. 217–225. Springer, Cham (2017). https://doi.org/10.1007/978-3-319-67425-4_13
20. Bandura, A., Kurilenko, N., Mazzara, M., Rivera, V., Safina, L., Tchitchigin, A.: Jolie community on the rise. In: SOCA, pp. 40–43. IEEE Computer Society (2016)
21. van Deursen, A., Klint, P., Visser, J.: Domain-specific languages: an annotated bibliography. SIGPLAN Not. **35**(6), 26–36 (2000)
22. Ward, M.: Language oriented programming. Softw. Concepts Tools **15**, 147–161 (1994)

23. Voelter, M.: Language and IDE modularization and composition with MPS. In: Generative and Transformational Techniques in Software Engineering IV, GTTSE 2011, pp. 383–430. International Summer School (2011)
24. Voelter, M., Pech, V.: Language modularity with the MPS language workbench. In: 34th International Conference on Software Engineering, ICSE 2012, pp. 1449–1450 (2012)
25. Campagne, F.: The MPS Language Workbench, vol. 1, 1st edn. CreateSpace Independent Publishing Platform, Hamburg (2014)
26. Campagne, F.: The MPS Language Workbench Volume II: The Meta Programming System, vol. 2, 1st edn. CreateSpace Independent Publishing Platform, Hamburg (2016)
27. Balalaie, A., Heydarnoori, A., Jamshidi, P.: Microservices architecture enables devops: migration to a cloud-native architecture. IEEE Softw. **33**, 42–52 (2016)
28. Knoche, H., Hasselbring, W.: Using microservices for legacy software modernization. IEEE Softw. **35**, 44–49 (2018)
29. Levcovitz, A., Terra, R., Valente, M.T.: Towards a technique for extracting microservices from monolithic enterprise systems. In: III Workshop de Visualização, Evolução e Manutenção de Software (VEM), pp. 97–104 (2015)
30. Balalaie, A., Heydarnoori, A., Jamshidi, P.: Migrating to cloud-native architectures using microservices: an experience report. In: Celesti, A., Leitner, P. (eds.) ESOCC Workshops 2015. CCIS, vol. 567, pp. 201–215. Springer, Cham (2016). https://doi.org/10.1007/978-3-319-33313-7_15
31. Balalaie, A., Heydarnoori, A., Jamshidi, P., Tamburri, D.A., Lynn, T.: Microservices migration patterns. Softw. Pract. Exp. **48**, 2019–2042 (2018)
32. Furda, A., Fidge, C., Zimmermann, O., Kelly, W., Barros, A.: Migrating enterprise legacy source code to microservices: on multitenancy, statefulness, and data consistency. IEEE Softw. **35**, 63–72 (2018)
33. Bucchiarone, A., Dragoni, N., Dustdar, S., Larsen, S.T., Mazzara, M.: From monolithic to microservices: an experience report from the banking domain. IEEE Softw. **35**(3), 50–55 (2018)

Anomaly Detection in DevOps Toolchain

Antonio Capizzi[1], Salvatore Distefano[1], Luiz J. P. Araújo[2],
Manuel Mazzara[2(✉)], Muhammad Ahmad[1,3], and Evgeny Bobrov[2]

[1] University of Messina, Messina, Italy
[2] Innopolis University, Innopolis, Respublika Tatarstan, Russian Federation
m.mazzara@innopolis.ru
[3] Department of Computer Engineering, Khwaja Fareed University of Engineering
and Information Technology, Rahim Yar Khan, Pakistan

Abstract. The tools employed in the DevOps Toolchain generates a
large quantity of data that is typically ignored or inspected only on
particular occasions, at most. However, the analysis of such data could
enable the extraction of useful information about the status and evolution of the project. For example, metrics like the "lines of code added
since the last release" or "failures detected in the staging environment"
are good indicators for predicting potential risks in the incoming release.
In order to prevent problems appearing in later stages of production,
an anomaly detection system can operate in the staging environment to
compare the current incoming release with previous ones according to
predefined metrics. The analysis is conducted before going into production to identify anomalies which should be addressed by human operators that address false-positive and negatives that can appear. In this
paper, we describe a prototypical implementation of the aforementioned
idea in the form of a "proof of concept". The current study effectively
demonstrates the feasibility of the approach for a set of implemented
functionalities.

1 Introduction

Evolution of software engineering spans over more than fifty years where different problems have been presented, and solutions explored [1]. From *structured
programming* to *"life cycle models"* and *"software development methodologies"*,
researchers and developers have better understood the software development process and its complexity. Meanwhile, a fast-speed growing technological progress
has transformed the usage of computers from devices for numerical and scientific
computation into every-day ubiquitous devices. This progress has not stopped,
and an increasing number of companies are moving to Agile methodologies, also
including in the software development process feedback from operational stages
in a DevOps [2,3] fashion.

Continuous delivery (CD) is an important concept part of the DevOps philosophy and practice as it enables organizations to deliver new features quickly
as well as to create a repeatable and reliable process incrementally improving to
bring software from concept to customer. The goal of CD is to enable a constant

© Springer Nature Switzerland AG 2020
J.-M. Bruel et al. (Eds.): DEVOPS 2019, LNCS 12055, pp. 37–51, 2020.
https://doi.org/10.1007/978-3-030-39306-9_3

flow of changes into the production via an automated software production line - the *continuous delivery pipeline*. The CD pipeline has a variable complexity and can be constituted by several phases supported by different tools. However, the core idea is always the same: when a developer integrates or fixes a functionality into the software, a set of software tools automatically builds the application, starts the automatic tests and, finally, delivers the new feature.

CD is made possible via automation to eliminate several manual routines during software production, testing, and delivery. CD pipeline automation involves in the toolchain different tools, each generating messages, data and logs. However, the amount of recorded data can prevent its manual inspection when one searches for a specific issue or traces back abnormal behavior. Inside a DevOps toolchain, data is generated and stored in different formats. The analysis of such data is a daunting task even for an experienced professional as well as its processing, recognition, mining and, consequently, addressing of critical aspects.

In this paper, we discuss how to automatically analyze the data generated during a DevOps toolchain integrated to anomaly detection (AD) methods for identifying potentially harmful software releases. As a result, software releases that can lead to potential malfunctioning during the normal system life could be identified. The implemented approach could still lead to false-positives and false-negatives since no approach can overcome this theoretical limitation [4]; however, developers are provided with an instrument to validate and maintain the code. This investigation focuses on an ongoing project structured according to the DevOps philosophy, and we will apply analytical techniques to gain insights for professionals involved in the software development process.

In Sect. 2, background is provided, with specific regard to DevOps toolchains and AD techniques and tools. In Sect. 3, we presented an approach for integrating AD into a project structured with DevOps. After that, Sect. 4 describes the case study, in details: the SpaceViewer application, the corresponding DevOps process and toolchain and the developed AD module, the SpaceViewer AD system - SVADS. Section 5 then reports on the experiments and obtained results, also compared against those obtained by offline tools on the full SpaceViewer dataset, demonstrating the effectiveness of the proposed approach. Section 6 summarises the key aspects of the proposed approach and future work.

2 Background

This section introduce some technical background for this work project and its implementation. This research is bringing together two different communities with research literature and vocabulary sporadically overlapping. Thus, we first discuss the details of DevOps toolchains, and then we report on data science techniques adopted in the software development process.

2.1 The DevOps Toolchain

DevOps [2] consists of a set of practices to promote collaboration between the developers, IT professionals (in particular sysadmin, i.e. who works on

IT operations) and quality assurance personnel. DevOps is implemented via a set of software tools [5] that enable the management of an environment in which software can be built, tested and released quickly, frequently, and a more reliable manner. In addition to CD, *continuous integration* (CI) stands as a key concept in DevOps approaches. A typical example of CI consists of continuously integrating changes made by developers into a repository, then a project build is automatically executed, if the build works well automatic tests are started. IF also automatic tests passes, the change is integrated into the code through CD and published in production environment.

One of the main objectives of DevOps is to mitigate problems in production, which is done by reducing the gap between development and testing environments with the production environment. Collaborations between "Dev" and "Ops" aiming to reduce this gap make use of a complex toolchain including, at least, some version control tool (e.g. Git), CI/CD automation tools (e.g. Jenkins), package managers (e.g. NPM) and test tools (e.g. JUnit). Other additional tools used in DevOps are configuration management tools (e.g. Ansible), monitoring tools (e.g. Nagios), security tools (e.g. SonarCube), team collaboration tools (e.g. Jira) and database management tools (e.g. Flyway). DevOps infrastructures are typically either fully implemented on cloud platforms. It is a good practice in DevOps to build the entire infrastructure using containers; therefore, tools for containerization (e.g. Docker) are employed, sometimes coupled by tools for containers orchestration (e.g. Kubernetes).

An outcome from the complex pipeline involved in a DevOps project is the generation of a large amount of data, in particular, log files and metrics generated in each stage. Examples of activities that generate considerable data on the project cycle include changes made by developers; the application building and its corresponding entries on the compilation and dependencies of the project; the execution of automatic tests; and software usage by end-users after release into the production.

A large amount of the data generated in a DevOps toolchain requires some form of automation and possibly dimensionality reduction and feature selection [6]. However, collecting, storing, and analysing such a high dimensional data could enable insights into how to improve the DevOps pipeline [7]. For example, historical data can be analyzed to estimate a probabilistic measure of the success of a new release.

2.2   Anomaly Detection in Software Development

The application of data science techniques to software development processes has become increasingly popular in the last decades, in part due to the availability of a growing amount of data generated during the development process. Methods like data preprocessing and machine learning have been used for tasks including estimating programming effort, predicting risks to the project and identifying defects in the produced artefacts [8].

In recent years, the term "AIOps" has been coined to refer to a set of techniques which employ machine learning and artificial intelligence to enable the analysis of data from IT operation tools [9]. As a result, there has been a noticeable improvement in service delivery, IT efficiency and superior user experience [10]. Applications of AIOps to DevOps processes, mainly to analyze data produced by the toolchain, specifically in operation, have been proposed in literature [11]. In another example, AIops has been used to support software development processes within an organization during the migration from waterfall processes to Agile/DevOps [12].

AD has been an increasingly popular approach for identifying observations that deviate from the expected pattern in the data. In data science, AD refers to a set of techniques used for identifying observations which occur with low frequency in the dataset, i.e. entries that do not conform to the expected distribution or pattern. Such data entries raise suspicion and represent potential risk depending on the context in which data has been collected. Examples of applications of AD in different problem domains include detection of bank frauds [13], structural defects in building construction [14], system health monitoring and errors in a text [15]. It is trustworthy mentioning that there has been limited literature demonstrating the application of AD methods in the context of DevOps. An example of AD applied to DevOps operations in a Cloud platform was reported in [16].

3   Integrating Anomaly Detection into DevOps

As mentioned previously, the vast amount of data generated by the DevOps toolchain enables the use of AD techniques to reduce the probability of software errors released in production. An AD system can compare the multivariate features of the prospective release with the collected data from previous versions. The DevOps study analyzed in this work is following the development, staging, and production model. In this model, the activities are sorted in three deployment environments, detailed as follows:

- **Development**: environment in which the developers work and can quickly test new features.
- **Staging**: testing environment to experiment and test the new features that have to be merged to the system.
- **Production**: environment in which the software is released and utilised by end-users.

The development and staging environments offer an opportunity for assessing the correctness of the prospective release. Moreover, the data collected during these stages enable the application of data science techniques such as AD for preventing software errors. The most suitable approach depends on the characteristics of the data. For example, if a considerable amount of labeled data is available, supervised learning techniques (e.g. support vector machine) can lead to satisfactory predictive accuracy. In case there is no information whether each observation in the training dataset is an anomaly, an unsupervised learning technique is the most suitable approach.

This study employs the local outlier factor (LOF) algorithm, which is an unsupervised AD technique which computes the local density deviation of a multivariate data point compared to its neighbors. This method enables the identification and plotting of anomalies in the data and supports better decision-making [17]. The LOF algorithm is used before a new version of the software is moved from the staging phase to the release phase. In other words, it identifies whether the prospective release significantly deviates from exiting distributions in the following set of metrics: the number of pushes, builds and errors, lines of code that have been changed and the number of failed tests. Figure 1 shows the operational flow, which consists of three macro-phases distinguishing development, AD and recovery activities.

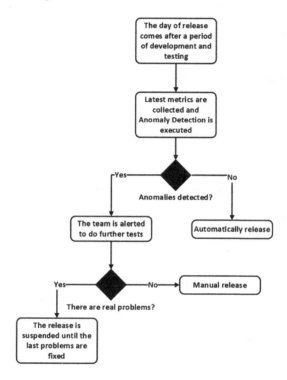

Fig. 1. The anomaly detection task in the proposed DevOps workflow.

In the development stage, software development and testing are implemented in the development and staging environments as described previously. These activities are performed between the current release and the next version. The activities in this stage are mostly executed by the development team. In the detection stage, AD using the LOF algorithm is employed and possibly coupled with advanced computational techniques like artificial intelligence and machine learning. Moreover, the comparison of distinct AD methods can provide more a well-informed decision in the recovery phase, when a human actor assesses the identified anomalies.

4   A Case Study: SpaceViewer

This section describes a proof-of-concept application developed by exploiting a DevOps approach and toolchain proposed in this work. It consists of a Web application developed by adopting a DevOps process: *Space Viewer* [18]. Space-Viewer is a ReactJS [19] project enabling queries for interacting and interfacing the NASA space archive exploiting their Open APIs [20]. A client-server app has been implemented where the server-side small back-end interface [21] (developed in Python 3.7 [22] using Flask 1.0.2 [23]) sends a token to the client app necessary to query the NASA DB. Figure 2 reports the SpaceViewer homepage with the main features implemented.

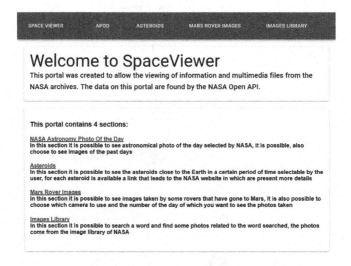

Fig. 2. SpaceViewer ReactJS web-application

4.1   DevOps Toolchain

The DevOps toolchain adopted in the SpaceViewer app development is composed of the following tools

- **Jenkins** [24]: CI/CD and automation
- **GitHub** [25]: version control
- **CodeClimate** [26]: assessment of the quality of the source code
- **Docker** [27]: deployment tool
- **Slack** [28]: team collaboration and management of automatic alerts from Jenkins Jobs
- **Node Package Manager - NPM** [29]: run build, deploy, and automatic test of the ReactJS application

– **SpaceViewer Anomaly Detection System - SVADS** [30]: this tool
   was created specifically for this experimentation, it will be described in the
   Sect. 4.2.

As discussed in Sect. 3, the deployment environments have been implemented as
follows:

– **Development environment**: local in developer machines.
– **Staging environment**: remote server deployed in a Docker container and
   triggered by Jenkins. Whenever a new version of the software is pushed on
   the GitHub repository, the staging environment is automatically rebuilt.
– **Production environment**: remote server in a Docker container triggered
   by Jenkins. Before a build in production, SVADS is triggered.

Fig. 3. SpaceViewer Jenkins Jobs (pipelines).

The Jenkins tool has been set up to manage such deployment environments. Figure 3 depicts the Jenkins Jobs created for the SpaceViewer case
study, thus establishing a Jenkins pipelines [31]. Jenkins jobs are mainly
instantiated for deploying in staging (SpaceViewer_Staging) and production
(SpaceViewer_Production), while additional jobs are created to run the back-end
process (SpaceViewer_Backend) and perform AD before launching the production job (SpaceViewer_AnomalyDetection).

Fig. 4. Staging/production pipelines stages

The pipelines for both the Staging and the Production deployments consist
of the stages shown in Fig. 4. An automatic system in Jenkins triggering the
rebuild in Staging at every Development push on the GitHub repository has been
deployed. As stated above, before deploying in Production, the AD job has to be
performed to detect any possible anomaly or issue in the DevOps development

process. Then, if no anomalies are detected, the Production job is automatically triggered and the SpaceViewer software version is released in Production. In the SpaceViewer DevOps pipeline, Jenkins is also connected through a specific plugin [32] to the messaging software Slack [28]. This way, the team can receive real-time automatic alerts regarding Jenkins jobs outcomes (e.g. failure and success).

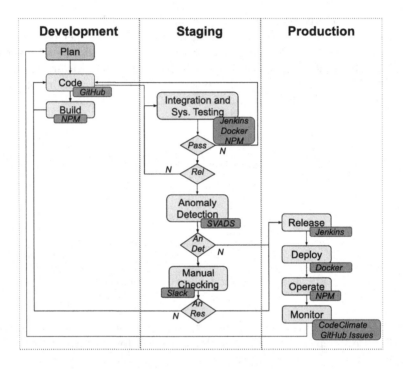

Fig. 5. SpaceViewer DevOps process and toolchain.

The overall SpaceViewer DevOps process and toolchain are shown in Fig. 5, highlighting the different stages of the process and the main tools involved. The swim-lanes identify the three environments taken into account, correlating their activities with the different stages of the process. As stated above, the latter two environments are deployed into two independent containers, while the Development one runs locally into the development/developer machines. The only step that is not directly involved in the SpaceViewer automated DevOps process is the initial Plan one. After planning, coding activities (Code) trigger the DevOps pipeline with specific metrics from the development environment and tools (ReactJS and GitHub), as discussed in the following section. Once implemented, SpaceViewer modules are ready for unit testing and building loop (Build exploiting the NPM tool) and, after that, they are automatically released to the Staging Environment for Integration and System Testing by the Jenkins SpaceViewer_Staging job, triggered by GitHub pushes into the repository. This stage loops until related activities, mainly testing ones, are performed and successfully passed, then triggering the release if ready for that, always orchestrated by the SpaceViewer_Staging job (see Fig. 3). If so, the AD job (SpaceViewer_AnomalyDetection) is launched and run the SVADS tool. In the case of anomaly the control is demanded to the people involved in project for further Manual Checking, automatically informing the team about the anomaly through a Slack chat, the procedure of release is suspended and in production remains the latest version of application. On the other hand, if there are no anomalies, the SpaceViewer_Production job (see Fig. 3) is triggered by SVADS, the production environment is rebuilt and the latest features are integrated (Release, Deploy, Operate, Monitor) through the corresponding tools in the pipeline.

4.2   Space Viewer Anomaly Detection System

The tool for AD - Space Viewer Anomaly Detection System, SVADS in short - has been developed in Python and, in the SpaceViewer case study [30], consists of a script launched by the Jenkins before the delivery in Production of a new version of the software. SVADS retrieves data relating to the last development period (i.e. since the day after the last release, to the day the new release is being executed), generated by the DevOps toolchain and collected by the system meanwhile, to perform AD. The SVADS algorithm is mainly tasked at detecting outliers in the SpaceViewer software release to Production, to avoid potential issues for the software in Production. It implements the Local Outlier Factor (LOF) algorithm [33] by exploiting the *scikit-learn* Python Library [34]. After executing the SVADS algorithm, the system fills the FLAG attribute indicating the presence/absence of an anomaly, and stores latest data in the dataset for future release AD.

Specifically, such a dataset is comprised of performance metrics collected via Rest APIs provided by the DevOps toolchain shown in Fig. 5. The parameters taken into account by the SVADS dataset are reported below and, as discussed above, are related to the modifications done exclusively in the last DevOps cycle:

- Number of lines of code ($NLoC$) added, modified or deleted divided by the number of commits ($NCom$) from GitHub in the Code stage - $P1 = NLoC/NComm$
- Number of builds that failed when executing the Jenkins pipeline to deploy in staging from the Integration and System Testing phase - $P2$
- Number of automatic tests that failed when executing the Jenkins pipeline to deploy in staging from the Integration and System Testing phase - $P3$
- Number of deliveries that failed when executing the Jenkins pipeline to deploy in staging from the Integration and System Testing phase - $P4$
- Number of issues reported by CodeClimate from the Code and Monitor phases - $P5$
- Number of issues reported in GitHub from Operation and Monitor phases - $P6$

Each entry in the dataset corresponds to a software release and the parameters $P1 - P6$ are the number of occurrences of related events since the last release. They are therefore reset by any new release. The values of such attributes are normalized according to the number of working days elapsed since the last release to mitigate the effects of longer periods of maintenance. It also reflects the good practice of performing regular "small" commits in contrast to doing few but substantial commits. The following attributes capturing meta-data of each entry are also added to the dataset:

- A unique identifier - ID
- The date of the release, i.e. when the parameter values are collected and written into the dataset - $DATE$

Some of the above DevOps toolchain metrics are often used to also support better decision-making regarding potential risks in a software release. For example, a high number of failed builds, automated tests and deliveries in Staging might be an indicator that a specific release requires additional management effort. It is trustworthy mentioning that such a dataset can also enable the observation of complex patterns involving different parameters related to the occurrence of software defects, errors or faults.

It is important to point out that the SVADS tool was created for this case study, but it can be used for any project that has a DevOps Toolchain like the one used in this study.

5   Experiments, Results and Discussion

The experimentation of the proposed approach for the DevOps toolchain in the SpaceViewer case study started in early July 2019 and took approximately one month. In this experimentation, data entries conforming the format defined in Sect. 4.2 were added to the SpaceViewer dataset at the moment of every software release in production by the SVADS tool. Table 1 reports the full dataset describing 25 subsequent releases between 4th of July and 8th of August, uniquely identified by the attribute ID.

Firstly, an initial dataset was generated to attend the requirement of a considerable quantity of observations to perform an unsupervised AD method. In this study, data concerning software releases were collected for ten days without being processed by the SVADS module. After this initial period, the AD system was then activated, thus starting operating on the SpaceViewer DevOps process, as shown in Fig. 5. For each new release, the LOF algorithm was trained with the dataset comprising previous releases and the current candidate release. Finally, the data describing the last release is appended to the dataset and available for future use. Figure 6 illustrates the output from the LOF model after the 25th release, i.e. the outlier scores for each observation. It should be noted that only two features are displayed in this graph (tests failed and commits), but in the elaboration performed during the experimentation, the algorithm used all the features.

Table 1. The SpaceViewer dataset.

P1	P2	P3	P4	P5	P6	ID	DATE
22.57	0.04	0.06	0.08	0	0	1	7/4/2019
59	2	3	5	0	1	2	7/5/2019
87	1	4	6	0	1	3	7/6/2019
13	1	3	6	0	0	4	7/7/2019
130	3	4	5	1	0	5	7/8/2019
135	3	6	8	3	0	6	7/9/2019
27	2	4	7	6	0	7	7/10/2019
10	2	4	6	4	0	8	7/11/2019
40	0	1	3	6	0	9	7/12/2019
21	3	5	6	6	0	10	7/13/2019
33	3	5	6	6	0	11	7/14/2019
65	6	8	10	8	0	12	7/15/2019
90	3	4	6	8	0	13	7/16/2019
114	6	7	10	13	0	14	7/17/2019
255	5	9	9	12	0	15	7/18/2019
44	3	4	5	13	0	16	7/19/2019
123	4	6	8	17	0	17	7/22/2019
171	5	7	8	23	0	18	7/24/2019
100	3	4	5	23	0	19	7/25/2019
42	1	5	6	23	0	20	7/26/2019
94	1	3	4	8	0	21	7/29/2019
243	29	30	31	13	0	22	7/30/2019
28	5	6	8	15	0	23	7/31/2019
244	45	48	50	0	0	24	8/1/2019
35	6	7	8	0	0	25	8/8/2019

Figure 6 enables the observation of several insights into the integration of AD into DevOps. First, SVADS supports the identification of data entries, i.e. software releases, that clearly fails to conform expected patterns in data. For example, IDs 15, 22 and 24 have higher outlier scores and easily distinguished from their peers. Second, SVADS requires some degree of human interference for labelling data with edging feature values. For example, the release with ID in Fig. 6 is closer to most of the releases than to the clearly identified anomalies. In larger projects in the real-world, SVADS would flag such releases as requiring further assessment by the project manager. Finally, the collection and analysis of such data enable the observation of patterns between features such as lines of codes, stages of development and occurrences of anomalies. In the implemented

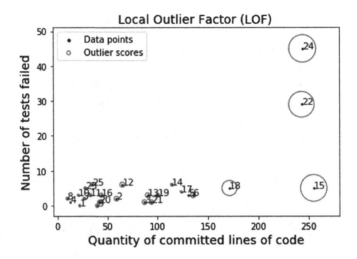

Fig. 6. Outlier scores for the dataset using LOF for anomaly detection on the full SpaceViewer dataset.

case study, for example, anomaly releases have been mostly identified by higher code volumes or Staging failures.

An interesting matter that deserves further consideration is whether an unsupervised AD (outlier detection) method should be employed instead of supervised AD (novelty detection). For the first case, at the moment of a new release, the AD model is trained with the entire dataset and outlier scores above a specified threshold indicate anomalies. In the second method, it is assumed that there is the availability of a significant number of software releases. Moreover, it is also necessary that each release has been labeled by a specialist (e.g. the project manager) whether it is an anomaly. Hence, the latter method can be noticed as closer to a policy-based approach for AD.

The implemented method was validated against other offline statistical and machine learning techniques. Several statistical methods can be utilised for identifying outliers, including the popular k-nearest neighbors and LOF. Moreover, some AD models outperform others depending on the characteristics of the data and the problem domain. Figure 6 illustrates four different AD models trained using the generated dataset.

These outcomes from the models in Fig. 7 reinforce the usefulness of the proposed SVADS approach. In fact, an ensemble of AD models enables a more precise and undisputed decision regarding software releases that are likely to result in an error in the production environment. Finally, some AD models can provide decision boundaries for classifying anomalies which enable one to gain insights regarding which features that are more likely yo result in a risk to the ongoing project.

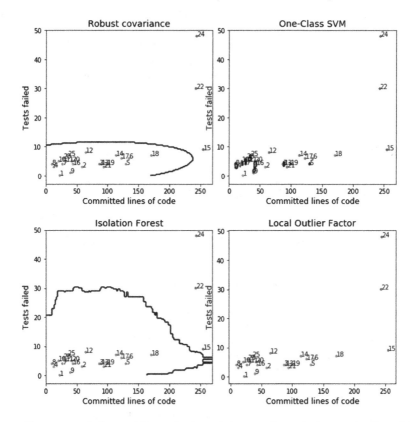

Fig. 7. Comparing different AD methods and decision boundaries on the SpaceViewer Dataset.

6   Conclusions

DevOps is becoming an increasingly adopted approach in software development, gaining attention from both industry and academia as per the rising number of projects, conferences, and training programs in this field [3, 35]. A DevOps toolchain typically generates a large amount of data that enables the extraction of information regarding the status and progress of the addressing project. In this paper, we described a prototypical implementation of a system for detecting anomalies in software release adopting DevOps development process.

Despite the small number of functionalities implemented in our SpaceViewer case study, this paper demonstrates the feasibility of the proposed workflow. Obtained results and their comparison against powerful solution integrating several AD models proves the validity of the proposed approach and its effectiveness as a tool for supporting decision-making and precise identification of potentially harmful candidate releases in the production. Furthermore, a dataset on AD for software release in the DevOps toolchain has been generated and made publicly available for the community.

Future work will approach the stabilization of the current implementation and broader experimentation in real-world production environments and an more extensive number of features, which has been scarcely reported in the literature. Moreover, future research will approach a broader discussion on how to consider the fluctuation of feature values can indicate anomalies through the project life-cycle.

References

1. Wasserman, A.I.: Modern software development methodologies and their environments. Comput. Phys. Commun. **38**(2), 119–134 (1985)
2. Bass, L., Weber, I., Zhu, L.: DevOps: A Software Architect's Perspective, 1st edn. Addison-Wesley Professional, Boston (2015)
3. Bruel, J.-M., Mazzara, M., Meyer, B. (eds.): DEVOPS 2018. LNCS, vol. 11350. Springer, Cham (2019). https://doi.org/10.1007/978-3-030-06019-0
4. Hopcroft, J.E., Motwani, R., Ullman, J.D.: Introduction to Automata Theory, Languages, and Computation, 3rd edn. Pearson International Edition, Addison-Wesley, Boston (2007)
5. Kersten, M.: A cambrian explosion of devops tools. IEEE Softw. **35**, 14–17 (2018)
6. Protasov, S., Khan, A.M., Sozykin, K., Ahmad, M.: Using deep features for video scene detection and annotation. SIViP **12**, 991–999 (2018)
7. Kontogiannis, K., et al.: 2nd workshop on DevOps and software analytics for continuous engineering and improvement. In: Proceedings of the 28th Annual International Conference on Computer Science and Software Engineering, CASCON 2018, Riverton, NJ, USA, pp. 369–370. IBM Corp (2018)
8. Akinsanya, B., et al.: Machine learning and value generation in software development: a survey. In: Software Testing, Machine Learning and Complex Process Analysis (TMPA 2019), pp. 1–10. Springer International Publishing (2019, forthcoming)
9. Li, Z., Dang, Y.: AIOps: Challenges and Experiences in Azure. USENIX Association, Santa Clara (2019)
10. Yang, Y., Falessi, D., Menzies, T., Hihn, J.: Actionable analytics for software engineering. IEEE Softw. **35**, 51–53 (2018)
11. Hoffman, J.: How AIOps Supports a DevOps World. https://thenewstack.io/how-aiops-supports-a-devops-world/
12. Snyder, B., Curtis, B.: Using analytics to guide improvement during an Agile-DevOps transformation. IEEE Softw. **35**, 78–83 (2018)
13. Guo, C., Wang, H., Dai, H., Cheng, S., Wang, T.: Fraud risk monitoring system for e-banking transactions. In: 2018 IEEE 16th Intl Conf on Dependable, Autonomic and Secure Computing, 16th Intl Conf on Pervasive Intelligence and Computing, 4th Intl Conf on Big Data Intelligence and Computing and Cyber Science and Technology Congress (DASC/PiCom/DataCom/CyberSciTech), pp. 100–105, August 2018
14. Chen, P., Yang, S., McCann, J.A.: Distributed real-time anomaly detection in networked industrial sensing systems. IEEE Trans. Industr. Electron. **62**, 3832–3842 (2015)
15. Chandola, V., Banerjee, A., Kumar, V.: Anomaly Detection, pp. 1–15. Springer, Boston (2016). https://doi.org/10.1007/978-1-4899-7502-7

16. Sun, D., Fu, M., Zhu, L., Li, G., Lu, Q.: Non-intrusive anomaly detection with streaming performance metrics and logs for devops in public clouds: a case study in aws. IEEE Trans. Emerg. Top. Comput. **4**, 278–289 (2016)
17. Hodge, V.J., Austin, J.: A survey of outlier detection methodologies. Artif. Intell. Rev. **22**, 85–126 (2004)
18. Capizzi, A.: SpaceViewer - a ReactJS portal for NASA Open API consultation. https://github.com/antoniocapizzi95/SpaceViewer/
19. Facebook: ReactJS - A JavaScript library for building user interfaces. https://reactjs.org/
20. NASA: NASA Open API. https://api.nasa.gov/
21. Capizzi, A.: SpaceViewer - little back end. https://github.com/antoniocapizzi95/SpaceViewer_BE/
22. P. S. Foundation: Python - Programming Language. https://www.python.org/
23. T. P. Projects: Flask is a lightweight WSGI web application framework. https://palletsprojects.com/p/flask/
24. Kawaguchi, K.: Jenkins - an open source automation server which enables developers around the world to reliably build, test, and deploy their software. https://jenkins.io/
25. Preston-Werner, S.C.P.J.H.T., Wanstrath, C.: GitHub - The world's leading software development platform. https://github.com/
26. CodeClimate: CodeClimate Quality. https://codeclimate.com/quality/
27. Docker, I.: Docker - Build, Share, and Run Any App, Anywhere. https://www.docker.com/
28. S. Technologies: Slack is where work flows. It's where the people you need, the information you share, and the tools you use come together to get things done. https://slack.com/
29. Schlueter, K.M.I.Z., Turner, R.: Node Package Manager. https://www.npmjs.com/
30. Capizzi, A.: Anomaly Detection System used for SpaceViewer DevOps Toolchain. https://github.com/antoniocapizzi95/SpaceViewer_ADS/
31. Kawaguchi, K.: Jenkins Pipeline Documentation. https://jenkins.io/doc/book/pipeline/
32. Jacomb, T.: Slack Notification Plugin for Jenkins. https://plugins.jenkins.io/slack
33. scikit learn: Novelty detection with Local Outlier Factor (LOF). https://scikit-learn.org/stable/auto_examples/neighbors/plot_lof_novelty_detection.html/
34. Pedregosa, F., et al.: Scikit-learn: machine learning in Python. J. Mach. Learn. Res. **12**, 2825–2830 (2011)
35. Mazzara, M., Naumchev, A., Safina, L., Sillitti, A., Urysov, K.: Teaching DevOps in corporate environments. In: Bruel, J.-M., Mazzara, M., Meyer, B. (eds.) DEVOPS 2018. LNCS, vol. 11350, pp. 100–111. Springer, Cham (2019). https://doi.org/10.1007/978-3-030-06019-0_8

From DevOps to DevDataOps: Data Management in DevOps Processes

Antonio Capizzi[1], Salvatore Distefano[1], and Manuel Mazzara[2(✉)]

[1] University of Messina, Messina, Italy
[2] Innopolis University, Innopolis, Respublika Tatarstan, Russian Federation
m.mazzara@innopolis.ru

Abstract. DevOps is a quite effective approach for managing software development and operation, as confirmed by plenty of success stories in real applications and case studies. DevOps is now becoming the mainstream solution adopted by the software industry in development, able to reduce the time to market and costs while improving quality and ensuring evolvability and adaptability of the resulting software architecture. Among the aspects to take into account in a DevOps process, data is assuming strategic importance, since it allows to gain insights from the operation directly into the development, the main objective of a DevOps approach. Data can be therefore considered as the fuel of the DevOps process, requiring proper solutions for its management. Based on the amount of data generated, its variety, velocity, variability, value and other relevant features, DevOps data management can be mainly framed into the BigData category. This allows exploiting BigData solutions for the management of DevOps data generated throughout the process, including artefacts, code, documentation, logs and so on. This paper aims at investigating data management in DevOps processes, identifying related issues, challenges and potential solutions taken from the BigData world as well as from new trends adopting and adapting DevOps approaches in data management, i.e. DataOps.

1 Introduction

DevOps [1,2] is an approach for software development and (IT) system operation combining best practices from both such domains to improve the overall quality of the software-system while reducing costs and shortening time-to-market. Its effectiveness is demonstrated by the quite widely adoption of DevOps approaches in business contexts, where there is a big demand of specific professionals such as DevOps engineers as well as data scientists, just partially, minimally covered by current offer.

The DevOps philosophy can be generalized as a way, a good practice for improving a generic product or service development and operation, by connecting these through a feedback from operation to development. An important feature of DevOps is the automation of such a process: *continuous delivery* (CD)

© Springer Nature Switzerland AG 2020
J.-M. Bruel et al. (Eds.): DEVOPS 2019, LNCS 12055, pp. 52–62, 2020.
https://doi.org/10.1007/978-3-030-39306-9_4

enables organizations to deliver new features quickly and incrementally by implementing a flow of changes into the production via an automated "assembly line" - the *continuous delivery pipeline*. This is coupled with *continuous integration* (CI) that aims at automating the software/product integration process of codes, modules and parts, thus identifying a CI/CD pipeline.

The tools adopted to implement this high degree of automation in the DevOps process identifies a *toolchain*. DevOps toolchain tools are usually encapsulated into different, independent containers deployed into physical or virtual servers (typically on Cloud), and then managed by specific scripts and/or tools (e.g. Jenkins), able to orchestrate and coordinate them automatically.

Such DevOps principles have been therefore either specialized to some specific software/application domains (security - SecOps, SecDevOps, DevSecOps [3], system administration - SysOps [4], Web - WebOps or WebDevOps [5]) or even adopted, rethought and adapted in other contexts such as artificial intelligence (AIOps [6]) and machine learning (MLOps, DeepOps [7]), and data management (DataOps [8]). The latter, DataOps, aims at mainly organizing data management according to DevOps principles and best practices. To this end, DataOps introduces the concept of *dataflow pipeline* and toolchain, to be deployed in containerized (Cloud) environment providing feedback on performance and QoS of the overall data management process, used to real-time tune the pipeline to actual operational needs and requirements.

As discussed above, the DevOps pipeline automation involves in the toolchain different tools, each continuously generating messages, logs and data including artifacts. To achieve DevOps aims and goals, such data has to be properly managed, collected, processed and stored to provide insights from operations to the development stages. DevOps data management could therefore be quite challenging, due to the large amount of data to be considered as well as its variety, variability and similar metrics usually identified as V properties in the BigData community, to which we have to refer to. BigData approaches, indeed, could be a good solution to consider in the management of a DevOps process and toolchain.

In light of these considerations, in this paper we focus on DevOps data management, proposing to adopt BigData approaches and solutions. More specifically, the main goal of this paper is to explore the convergence between DevOps and DataOps approaches, defining a possible (big)dataflow pipeline for DevOps processes and toolchains and organizing it following a DataOps process, towards DevDataOps. This way, we investigate on the adoption of DataOps, mainly implementing a BigData pipeline and toolchain, in DevOps contexts, i.e. for improving the development and operation of a software architecture.

To this extent, Sect. 2 describes the DevOps and DataOps processes and toolchains. Section 3 discusses about DevOps artifacts and data in the BigData context. Then, Sect. 4 proposes a DevOps (big) dataflow pipeline and related implementation in the DataOps philosophy. Section 5 summarises the key aspects of the proposed approach and future work.

2   DevOps and DataOps

2.1   The DevOps Process and Toolchain

DevOps [1] consists of a set of practices to promote collaboration between the developers, IT professionals (in particular sysadmin, i.e. who works on IT operations) and quality assurance personnel. DevOps is implemented via a set of software tools [2] that enable the management of an environment in which software can be built, tested and released quickly, frequently, and a more reliable manner. In addition to *continuous delivery* (CD), which aims at developing "small" software releases in reasonably short cycles, *continuous integration* (CI) stands as a key concept in DevOps approaches. A typical example of CI consists of continuously integrating changes made by developers into a repository, then a project build is automatically executed, and if the build the modifications are integrated into the code through CD and published in the production environment.

A DevOps process is usually composed of different stages and phases, which can be periodically reiterated for proper development and operation of the software architecture, in an evolutionary fashion able to caught new requirements, features and behaviors arising from operation. This way, a DevOps process belongs to the category of agile process, not plan driver, where the number of development cycle is unknown a-priori. Consequently, the amount of data generated by a DevOps process is usually unpredictable and could be really high. There is no standard definition of a DevOps process, but several different versions and implementations have been provided by the related community. Among them, main DevOps stages can be summarized below.

- *Plan*: activity planning and task scheduling for the current release. This step is usually dealt with by project managers in collaboration with the team and exploiting project management tools such as Trello, Asana, Clarizen, Jira, Azure DevOps, to name a few.
- *Code*: code development and code review. Developers are the most closely involved in this activity using IDE and tools for source code management such as GitHub, Artfactory, CodeClimate, etc.
- *Build*: is when source code is converted into a stand-alone form that can be run on a computer system. In this activity are involved various professional figures, mainly developers and sysadmins. The tools used in this phase are: CI tools (for example Jenkins, TravisCI), build tools (for example Maven) etc.
- *Test*: in this phase the software is tested by the quality assurance staff using tools for (automatic) testing and similar. Examples of such kind of tools are JUnit, Jmeter, Selenium, etc.
- *Release*: triggered when a new version of software is ready to be released to end users. In this activity, various professionals of the development team are involved, primarily developers and sysadmins. Release management tools (such as Spinnaker) or similar support such an activity.

- *Deploy*: it deals with the installation and execution of the new software release in the production environment and infrastructure. At this stage, the collaboration between developers and syadmins is mandatory. The tools used for deployment depend on the target infrastructure (physical or virtual nodes, Cloud, etc.) as well as on the adopted system software (OS, virtualization, containerization, middleware, compilers, libraries), thus identifying a wide set of possible options for deployment management (VmWare, Virtualbox, Docker, LXD, Kubertenes, AWS CodeDeploy, ElasticBox etc.).
- *Operate*: is the activity that maintains and adapts the infrastructure in which the software is running. This activity is mainly driven by sysadmins, supported by configuration management tools (such as Ansible, Puppet, Chef), security tools (such as Sonarqube, Fortify SCA, Veracode), database management tools (such as Flyway, MongoDB), recovery tools (PowerShell, Ravello), etc.
- *Monitor*: in this activity the software in production is monitored by mainly sysadmins, operators and others managing the project. The tools used are: tools that monitor the performance of the service, tools that analyze the logs (for example Logstash, Nagios, Zabbix), tools that analyze the end user experience (Zenoss).

One of the main objectives of DevOps is to mitigate issues in production, which is done by reducing the gap among development and testing environments to the production one. To this purpose, several tools as the one mentioned above are usually used and combined into a set identified as the "DevOps Toolchain", which can be considered as a scaffold built around the development project. To compose a Toolchain, in general, there are no fixed rules, it is necessary to follow the DevOps principles and best practices to choose the tools according to the project characteristics. For a small project 3 or 4 tools might be enough, while in a larger project 10 or more tools might be necessary. A minimal (CI/CD) DevOps toolchain might include, at least, some version control tool (e.g. Git), automation tools (e.g. Jenkins), package managers (e.g. NPM) and test tools (e.g. JUnit). DevOps infrastructures are typically fully implemented on Cloud platforms. It is a good practice in DevOps to build the entire infrastructure using containers to minimize portability issues. For that, containerization technologies such as Docker, LXD or similar are adopted, sometimes coupled by tools for containers orchestration (e.g. Kubernetes or Swarm).

2.2 DataOps

DataOps is a new approach that aims to improve quality and responsiveness of data analytics life-cycle [8–10]. This approach is based on DevOps rules, in particular DataOps aims to bring DevOps benefits to data analytics, adopting Agile rules and Lean concepts. When the volume of data is larger and larger, the purpose of DataOps is to improve the life cycle of analytics by taking advantage of DevOps principles such as communication between teams (data scientists, ETL, analysts, etc.), cooperation, automation, integration, etc. To achieve this it is necessary to apply a set of human practices and dedicated tools. With DataOps a new professional figure called "DataOps Engineer" was born, to deal with the automation and orchestration of the process. A large DataOps community issued a Manifesto[1] that contains 18 rules, the mission and best practices to apply DataOps. However, this is the most concrete activity behind DataOps, that is still mainly a set of rules, concepts and ideas to be applied to data management. There is, indeed, a lack of examples, dataflow pipelines, toolchians and standard process for DataOps.

However, despite the DataOps approach is still mainly abstract, it can be mostly summarized with the DataOps principles detailed in the Manifesto, some implementations of the DataOps idea start to be defined and fixed. For example, a DataOps process can be broadly organized into three steps[2]:

- *Build* - In this step, the data is taken from a source point (e.g. a database, a log file, etc.), transformed by applying one or more actions, and then written to a destination point. The flow executed by these actions is called "dataflow or DataOps pipeline". In the Build phase you can also have multiple pipelines connected to each other.
- *Execute* - at this stage the build pipelines are put into production in a running environment e.g. clusters, datacenters, Clouds. It is important, for a company adopting DataOps, to be able to use the existing infrastructure to run the pipeline, in order to avoid incurring in additional costs.
- *Operate* - When this step is reached, the system is running on an environment, it is necessary to monitor it and react to any change (for example when larger volumes of data arrive and it is required to scale the infrastructure to cope with burst). One approach used in DataOps (borrowed from Agile) is to start with small instances and increase their resources when the demand grows.

3   DevOps Data

An outcome from the complex pipeline involved in a DevOps project is the generation of a large amount of data, considering the process artefacts and the log files generated in each stage. Examples of activities that generate considerable data on the project cycle include changes made by developers; the application building and its corresponding entries on the compilation and dependencies of the project; the execution of automatic tests; software usage by end-users after release into the production. Furthermore, the number of cycle of a DevOps process is usually unknown, and typically lasting years, so reaching hundreds, or even thousands of releases each generating a considerable amount of data that should be adequately preserved and managed for gaining insights and the process.

Artifacts and data produced in a DevOps process are quite large and widely different. These can include software artifacts (code, documentation, test, executable, prototypes) and other information generated by the DevOps toolchain

---

[1] https://www.dataopsmanifesto.org/.

[2] https://dzone.com/articles/dataops-applying-devops-to-data-continuous-dataflo.

(logs, configuration files, traces,...). More specifically, based on the above DevOps reference process, the data associated to each stage is reported below.

- *Plan*: planning artifacts and data are software design blueprint, requirement documentations (UML or similar, if any), project environment information including user stories, tasks, activities, backlog, and statistics.
- *Code*: development artifacts include codes, versions, prototypes and related info such as lines of code, version differences and relevant parameters.
- *Build*: mainly executable files, packages, logs and metrics that contain information about builds and may indicate compilation errors, warnings, successes, failures etc.
- *Test*: code for automatic tests, logs from automatic test tools that indicates unit tests failed or passed, system tests results, or documentation written by Quality Assurance staff about verification on software in development.
- *Release*: documentation about releases (for example new features introduced), new final version of executable files or packages, logs and metrics from release orchestration tools.
- *Deploy*: configuration files, scripts and logs originating from Deploy tools that may contain errors or warnings.
- *Operate*: data generated by the software, logs from the tools involved in this stage and system logs from (physical or virtual) servers.
- *Monitor*: logs, metrics and other information from monitoring tools, the data retrieved in this phase is important to obtain a feedback from users.

It could be worth to invest in a data management system for a DevOps process, where the high volume of generated data is not only properly collected and stored but also managed, filtered, aggregated and possibly made available for further processing, to gain insights on the overall process to achieve essential DevOps aims and goals. This calls for proper data management techniques, providing mechanisms for collection, aggregation, storage filtering, aggregation, fusion, archival, mining and feature extraction, local and global analytics preferably in an automated manner [11], to improve the DevOps pipeline [12]. For example, historical data can be analyzed to estimate a probabilistic measure of the success of a new release, or for identifying potential source of bugs (root-cause analysis) or even to prevent them.

From a data/information-oriented perspective therefore, a DevOps process can be considered as a data-intensive process, in the sense that it could generate large amount of data. To this purpose, DevOps data management issues and challenges can be framed into the BigData context. Considering the reference DevOps process and toolchain described in Sect. 2.1, it could be interesting to characterize such a process in BigData terms. To this purpose, we refer to well-known and widely used Bigdata metrics: the "Vs". BigData V properties are usually used in the community to categorize an application, and range in number from original 3 (Volume, Velocity, Variety) to 10 or even more. Shortly, *volume* is probably the best known characteristic of big data, quantifying the amount of data generated; *velocity* refers to the speed at which data is being generated, produced, created, or refreshed; *variety* is related to the "structured-ness" of data: we don't only have to handle structured data (logs, traces, DB) but also semistructured and mostly unstructured data (images, multimedia files, social media updates) as well; *variability* refers to inconsistencies in the data, to the multitude of data dimensions resulting from multiple disparate data types and sources and to the inconsistent speed at which big data is loaded into DB; *veracity* is the confidence or trust in the data, mainly referring to the prove-nance or reliability of the data source, its context, and how meaningful it is to the analysis based on it; *validity* refers to how accurate and correct the data is for its intended use; *vulnerability* is concerned with big data security, privacy and confidentiality; *volatility* refers to data "lifetime", i.e. the amount of time needed for data to be considered irrelevant, historic, or not useful any longer; *visualiza-tion* faces technical challenges due to limitations of in-memory technology and poor scalability, functionality, and response time to represent big data (billion data points) such as data clustering or using tree maps, sunbursts, parallel coor-dinates, circular network diagrams, or cone trees; *value* is the property to be derived from the data through processing and analytics. In the DevOps context, the process data value is exploited to support decision making in development. This way, Table 1 reports the characterization of a DevOps pipeline from a Big-Data perspective, expressed in terms of V metric values ranges for a "mid-size" DevOps reference process.

Table 1. DevOps project Bigdata Vs.

Stage/Vs	Volume	Velocity	Variety	Variability	Veracity	Validity	Vulnerability	Volatility	Visualization	Value
Plan	10 KB–1 GB	Week	UnStr.	Medium/High	High	Low	Low	Week/Days	Poor	High
Code	1–100 MB	Hours	SemiStr.	High	High	High	Medium	Hours	Poor	High
Build	1–10 GB	Hours	SemiStr	Medium	Low	Low	Medium	Hours	High	High
Test	10 KB–1 GB	Minutes	Str	Medium	High	High	Medium	Days	High	Medium
Release	1–10 GB	Week	UnStr	High	Medium	Medium	Medium	Week/Month	Medium	High
Deploy	1–100 MB	Week	UnStr	High	Medium	Medium	Medium	Week/Month	Medium	High
Operate	10 KB–1 GB	Hours	SemiStr	High	High	High	Medium	Hours	Medium	High
Monitor	10 KB–1 GB	Seconds/Minutes	SemiStr	High	High	High	High	Hours	High	High

4   DevDataOps

4.1   DevOps Dataflow Pipeline

The data generated by a DevOps pipeline is therefore quite complex and hetero-geneous, and consequently quite hard to manage and maintain [13]. The DevOps data life-cycle and workflow can be decomposed into different stages and steps identifying the dataflow pipeline shown in Fig. 1. This could be considered as

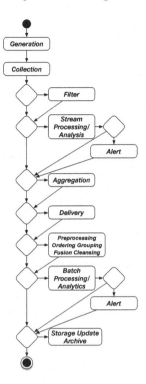

Fig. 1. DevOps dataflow pipeline

a quite generic DataOps pipeline that can be generally applied to any DevOps process, after adaptation, represented in Fig. 1 by the conditional diamonds modeling the presence or absence of a specific step in the DevOps dataflow-DataOps pipeline.

- **Generation**: Each module of the DevOps pipeline generates a log stream reporting its operation through a specific monitoring process.
- **Collection**: The generated logs are collected, reordered according to their timestamps, and grouped altogether to provide a snapshot of the whole DevOps process for each time interval.
- **Filtering**: Logs are then filtered to remove outliers, replicas, or observations that may contain errors or are undesirable for analysis. Logs filters are usually based on temporal statistics, i.e. based on previously logs average or similar statistical moments.
- **Stream processing, analysis and alerting**: The processing of single logs streams is locally performed in nearly real-time to identify potential flaws, defects or errors in a particular DevOps pipeline stage. In such cases, warning, error messages or activities are triggered by the alerting tool.

- **Aggregation**: The logs are aggregated and expressed in a summary form for statistical analysis. The main goal of the aggregation is to compress the volume of data.
- **Delivery**: The logs are made available to end-users and applications. This data is typically transmitted through networks using related protocols to physical and virtual servers.
- **Preprocessing, ordering, grouping, cleansing, and fusion**: The logs are reordered according to their timestamp and grouped to provide a snapshot of the DevOps process at each time interval. Next, the logs have to be cleaned, that is, having redundancies removed and being integrated with different sources into a unified schema before storage. The schema integration has to provide an abstract definition of a consistent way to access the logs without having to customize access for each log source format. Still during the preprocessing stage, logs undergo through a fusion process aiming to integrate multiple sources to produce a more consistent and accurate information.
- **Storage, update and archiving**: This phase aims the efficient storage and organization as well as a continuous update of logs as they become available. Archiving refers to the long-term offline storage of logs. The core of the centralized storage is the deployment of structures that adapt to the various data types and the frequency of the capture (e.g. relational database management systems).
- **Processing and analytics**: Ongoing retrieval and analysis operations on stored and archived logs, mainly offline for root cause analysis, to identify any correlation among stages, predict behaviors and support decisions. Analytics is the discovery, interpretation, and communication of meaningful patterns in data in the logs and can be performed at different levels with different objectives: *descriptive* (what happened), *diagnostic* (why something happened), *predictive* (what is likely to happen) and *prescriptive* (what action to take).

4.2   DataOps Implementation

The DevOps dataflow pipeline should be then implemented according to a DataOps approach, as reported below

Build - To implement the DevOps dataflow pipeline of Fig. 1 in a DataOps fashion, following the process described in Sect. 2.2, we have to start with building the toolchain, thus identifying the tools associated with each of the pipeline step. In this case, the real benefit of adopting BigData solutions in DataOps is clearly manifested: this way, the DevOps dataflow pipeline of Fig. 1 can be just considered as a BigData workflow to be deployed exploiting a tool among the plethora available to manage BigData workflow (Hadoop, Spark, Storm, Flink, Samza, NiFi, Kafka, NodRed, Crosser.io, to name but a few). Mainly belonging to the Apache (big) family, they allows to define and manage BigData workflows composed of different tasks or processes, highly customizable and configurable, then linked through specific mechanisms and tools able to enforce the workflow topology, or even to further parallelize and optimize it.

Execute - Once built as a BigData workflow, the DataOps toolchain needs to be deployed and executed. At this stage, therefore, automation tools such as Jenkins and deployment tools such as Docker or Jupiter could be used to support and further automate the BigData one, by for example containerising tasks or connecting them with tools (monitoring) external to the BigData workflow. Usually, the target deployment infrastructure for a DataOps toolchain is the Cloud, public as Microsoft Azure and Amazon EC2, or private such as those managed locally by OpenStack or similar middleware.

Operate - The operation stage is mainly tasked at providing a feedback on the DataOps toolchain to the DataOps engineers that have to tune it based on this feedback. Both the process and the underlying infrastructure running the toolchains have to be monitored. Metric of interest to be benchmarked in this case could be system parameters (CPU, memory, storage utilization), process non functional properties (response time, reliability, availability, energy consumption), or even specific V properties (volume, velocity, variety, etc, see Sect. 3) In this step, tools for monitoring such as Prometheus or Nagios, and for managing the infrastructure such as Chef, Puppet etc. can be exploited.

5   Conclusions

DevOps is a modern approach to software development aiming at accelerating the build lifecycle via automation. Google, Amazon and many other companies can now release software multiple times per day making the old concept of "release" obsolete. Data is at the centre of all the DevOps process and requires BigData solutions to be managed. Despite of the growing importance of DevOps practices in software development, management of the data generated by the toolchain is still undervalued, if not entirely neglected.

In this paper we investigated this cutting-edge aspect of software development identifying related issues, challenges and potential solutions. Solutions do not need to be entirely new since large literature has been already published in the field of BigData. This emerging field of research is often referred to as *DataOps*. While DevOps was created to serve the needs of software developers, DataOps users are often data scientists or analysts.

The current work has just started scratching the surface of such a complex subject, and in the limited space could not explore all the detailed aspects of analytics. One of the project on which our team is working at the moment is the analysis of data generated by the DevOps toolchain in order to identify anomalies in the incoming releases [14]. The same idea can be applied to Microservices monitoring, and this is exactly our next goal towards NoOps.

References

1. Bass, L., Weber, I., Zhu, L.: DevOps: A Software Architect's Perspective, 1st edn. Addison-Wesley Professional, Reading (2015)

2. Kersten, M.: A cambrian explosion of DevOps tools. IEEE Softw. **35**, 14–17 (2018)
3. Mohan, V., Othmane, L.B.: SecDEVOps: is it a marketing buzzword?-mapping research on security in DevOps. In: 2016 11th International Conference on Availability, Reliability and Security (ARES), pp. 542–547. IEEE (2016)
4. Burgess, E., et al.: DevOps the future of sysadmin? vol. 38, no. 2 (2013). Usenix.org login
5. Sacks, M.: DevOps principles for successful web sites. In: Sacks, M. (ed.) Pro Website Development and Operations. Apress, Berkeley (2012). https://doi.org/10.1007/978-1-4302-3970-3_1
6. Hoffman, J.: How AIOps supports a DevOps world. https://thenewstack.io/how-aiops-supports-a-devops-world/
7. Lim, J., Lee, H., Won, Y., Yeon, H.: MLOP lifecycle scheme for vision-based inspection process in manufacturing. In: 2019 USENIX Conference on Operational Machine Learning (OpML 2019), pp. 9–11 (2019)
8. Khalajzadeh, H., Abdelrazek, M., Grundy, J., Hosking, J., He, Q.: A survey of current end-user data analytics tool support. In: 2018 IEEE International Congress on Big Data (BigData Congress), pp. 41–48. IEEE (2018)
9. Ereth, J.: DataOps - towards a definition, November 2018
10. Kale, V.: Big Data Computing: A Guide for Business and Technology Managers. Chapman and Hall/CRC, Boca Raton (2016)
11. Protasov, S., Khan, A.M., Sozykin, K., Ahmad, M.: Using deep features for video scene detection and annotation. Signal, Image Video Process. **12**, 991–999 (2018)
12. Kontogiannis, K., et al.: 2nd workshop on DevOps and software analytics for continuous engineering and improvement. In: Proceedings of the 28th Annual International Conference on Computer Science and Software Engineering, CASCON 2018, Riverton, NJ, USA, pp. 369–370, IBM Corp. (2018)
13. Chen, B.: Improving the software logging practices in DevOps. In: 2019 IEEE/ACM 41st International Conference on Software Engineering: Companion Proceedings (ICSE-Companion), pp. 194–197, May 2019
14. Capizzi, A., Distefano, S., Bobrov, E., Araújo, L.J.P., Mazzara, M., Ahmad, M.: Anomaly detection in DevOps toolchain. In: Bruel, J.-M., et al. (eds.) DEVOPS 2019, LNCS, vol. 12055, pp. 37–51 (2019)

Exploiting Agile Practices to Teach Computational Thinking

Paolo Ciancarini[1,2(✉)], Marcello Missiroli[1], and Daniel Russo[3]

[1] DISI, University of Bologna, Bologna, Italy
`paolo.ciancarini@unibo.it`
[2] Innopolis University, Innopolis, Russian Federation
[3] Department of Computer Science, Aalborg University, Aalborg, Denmark

Abstract. Computational Thinking has been introduced as a fundamental skill to acquire, just like basic skills like reading, writing, and numeracy. The reason is that Computational Thinking is one of the most important skills for XXI century citizens, in particular for programmers and scientists at large. Currently, Computer Science teaching practices focus on individual programming and Computational Thinking first, and only later address students to work in teams. We study how Computational Thinking can be enhanced with social skills and teaming practices, aiming at training our students in Computational Thinking exploiting Agile values and practices. Based on prior studies, we describe and compare the four traditional software development learning approaches: solo programmer, pair programmers, self-organized teams, and directed teams. Such approaches have been explored in a number of teaching experiments, involving a significant number of students, over several years. Accordingly, we induced a model that we call Cooperative Thinking, based on such previous evidence and grounded in literature. This paper provides a research synthesis of previous works contextualized in a pedagogical framework, and proposes a new learning paradigm for software engineering education.

Keywords: Computer education · Agile methods · Computational Thinking · Meta–analysis · Cooperative Thinking

1 Introduction

Computational Thinking is a new form of literacy [62]. It is a concept that has enjoyed increasing popularity during the last decade, especially in the educational field. Computational Thinking is usually considered an individual skill, and practiced and trained as such [31,63].

However, such an approach does not match current teaming structures of both science and business, where problems and projects have become so complex that a single individual cannot handle them within a reasonable time frame. To handle the increasing complexity, especially in engineering software systems, developers should be educated to act and operate as a team [17]. This

© Springer Nature Switzerland AG 2020
J.-M. Bruel et al. (Eds.): DEVOPS 2019, LNCS 12055, pp. 63–83, 2020.
https://doi.org/10.1007/978-3-030-39306-9_5

is already happening in the business world. In fact, teaming is considered the key driver to Digital Transformation, where solutions are not provided by individuals but by self-organizing teams [18]. Digital Transformation is often subject to "wicked problems", which do not have an unique solution but many Pareto-optimal ones [47]. This also applies to software development when complexity becomes very high [20]. Moreover, the DevOps technological trend needs specific approaches to support the training of developers/operators [5]

In Software Engineering, the role of the team and teamwork in general is especially crucial when Agile methods are used. The Agile principles acknowledge that important information and know-how might not be available at the beginning of a project [46]. Reaching the development goal requires several iterations, to build incremental solutions of increasing value for the users.

A key agile team–building factor is *self-organization*, meaning that any member of the developing team contributes with her knowledge, ability, and technical skills in order to work out a solution. Since each team member is responsible for the project as a whole, it is in everybody's interest to organize work at best – not bounce responsibilities. Moreover, teams are not static but they modify their structure according to necessities, which change over time. Not surprisingly, some organizations have built their competitive advantage and success on this model [1]. They comply with Conway's Law, according to which "organizations which design systems [...] are constrained to produce designs which are copies of the communication structures of these organizations" [10]. A consequence of this observation is that organizations have to modify their *communication structures* accordingly to the problem which need to be solved. Therefore, flexible and self-organizing teams are best suited to comply with such pivotal evidence for any organization.

We argue that Agile principles and values should enrich the current efforts to establish Computational Thinking as a fundamental literacy ability. We call such a combination Cooperative Computational Thinking, or *Cooperative Thinking* for short. From a pedagogical perspective, it is grounded in Johnson & Johnson's Cooperative Learning approach, where students must work in groups to complete tasks collectively toward academic goals [28]. We suggest a team-oriented approach to educate software engineers in Computational Thinking. Educators should not just promote some good software engineering practices; rather, they should foster collaboration skills and train student teams to cooperate on wicked problems. Programming skills are usually considered personal ones; in most cases—job interviews, university exams, official certifications—the focus is always the performance of the *individual*. We lack a general approach to enable group skills in this context. Even if this idea may be widely shared by the community, we did not find any evidence of a comprehensive approach to it. This is probably due to the lack of explicit awareness of such concept as enabler of Digital Transformation processes: we may use it implicitly without recognizing it.

In this paper we analyze processes and interactions in four different learning modalities that mirror some standard software development models: solo programmer, pair programmers, self-organized teams, and directed teams. We report differences, practical and educational issues, their relative strengths with respect to developing Computational Thinking skills on one hand and how they impact Agile team-related skills, that form the base of Cooperative Thinking, on the other.

As a result, we developed a model for Cooperative Thinking, contextualizing in relevant pedagogical theories. We provide results based on empirical and theoretical evidence; they can be applied to daily teaching practices.

This paper is organized as follows. Section 2 provides background information on related research on Computational Thinking and Agile education. In Sect. 3 we present the methodological framework used for this research synthesis. Section 4 presents the investigations we performed in teaching Cooperative Thinking comparing four modalities for organizing software development classes. Aggregated insights from our synthesis are presented in Sect. 5, where we propose actionable solution for educational practitioners. We discuss the synthesis of our research in Sect. 6, presenting the details of the extension of Computational Thinking with Agile practices, that we call *Cooperative Thinking*: self-organized teams are an effective way to enact and support Cooperative Thinking. Finally, in Sect. 7, we summarize our vision, outline our future research, and draw our conclusions.

2   Related Works

Computational Thinking has generated a lot of interest in the scientific community [62]. It is related to problem solving [44] and algorithms [33], because it is the ability of formulating a problem and expressing its solution process so that a human or a machine can effectively find a solution to the stated problem.

However, several scholars argue whether the Computational Thinking concept is too vague to have a real effect. For instance, a recent critique has been advanced by [15]. He claims that Computational Thinking is too vaguely defined and, most important in an educational context, its *evaluation* is very difficult to have practical effects. This same idea can be found in the CS Teaching community. [2] and [24] for example, try to decompose the Computational Thinking idea itself, in order to have an operative definition. [23] notes that computing education has been too slow moving from the computing programming model to a more general one. [4] even wonders if the Computational Thinking concept is at all useful in Computer Science, since it puts too much importance on abstracts ideas. It is also remarkable that there is some research trying to correlate CS and learning styles [25,57], but generally inconclusive.

Though the Agile approach to software development is eventually going mainstream in the professional world, *teaching* the Agile methodology is still relatively uncommon, especially at the K-12 level. Moreover, a Waterfall-like development model is often the main development strategy taught in universities [35]. Moreso, it is usually limited to an introductory level and rarely tested firsthand. In practice, Agile is learned "on the field", often after attending *ad hoc* seminars. Interest in the field is however rising, and curricula are being updated to reflect this [36,55]. An interesting and complete proposal has been proposed by [37]. The paper presents the "Agile Constructionist Mentoring Methodology" and its year-long implementation in high school; it considers all aspects of software development, with a strong pedagogical support.

To summarize, programming remains a difficult topic to learn and even to teach, both at university and high school level; the ability to design and develop software remains an individual skill and taught as such.

Some studies, however, tackle the idea that hard skills expertise should be complemented with soft skills, possibly introducing active and cooperative learning [30]. For example, in [48], a long list of so-called soft skills expertise is paired with various developer roles. In [8] the problem is well analyzed, but arguably the proposed solution is not comprehensive. [38] presents an example of how to promote cooperation within a software project; however generalizing the proposed scheme seems difficult. We note however that the approach is hardly systematic, and no general consensus exists on how to proceed along this line.

3   Research Methodology

Meta-analysis is a widely known and old research procedure, firstly methodologically supported by the work of [21]. The first meta-analysis was probably carried out by Andronicus of Rhodes in 60 BC, editing Aristotle's 250 year older manuscripts, concerning the work *The Metaphysics*. The prefix meta- was then used to design studies whose aim is to provide new insights by grouping, comparing, and analyzing previous contributions. Accordingly, we use the term meta-analysis to indicate an analysis of analyses. In this sense, there are a variety of analysis of analyses, like systematic literature reviews, systematic mapping studies, and research synthesis.

According to [12], a research synthesis can be defined as the conjunction of a particular set of literature review characteristics with a different focus and goal. Research synthesis aim to integrate empirical research in order to generalize findings. The first effort to systematize from a methodological perspective a research synthesis was performed by [11], building on the work of [27], proposing a multi-stage model. The stages are the following: (i) problem definition, (ii) collection of research evidence, (iii) evaluation of the correspondence between methods, (iv) analysis of individual studies, (v) interpretation of cumulative evidence, and (vi) presentation of results.

Following the multi-stage framework suggested in [11], we provide our problem definition, set as Research Question (RQ).

RQ: Is Computational Thinking scalable to teamwork?

To answer this question, we looked back to some previous works investigating the phenomenon on different perspectives.

All analyzed papers are both homogeneous and comparable, as depicted in Table 1.

We both provided insights on single papers in Sect. 4, and provide an interpretation of cumulative evidence in Sect. 5.

Table 1. Investigation list

Title	Focus of experiment	# Subjects	Ref
Learning Agile software development in high school: an investigation	Pair Programming, Timeboxing, User Stories, Team Development	84	[39]
Teaching Test-First Programming: assessment and solutions	Pair Programming, Social dynamics	102	[41]
Agile for Millennials: a comparative study	User Stories, Scrum, Waterfall, Team Development, Timeboxing	160	[40]

As an outcome we propose a new educational framework, namely Cooperative Thinking, which we use to answer to our research question in Sect. 6.

4   Results

We performed some experiments collecting several insights regarding teaming for solving computational problems, as listed in Table 1.

For the purpose of this research synthesis, we abstracted empirical knowledge and mapped learning models to learner types. To do so, we used the well–known Kolb's learning style inventory [32, 34], consisting in:

- Individual learning (best suited to Assimilators)
- Paired learning (best suited to Convergers)
- Directed group learning (best suited to Divergers)
- Self-determined group learning (best suited to Accommodators)

This classification supports our inductive epistemological approach, allowing us to contextualize already collected evidence into a broader theoretical framework. Hereafter, we make our considerations for the four learner groups.

4.1   Individual Learning

Directed Individual learning (short: Individual Learning) corresponds to the most common form of teaching, practiced everywhere in practically every subject and most often associated to Directed Instruction. The typical form consists of a lecture on a new topic, followed by individual study and exercises, then finalized in some kind of assessment (test and/or capstone project); teaching is generally sequential, each concept built on previously acquired knowledge. The main advantages of this model are its simplicity and efficiency; a single individual can teach a full class of people at the same time; moreover, we all already have plentiful experience with this method. More recently, by using modern technology this model can scale almost indefinitely. Practical examples include the Khan Academy, Udacity, and other MOOCs. An interesting aspect is that the sequential progression is ideal for stimulating Computational Thinking concepts—especially Problem Solving. Once a topic is mastered, it can be used to tackle more complex concepts or deepen and reinforce the significance of an acquired one. Another advantage is assessment; for instance, it is very easy to evaluate a program written by a student thanks to standard testing frameworks, to the point that automatic evaluation is becoming more and more common—a decisive point in case of e-learning on very large classes.

This model is dominant, however it has several limitations. One of most important ones is the fairness of the assessment. The difficulty of the assessment test is usually tailored upon the average student, resulting in a Gaussian curve grade distribution. In this model, students falling behind at the beginning of the course rarely have the capacity to catch up, as the time allotted is the same for every student; additional information, requirements, time–demanding exercises pile up very quickly. People experiencing learning difficulties have very few options. Those who can afford it resort to privately paid tuition, but for the rest the road a failing grade is almost certain. A consequence is the so called "Ability Myth": it states that each of us is born with a set of abilities that hardly change during our lifetime [56]; in fact, this phenomenon is in most cases the effect of accumulated advantages [54].

Another drawback is the absence of positive social interaction. Direct teacher/student communication is constrained by the available time. Student/ student interaction rarely includes exchanges of ideas or effective cooperation; more often than not, it results in direct competition or in nonconstructive and illegal help (i.e. cheating). All of this might have a negative influence on overall motivation, especially in less-than-average performing students.

In experiments [39,40], we simulated a working day in a software house; the teacher assumed the role of the software house boss, and selected a number of students who were previously categorized as either "good", "average" or "poor" programmers. Each student was given a moderately difficult task using a new work methodology (either TFD or User stories) within a limited time-frame. Without much surprise, both performance and the perceived utility of the activity mirrored their current skill level.

Individual learning help foster Computational Thinking but it is not useful (or maybe detrimental) to develop social skills needed for Cooperative Thinking. According to Kolb's learning inventory [34], this teaching model best suits *Assimiliative* learners, since they like organized and structured understanding and respect the knowledge of experts. They also prefer to work alone.

4.2 Paired Learning

Paired learning (also called *Dyadic Cooperative Learning Strategy* [53]) is also a common technique but far less popular than the previous one. The basic principle involves the teacher posing a question or presenting a problem, then the students discuss in pairs and find their own way toward the solution; pair members are often switched, sometimes even during the activity.

The role of the teacher in this case is quite limited, as she acts as a general coordinator and facilitator of the class of pairs. In the software development field, we find an obvious transposition of this model in Pair Programming, one of the key Agile programming practices and, to a lesser extent, in some training techniques (Randori and Code Retreats among others [50]).

According to [14], this model has beneficial influence on retention, understanding, recall, and elaborate skills at the cognitive level; it is particularly effective on mood and social skills, and introduces the idea of software being an iterative, evolutionary process. As it promotes knowledge sharing, it can help less skilled individuals to improve themselves taking inspiration from their partners. However, it is more difficult to develop a teaching progression using only this model, and in any event, it would be rather slow. In addition, psychological and personal factors become important, since partner incompatibilities and social difficulties might dramatically change both the learning outcomes and the quality of the code produced. Assessment is more difficult than in the previous case; though automatic evaluation is still possible, some extra steps are required by the teacher to deduce the effective contribution of each member of the pair to the final work.

We tested firsthand this effect in experiments [39, 41]. We proposed the same method and problems stated in Sect. 4.1, but in this case we paired students according to six possible pair types, classified as homogeneous (good-good, average-average, poor-poor) or as non-homogeneous (good-average, average-poor, good-poor).

According to results, homogeneous pairs performed generally equal or worse than their solo counterparts, but non-homogeneous pairs had statistically better results. In the latter case a form of epistemic curiosity [29] appeared, possibly unconsciously, and was a key motivating factor for the pair; the resulting interaction helped both to solve the task at hand and to develop social skills. Computational Thinking was also stimulated, but a little less than with the previous model, since the "effort" was split and each single task was not really challenging, requiring expertise more than logical reasoning.

In addition, both students and teachers praised the new methodology and its positive effect on mood. However, the retention rate was very low, much worse than expected; in an interview conducted some time after the experiment was over, students generally only had a vague idea of the techniques used and only about 5% of them was able to name them correctly.

To summarize, paired learning has beneficial effects on social skills related to Agile development, and generally is useful in leveling skills upwards. Knowledge building will however be much slower than in the traditional approach. This teaching model better suits *Convergent* learner types, since they want to learn by understanding how things work in practice, like practical activities and seek to make things efficient by making small and careful changes.

4.3   Directed Group Learning

Group learning is one of the many facets of Cooperative Learning, which is becoming fairly common in modern, constructivist-influenced education [6]. It is also a common practice in some working environments, notably in the health context for nurses [61]. Group learning in a software engineering lab class is best exploited by developing a full software project, not simple exercises or abstract analyses. So, it is natural to join Group Learning and Project-Based Learning strategies, especially using the Jonassen variant [26]: a complex task taken from real-life with authentic evaluation, comprehensive of all phases of development.

We are aware that many software development methodologies exist, and each of them can be transposed in an educational context promoting different behaviors and skills. One of them is the Waterfall model, probably the oldest one but still quite popular in the industry.

Waterfall embodies in many ways all the tenets of our prevailing culture, such as linear hierarchies, top-down decision making, accepting the assumptions, acquire all information in order to prepare a detailed plan and then following it—values that have forged the way traditional education was conceived and in most cases is still carried out.

A Waterfall school project will see the teacher assume the role similar to that of a senior project leader, assigning tasks and roles to students according to their skill, knowledge, and ability and applying a certain degree of control. The teacher's role will be very important at the beginning of the project, as students generally lack the ability to perform a thorough analysis and comprehensive design phase. As the project continues its course, the role will be more oriented to control, checking that documents are properly written, modules developed and tested, directing the flow of the entire operation. Assessing a group project is considerably more complex that both previous model, since it involves not only the final product, but also the process used and the interaction among the student and their relative contributions. To resolve it, usually a combination of traditional evaluation (automated or not), direct teacher observation and peer evaluation is used, forcing students to evaluate and reflect on the quality of their work.

In a different experiment, we decided to give students a very challenging task, almost impossible to solve. They had to build from scratch a complete dynamic website, a task we estimated in about 30 man-hours to complete when handled by experts. We only gave them 6 h. This forced teams to make hard decision as to what was the most suitable course of action in order to make the best use of the allotted time and resources.

Then some extra restraints were imposed on the group, such as:

- A rich set of artifacts, such as a complete SRS, ER-diagrams, management priorities, UI-Mockups.
- Specific roles (programmer, UI-expert, tester, ...) and hierarchies (chief programmer, for example) were imposed.
- A predefined time schedule.

From an educational viewpoint, the target product was definitely outside a single student's zone of proxymal development [59], but was theoretically doable as a team effort. From a different viewpoint, such a target looks like a wicked problem, since students lacked the knowledge and the competence to complete the task, and were requested to acquire them along the way [60]. The great amount of information and in general the directive role of the teacher gives the opportunity to highlight whatever learning goal is deemed important.

Results show that, under these conditions, groups tend to concentrate on non-functional requirements and process-related goals instead of pursuing the main goal: delivering a working product to the "customer". The products, on average, had very few working features, but the defects were hidden under a pleasant user interface, close to the one proposed by the "management". Roles were interpreted rather closely to the given instructions (barring a few cases of internal dissent), timing was impeccable, and even the documentation was acceptable. Teacher-student interactions were not intense, but rather limited to simple yes-no questions. Students reported great satisfaction for both the activity and the product realized, asserting it was an activity both useful and fun [40].

To summarize, this teaching model promotes the use of social skills, while leaving the steering wheel in the hand of the teacher. This power can be used to provide a meaningful learning path, though slower that Individual Learning and with a non-trivial evaluation method. It also does not seem to stimulate enough other interesting skills, such as decision making. It better suits *Divergent* learner types, since they and will start from detail to logically work up to the big picture. They like working with others but prefer things to remain calm.

4.4 Self-directed Group Learning

This model is a different version of Group Learning, radically different than the previous one in that students have a strong degree of autonomy. It applies to K-12, adult education and business/industrial environments, for example [22].

In this case, the teacher becomes a mentor and a facilitator, and invests a large amount of trust on the learners.

Most of what we said on Project-Based Learning in the previous subsection holds. In this case, the granted freedom can be a powerful weapon in the hands of the group, but it might also backfire.

It is easy to see that several Agile values are connected to this learning model: most prominently, shared responsibility and courage. Agile strongly promotes an adaptive approach to software development, where each iteration acts as a feedback for the next one. Teams should be self-organized, and great emphasis is put on communication, both within the team and with the stakeholders. This means that the teacher must *become part of the team* in order to maintain a high level of communication. It also means that the teacher cannot distribute grades in a standard way, as he will be directly involved in the process (effectively becoming a 'pig', and not a 'chicken', referring to the classic Agile metaphor). Grades should therefore come from reflections, group and/or personal and peer evaluation, and must include an evaluation of teacher work, as any other team member.

In experiment, we kept the same general structure outlined in Sect. 4.3, but within the same class we assigned the same project to a different, potentially equivalent, team. This allowed for a direct comparison of results, since it ruled out biases due to different teachers, learning environments, or curricula. We have chosen the Scrum methodology, because it is arguably very different from Waterfall and it does not really mandate any practices, giving maximum freedom to the teams [52]. The teacher assumed the role of the Product Owner in this specific case; alternatively, the Scrum Master role could be chosen as well [40].

The teams were given much less information and limitations with respect to Waterfall teams:

- A list of prioritized user stories.
- A 'definition of done' (as in Scrum): it is a definition of how a result can be considered to have some value, in terms of simple activities like writing code in a standard format, adding comments, performing unit testing, etc.
- The sprint length.

Everything else was to be decided by the team. Scrum teams also had the additional difficulty of having no experience with self-organization, whereas traditional Waterfall methodologies and roles were taught as part of standard curriculum.

Results show that Agile teams performed generally better than their Waterfall counterpart in the same class with respect to overall product completion and number of featured delivered. This is not surprising, since Agile privileges the functional dimension over the non-functional ones. It is interesting to note that many chose challenging but interesting tasks, possibly failing along the way. However, with respect to code quality, Agile teams fared worse than their counterparts. First, code was less readable and with worse Cyclomatic Complexity evaluation; second, the final product on average had severe usability problems, since this was not an explicitly stated goal. In general, teams underestimated the effort needed on the first sprint but guessed much better their second sprint, during which they were much more productive. Teacher-student interaction was also not very intense – suddenly cooperating at peer level with an older, experienced superior is not an easy task for anyone. Students reported great satisfaction for this activity, slightly more than for the previous model.

So, both types of Group learning (directed like Waterfall and self-directed like Scrum) missed the main point of the activity, which was to provide a valuable product for the customer. What is interesting is the motivation for such failures. Scrum teams concentrated their effort to reach a goal, possibly a difficult one, displaying Courage, a key XP value. Waterfall groups tended to "play safe", and concentrated on less risky objectives (user interface, process oriented goals) and working on what they most comfortable with, a pattern more in line with logical reasoning.

The self-directed group model strongly promotes the use of social skills and other qualities relevant to Cooperative Thinking. However, the learning rate could be exceedingly slow; moreover, evaluation requires great attention and

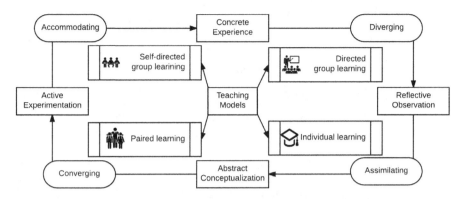

Fig. 1. Teaching activities mapped to learner types, following the taxonomy of [34]

balance. It better suits *Accomodative* learner types, since they display a strong preference for doing rather than thinking. They do not like routine tasks and will take creative risks to see what happens.

5 Implications for Practice

Kolb's model identifies four basic types of learning experiences (Active Experimentation, Concrete Experience, Reflective Observation) and four basic types of learners (Converging, Accommodating, Diverging, Assimilating). Kolb suggests to alternate these learning modalities in order to stimulate different aspects of the learners' mind, even if an individual is more oriented to a specific king of learning activity. We therefore classified four types of learning experiences specifically related to lab classes that can be appealing to a particular learner type, as shown in Fig. 1.

Table 2 summarizes the content of this section. Traditional teaching concentrates on individual learning, thus favoring Assimilating students; we argue that a more balanced approach is beneficial in general, and in particular can stimulate and develop focused social skills that are essential for developing an effective Cooperative Thinker.

Table 2. Learning model influence on learner and teacher's role

	Teacher role	Learning path	Computational thinking	Social skills	Agile skills	Ease of evaluation	Preferred Kolb learner type
Individual learning	Boss	+++	++	−	−	++	Assimilator
Paired learning	Facilitator	−	+	+	++	+	Convergent
Directed group learning	Project leader	+	=	++	+	−	Divergent
Self-directed group learning	Teammate	−	=	+++	+++	−	Accommodator

We understand that Kolb's classification is crude, as it cannot capture the complexity of teaching and learning in a social environment, be it at school or on the workplace; yet, even this simple model is powerful enough to analyze the situation and plan activities to reach our goals.

Cooperative Thinking is a general theoretical concept, just like Computational Thinking. Educators should do their best in order to have students understand and be able to put theory into practice. Is the educational system able to accept this change? Our discussion concentrates on teaching software development lab classes.

Usually, only individual performances are evaluated in lab classes of both high schools and colleges alike: it is less common to evaluate the teamwork. We will now describe some teaching models that can be used to promote the emergence of the two pillars of Cooperative Thinking: Computational Thinking and Agile practices. We have evaluated the impact on students designing and performing a series of learning experiments that exposed software development students to Agile practices and values.

In this article we analyzed a series of teaching strategies for software development, each with advantages and disadvantages and having a different impact on cognitive, reasoning and social skills that collectively concur to create what we called Cooperative Thinking.

Traditionally, education has considered literacy and knowledge in a broad sense. Consequently, the quality of education is often tied to fundamental skill expertise; one of the most recognized indicator is the result of the international PISA test, that evaluates how effective a country has been at deploying their prescribed math, science, and reading curricula. In this perspective, it makes perfect sense for educational institutions worldwide (and universities foremost) to favor individual learning as the primary – if not only – teaching strategy. For instance, a consequence of this is that several efforts are spent in schools on overcoming individual differences among students: see for instance the well known discussion of the "Matthew effect" in [54], which is a social selection process resulting in a concentration of resources and talent.

However, in the future, "pure" knowledge might become less important, even to the point of becoming a commodity, and soft skills could raise in importance. An educational system focusing on hard, technical skills could have difficulties in promoting soft skills. As [64] pointed out, there is an inverse correlation between PISA test scores and entrepreneurial capacity, a measured by the Global Entrepreneurship Monitor (GEM), the world's largest entrepreneurship study. Specifically, the countries with the top PISA scores had an average GEM:PISA ratio of less than half of the mid- and low-scoring countries, indicating a potential shortfall in PISA's measuring purpose to understand if students are "well-prepared to participate in society" [42]. And this might as well be true in Computer Science.

Notably, the ability to solve complex issues or *wicked problems*, is a requirement for new product development and innovation & entrepreneurship in general [7]. Wicked problems usually have no single perfect solution but many Pareto-optimal solutions. The traditional educational paradigm is not tailored to train people able to handle similar situations; PISA-like evaluations are meaningless to determine the educational system's efficiency, since the only offers an evaluation of the *individual*.

So, the gap between a formal educational background and real-life wicked and complex problems becomes larger. Actually, it will increase along with Digital Transformation processes, where the level of predictability decreases and uncertainties increases [45].

Therefore, the introduction of other teaching strategies that foster social skills and cooperation is very important, and should also be factored in grading activities. Note that we do not advocate a complete suppression of the Individual Learning strategy; on the contrary, it should be *complemented* with other strategies in order to obtain an overall balanced and blended mix tailored to specific situations – there is no silver bullet in education. This proposal will also have the extra bonus of potentially appeal to all learner types, even those that traditionally are less inclined to pick Computer Science as their course of study.

Given all the above considerations, we recommend all strategies we mentioned be used in teaching software development, in order to promote different but equally important skills and possibly favoring different learning styles. This strategy mix should begin as soon as possible and continue throughout the entire study path, up to and including the university tier. Otherwise, it might be too late to develop the full potential of Agile-related skills and, consequently, Cooperative Thinking.

5.1 Learning Path

Most CS courses are strongly oriented toward individual learning, the goal being to introduce and grasp the basic elements of CS and, specifically, programming [49]; a short to medium-length programming project of average difficulty is usually included.

As soon as possible, Pair Learning should also be presented. Specifically, Pair Programming should be introduced first and actively enforced as one of the main practices for class exercises throughout the course. Other Agile practices could be introduced (such as Test-First Development, Continuous integration, ...) along with the necessary software tools (like git or Jira). A project that verifies what students learned should be simple in terms of programming complexity but rich in process experiences, in that elements of Agile must be used and their use verified.

Next, forming the team is an important factor. We know that simply putting together people and telling them to work on a project is not enough to have an even decently efficient group. Preparation is in order, requiring some careful people selection, team-building exercises, and some short project to test how the teams work. Finally, a team-oriented project of moderate to high difficulty and length should be realized by the students.

The final step is, of course, proposing a demanding project to the teams and give them ample freedom. At this point students should have a solid knowledge of the programming language and development methods, a grasp of basic Agile practices, and some working experience with all necessary tools; moreover teams should know their strengths and weaknesses. This activity can actually be a course capstone project and should contribute significantly to the students' grade.

Our proposal requires formalization, testing, and formal validation. Though every step is nothing new or complicated, the overall teach process is. Our research group is currently working on a comprehensive proposal and its field testing in both K-12 and university classes.

5.2 The Influence of the Context

We discuss now the validity of this study in the different contexts of High School and University classes.

First, we examine some distinctive features of learning in high school:

- The learning activities encompass several years. During this long time period, teachers and learners get to know well each other and develop a relationship that has strong effect on the quality of their cooperation.
- The evaluation of the students is based on several factors. One is certainly the overall performance (tests, lab results), but many other aspects are factored in: initial level, handicaps, effort, proper behavior. This implies that the teacher must exert some form of control and surveillance, even due to age considerations.
- Learning goals tend to be broad-scoped, leaving advanced topics only to the best students.

The University learning context *seems* to be completely different. Instructors usually teach for a single semester, a time insufficient to establish a personal relationship. Performance evaluation is far more important, overshadowing other factors; standardized tests and procedures are used, focused on both general and specific topics. Higher levels of personal responsibility and self-organization are expected, so teacher control is generally limited.

However, in the specific case at hand, differences are not so well marked. We performed our experiments in high school courses (total: about 250 students) which are programming intensive, featuring around nine programming hours - labs included - per week for three full years. They cover basic and intermediate programming issues, including dynamic data structures, recursion, and databases for an average of 300 programming class hours per year, personal study not included. While we do not claim that this kind of education to software development is equivalent to a standard undergraduate level lab class in software development, it is undoubtedly comparable, on average compensating subject depth and personal motivation with more time spent in practical experiences. Our experiments on undergraduate students (total: about 90 students) confirm these impressions.

Not surprisingly, we found that our teaching strategies had to be adapted to the different educative levels. For example, students in high schools require learning activities on Agile to be repeated and, at least partially, integrated into standard teaching activities. Failing to do so inexorably results in limited long-term retention, as some interviews sadly demonstrated. Moreover, students must concentrate on Agile practices rather than on the overall development process; they are only able to handle a software project of limited scope and complexity, so setting up a full-fledged development environment (be it Agile or else) looks like an overkill.

Conversely, undergraduates are able to make the most out of one-shot activities; they are expected to reinforce their knowledge and skills with personal work, and most of them indeed do. They have sufficient capabilities and time to properly apply a standard Agile development cycle, especially in capstone projects. The problem in this case is the large amount of topics to cover: the instructor has the responsibility to select the topics that must be taught. In addition, undergraduates have a higher degree of freedom, so they cannot be forced to adopt a given method or practice. The effective use of Agile by students depends on their personal and, for some part, on the charisma of the instructors.

6 Discussion

In 2006, Jeannette Wing's paper defined and popularized the concept of Computational Thinking [62], portrayed as a fundamental skill in *all* fields, not only in Computer Science. It is a way to approach complex problems, breaking them down in smaller problems (decomposition), taking into account how similar problems have been solved (pattern recognition), ignoring irrelevant information (abstraction), and producing a general, deterministic solution (algorithm).

Even after more than a decade, the impact of this idea is strong. Eventually, some governments realized that future citizens should be *creators* in the digital economy, not just consumers, and also become *active citizens* in a technology-driven world.

Computational Thinking needs to be properly learned and, therefore, is being inserted as a fundamental topic in school programs worldwide. This is a welcomed change away from old educational policies that equated computer literacy in schools to the ability of using productivity tools for word processing, presenting slide shows, rote learning of basic concepts. Though useful in the past, they are currently outdated and even possibly harmful. The US initiatives *"21st Century Skills"* [58] and curriculum redefinition, along with *"Europe's Key Skills for Lifelong Learning"* [19] should be viewed in this perspective.

However, these approaches might not be sufficient in the long run. Current educational approaches concentrate on coding (as an example, consider the *Hour of Coding* initiative), but this it not the end to it. Computational Thinking is made of complex, tacit knowledge, that overcomes limited resources and requires deep engagement, lots of deliberate practice, and expert guidance. Coding is one aspect, and not necessarily the most important one.

Tasks solved by software systems are becoming more complex by the day, and many of these in the real world could be classified as *wicked problems* [47].

There is no single "best solution" to many such problems, only Pareto-optimal ones which may change over time. In this situation, satisfying expectations and requirements becomes harder and harder as they are beyond the limit of solvability for any single programmer.

This is well known in the fields of Science and Business. The most common approach to trying to solve wicked problems in these fields is by forming teams including people with complementary backgrounds, trained to face problems and reach the goal – together. These new cooperative entities benefit from a high degree of independence and autonomy to deal with the assigned task; the idea is to solve a problem attacking it from different points of view.

Even if Computational Thinking has been defined as a problem-solving skill, and has benn taken as the basis for several ongoing activities, by itself alone it does not offer the variety of viewpoints required to solve difficult or wicked problems. Computational Thinking has traditionally been considered an individual skill, and taught as such. Teamwork and soft skills are generally not factored in, and even shunned as "cheating" in some introductory programming courses.

In our view, the general approach to Computational Thinking needs to be updated, by enhancing it with a complementary concept: Agile values and practices. The Agile Manifesto was published in 2001, just a few years before Wing's paper. In just 68 words, it proposed a quite original perspective on software development, recalling values that clashed with the established culture of time, based on top-down hierarchies, linear decision making and, in general, pursuing unsustainable management plans. The most significant change introduced by the Agile movement is the paramount importance assigned to face-to-face communication and social interaction, superseding the internal organizational rigidity, documentation, contracts, roles, and more [46].

Including some Agile principles and learning-as-execute experiences in training for Computational Thinking is beneficial. We name *Cooperative Thinking* this Agile extension of Computational Thinking, and define it as follows:

"Cooperative Thinking is the ability to
describe, recognize, decompose, and computationally solve problems
teaming in a socially sustainable way"

This definition joins the basic values of both Computational Thinking and the Agile Manifesto.

Computational Thinking is based on the power of abstraction, problem recognition and decomposition, and algorithms. Agile principles include self-organizing teams, interaction and communication, and shared responsibility. Both Computational Thinking and Agile value the concepts of evolution and reflection of problems and solutions. Both approaches share the idea of problem solving by incremental practices based on learning by trial and error. Moreover, our definition of Cooperative Thinking underlines *sustainability*, since "solutions" as such have little impact, if not related to the available resources.

In sum, Computational Thinking is *the* individual skill to solve problems in an effective way. We found that Agile values are central not only for developers

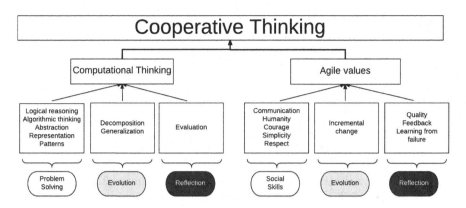

Fig. 2. Cooperative Thinking, Computational Thinking and Agile values breakdown (according to *Computing at School* [13] and [3])

but also for educating individuals. Cooperative Thinking adds a variety of points of view required to solve really demanding and complex tasks, like for instance developing critical systems [9,43,51]. Enhancing Computational Thinking with Agile values and principles allows to exploit the power of a team of diverse backgrounds towards a common goal. Being mentally flexible, understanding the others' points of view and synthesizing a common solution are crucial skills for teaming developers.

7   Conclusions

In this paper we explored Cooperative Thinking, a concept that expands Computational Thinking embracing Agile values. The proposal is graphically summarized in Fig. 2.

Cooperative Thinking is the extension of Computational Thinking with Agile Values. We considered the skill breakdown proposed for Computational Thinking by *Computing at School* [13] and grouped the skills into three broad categories: Problem solving, Evolution, and Reflection. Correspondingly, we considered Kent Beck's XP values and practices list [3] as representative of Agile values and practices in general; list items were also grouped in three categories: Social Skills, Evolution, and Reflection.

Cooperative Thinking is a complex skill to acquire and master, but in our view, is the way to go to obtain teaming individuals able to tackle and resolve the challenges and questions that the future will present them.

We examined four different learning models, each with a different balance of traditional, Agile, and Cooperative learning, showing the impact they had on students in developing Cooperative Thinking. Specifically, Individual learning is strongly related to Problem Solving, Social Skills to Self-directed group learning; all other aspects have a varying degree of relationship to the different models.

Experiments showed a significant effect on the learning outcomes. Cooperative Thinkers will enjoy an edge on the job marketplace, making them more flexible, socially aware, and more able to handle future challenges, be they related to software development or not.

In order to educate students to Cooperative Thinking, we suggest that a mix of learning strategies be used, in order to expose students to Agile practices and values and develop teaming skills without forgetting basic Computational Thinking skills, such as abstraction. While we do not claim the superiority of Agile practices as such, we do observe their effectiveness as *enablers* of Cooperative Thinking, since they promote interaction, force efficient resource handling, and are strongly goal-oriented, substantially more than individual learning.

We propose to define and evaluate innovative educational programs promoting Cooperative Thinking. Mixed methods assessments for educational construct validation with Structural Equation Modeling as also fine granular performance indicator for Pareto-optimal solutions need to be validated. However, finding the exact blend of teaching strategies will be the real challenge for the software engineering community; this is exactly what we are investigating now, both at K-12 and undergraduate level.

Another line of research that we intend to pursue concerns the constructs which constitute Cooperative Thinking, especially concerning teaming [16]. For instance, the dynamic structure of teams is interesting: we have seen in the experiments that in pair programming asymmetry of competences is quite effective. In teams including more people, say four or five students, we intend to study the emergence of mentors as facilitators rather than leaders, and the impact of such figures on self-organization of teams.

References

1. Amabile, T., Fisher, C., Pillemer, J.: Ideo's culture of helping. Harv. Bus. Rev. **92**(1–2), 54–61 (2014)
2. Barr, V., Stephenson, C.: Bringing computational thinking to K-12: what is involved and what is the role of the computer science education community? ACM Inroads **2**(1), 48–54 (2011)
3. Beck, K., Andres, C.: Extreme Programming Explained: Embrace Change, 2nd edn. Addison Wesley, Boston (2004)
4. Blackwell, A., Church, L., Green, T.R.: The abstract is 'an enemy': alternative perspectives to computational thinking. In: Proceedings of the 20th Annual Workshop of the Psychology of Programming Interest Group, vol. 8, pp. 34–43 (2008)
5. Bobrov, E., et al.: DevOps and its philosophy: education matters! CoRR abs/1904.02469 (2019). http://arxiv.org/abs/1904.02469
6. Brown, S.: 500 Tips on Group Learning. Routledge, New York (2014)
7. Buchanan, R.: Wicked problems in design thinking. Des. Issues **8**(2), 5–21 (1992)
8. Carter, L.: Ideas for adding soft skills education to service learning and capstone courses for computer science students. In: Proceedings of the 42nd ACM Technical Symposium on Computer Science Education, SIGCSE 2011, pp. 517–522. ACM, New York (2011). https://doi.org/10.1145/1953163.1953312. http://doi.acm.org/10.1145/1953163.1953312

9. Ciancarini, P., Messina, A., Poggi, F., Russo, D.: Agile knowledge engineering for mission critical software requirements. In: Nalepa, G.J., Baumeister, J. (eds.) Synergies Between Knowledge Engineering and Software Engineering. AISC, vol. 626, pp. 151–171. Springer, Cham (2018). https://doi.org/10.1007/978-3-319-64161-4_8

10. Conway, M.: How do committees invent. Datamation **14**(4), 28–31 (1968)

11. Cooper, H.: Scientific guidelines for conducting integrative research reviews. Rev. Educ. Res. **52**(2), 291–302 (1982)

12. Cooper, H., Hedges, L., Valentine, J.: The Handbook of Research Synthesis and Meta-Analysis. Sage, New York (2009)

13. Csizmadia, A., et al.: Computational thinking: A guide for teachers. Computing at Schools (2015)

14. Dansereau, D.F.: Cooperative learning strategies. In: Weinstein, C., Goetz, E., Alexander, P. (eds.) Learning and Study Strategies: Issues in Assessment, Instruction, and Evaluation, pp. 103–120. Academic Press, Cambridge (1988)

15. Denning, P.: Remaining trouble spots with computational thinking. Commun. ACM **60**(6), 33–39 (2017)

16. Dingsøyr, T., Fægri, T.E., Dybå, T., Haugset, B., Lindsjørn, Y.: Team performance in software development: research results versus agile principles. IEEE Softw. **33**(4), 106–110 (2016)

17. Edmonson, A.: Teaming to Innovate. Wiley, Hoboken (2013)

18. Edmonson, A.: Wicked problem solvers. Harv. Bus. Rev. **94**(June), 52 (2016)

19. European Community: Key competences for lifelong learning: European Reference Framework (2007). http://eur-lex.europa.eu/legal-content/EN/TXT/HTML/?uri=LEGISSUM:c1109

20. France, R., Rumpe, B.: Model-driven development of complex software: a research roadmap. In: Future of Software Engineering, FOSE 2007, pp. 37–54. IEEE Computer Society, Washington, DC (2007)

21. Glass, G.: Primary, secondary, and meta-analysis of research. Educ. Researcher **5**(10), 3–8 (1976)

22. Guglielmino, L.M., Guglielmino, P.J.: Practical experience with self-directed learning in business and industry human resource development. New Dir. Adult Continuing Educ. **1994**(64), 39–46 (1994)

23. Henderson, P.B.: Ubiquitous computational thinking. IEEE Comput. **42**(10), 100–102 (2009)

24. Hoskey, A., Zhang, S.: Computational thinking: what does it really mean for the K-16 computer science education community. J. Comput. Sci. Coll. **32**(3), 129–135 (2017)

25. Howard, R.A., Carver, C.A., Lane, W.D.: Felder's learning styles, Bloom's taxonomy, and the Kolb learning cycle: tying it all together in the CS2 course. In: ACM SIGCSE Bulletin, vol. 28, pp. 227–231. ACM (1996)

26. Hung, W., Jonassen, D.H., Liu, R., et al.: Problem-based learning. In: Handbook of Research on Educational Communications and Technology, vol. 3, pp. 485–506 (2008)

27. Jackson, G.: Methods for integrative reviews. Rev. Educ. Res. **50**(3), 438–460 (1980)

28. Johnson, D., Johnson, R.: Learning Together and Alone: Cooperative, Competitive, and Individualistic Learning. Prentice-Hall, Upper Saddle River (1987)

29. Johnson, D., Johnson, R., Smith, K.: Active Learning: Cooperation in the College Classroom. ERIC (1998)

30. Johnson, D., et al.: Cooperative Learning in the Classroom. ERIC (1994)

31. Johnson, M.: Should my kid learn to code? (2015). http://googleforeducation.blogspot.gr/2015/07/should-my-kid-learn-to-code.html
32. Joy, S., Kolb, D.A.: Are there cultural differences in learning style? Int. J. Intercultural Relat. **33**(1), 69–85 (2009)
33. Katz, D.L.: Conference report on the use of computers in engineering classroom instruction. Commun. ACM **3**(10), 522–527 (1960)
34. Kolb, D.: Learning Style Inventory Technical Manual. McBer, Boston (1976)
35. Kropp, M., Meier, A.: Teaching agile software development at university level: values, management, and craftsmanship. In: Proceedings of the 26th IEEE Conference on Software Engineering Education and Training (CSEE&T), pp. 179–188 (2013)
36. Kropp, M., Meier, A.: New sustainable teaching approaches in software engineering education. In: Proceedings of the IEEE Global Engineering Education Conference (EDUCON), pp. 1019–1022 (2014)
37. Meerbaum-Salant, O., Hazzan, O.: An agile constructionist mentoring methodology for software projects in the high school. ACM Trans. Comput. Educ. **9**(4) (2010)
38. Meier, A., Kropp, M., Perellano, G.: Experience report of teaching agile collaboration and values: agile software development in large student teams. In: Proceedings of the 29th IEEE Conference on Software Engineering Education and Training (CSEE&T), pp. 76–80 (2016)
39. Missiroli, M., Russo, D., Ciancarini, P.: Learning agile software development in high school: an investigation. In: Proceedings of the 38th International Conference on Software Engineering (ICSE), pp. 293–302 (2016)
40. Missiroli, M., Russo, D., Ciancarini, P.: Agile for Millennials: a comparative study. In: Proceedings of the 1st International Workshop on Software Engineering Curricula for Millennials, pp. 47–53. IEEE Press (2017)
41. Missiroli, M., Russo, D., Ciancarini, P.: Teaching test-first programming: assessment and solutions. In: COMPSAC, 2017. IEEE (2017)
42. Pasupathy, S., Asad, A., Teng, P.Y.: Rethinking k-20 education transformation for a new age (2016). www.atkearney.com/about-us/social-impact/related-publications-detail/-/asset_publisher/EVxmHENiBa8V/content/rethinking-k-20-education-transformation-for-a-new-age/10192
43. Poggi, F., Rossi, D., Ciancarini, P., Bompani, L.: An application of semantic technologies to self adaptations. In: Proceedings of International Conference on Research and Technologies for Society and Industry Leveraging a Better Tomorrow (RTSI), pp. 1–6. IEEE (2016)
44. Polya, G.: How to Solve It: A New Aspect of Mathematical Method. Princeton University Press, Princeton (1957)
45. Raskino, M., Waller, G.: Digital to the Core: Remastering Leadership for Your Industry, Your Enterprise, and Yourself. Routledge, New York (2016)
46. Rigby, D., Sutherland, J., Takeuchi, H.: Embracing agile. Harv. Bus. Rev. **94**(5), 40–50 (2016)
47. Rittel, H., Webber, M.M.: 2.3 planning problems are wicked. Polity **4**, 155–169 (1973)
48. Rivera-Ibarra, J.G., Rodríguez-Jacobo, J., Serrano-Vargas, M.A.: Competency framework for software engineers. In: Proceedings of the 23rd IEEE Conference on Software Engineering Education and Training (CSEE&T), pp. 33–40 (2010)
49. Robins, A., Rountree, J., Rountree, N.: Learning and teaching programming: a review and discussion. Comput. Sci. Educ. **13**(2), 137–172 (2003)

50. Rooksby, J., Hunt, J., Wang, X.: The theory and practice of Randori coding Dojos. In: Cantone, G., Marchesi, M. (eds.) XP 2014. LNBIP, vol. 179, pp. 251–259. Springer, Cham (2014). https://doi.org/10.1007/978-3-319-06862-6_18

51. Rossi, D., Poggi, F., Ciancarini, P.: An application of semantic technologies to self adaptations. In: Proceedings of the 33rd Symposium on Applied Computingm, pp. 128–137. ACM (2018)

52. Rubin, K.: Essential Scrum: A Practical Guide to the Most Popular Agile Process. Addison Wesley, Boston (2012)

53. Slavin, R.: Cooperative learning. In: Learning and Cognition in Education, pp. 160–166 (2011)

54. Stanovich, K.: Matthew effects in reading: some consequences of individual differences in the acquisition of literacy. Read. Res. Q. **22**, 360–407 (1986)

55. Steghöfer, J.P., Knauss, E., Alégroth, E., Hammouda, I., Burden, H., Ericsson, M.: Teaching Agile: addressing the conflict between project delivery and application of Agile methods. In: Proceedings of the 38th International Conference on Software Engineering (ICSE), pp. 303–312. ACM (2016)

56. Stobart, G.: The Expert Learner. McGraw-Hill Education, New York (2014)

57. Thomas, L., Ratcliffe, M., Woodbury, J., Jarman, E.: Learning styles and performance in the introductory programming sequence. In: ACM SIGCSE Bulletin, vol. 34, pp. 33–37. ACM (2002)

58. Vv.Aa.: The Glossary of Education Reform: 21st century skills (2016). http://edglossary.org/21st-century-skills/

59. Vygotsky, L.: Zone of proximal development. In: John-Steiner, V., Scribner, S., Souberman, E. (eds.) Mind in Society: The Development of Higher Psychological Processes, vol. 5291, p. 157. Harvard University Press, Cambridge (1987)

60. Weber, E.P., Khademian, A.M.: Wicked problems, knowledge challenges, and collaborative capacity builders in network settings. Public Adm. Rev. **68**(2), 334–349 (2008)

61. White, P., Rowland, A., Pesis-Katz, I.: Peer-led team learning model in a graduate-level nursing course. J. Nurs. Educ. **51**(8), 471–475 (2012)

62. Wing, J.: Computational thinking. Commun. ACM **49**(3), 33–35 (2006)

63. Yadav, A., Good, J., Voogt, J., Fisser, P.: Computational thinking as an emerging competence domain. In: Mulder, M. (ed.) Competence-based Vocational and Professional Education. TVETICP, vol. 23, pp. 1051–1067. Springer, Cham (2017). https://doi.org/10.1007/978-3-319-41713-4_49

64. Zhao, Y.: World Class Learners: Educating Creative and Entrepreneurial Students. Corwin Press, Thousand Oaks (2012)

Towards a Model-Based DevOps
for Cyber-Physical Systems

Benoit Combemale[1]([⊠]) and Manuel Wimmer[2]

[1] University Toulouse & Inria, Rennes, France
`benoit.combemale@irisa.fr`
[2] Johannes Kepler University Linz & CDL-MINT, Linz, Austria
`manuel.wimmer@jku.at`

Abstract. The emerging field of Cyber-Physical Systems (CPS) calls
for new scenarios of the use of models. In particular, CPS require to
support both the integration of physical and cyber parts in innovative
complex systems or production chains, together with the management
of the data gathered from the environment to drive dynamic reconfig-
uration at runtime or finding improved designs. In such a context, the
engineering of CPS must rely on models to uniformly reason about various heterogeneous concerns all along the system life cycle. In the last
decades, the use of models has been intensively investigated both at
design time for driving the development of complex systems, and at runtime as a reasoning layer to support deployment, monitoring and runtime
adaptations. However, the approaches remain mostly independent. With
the advent of DevOps principles, the engineering of CPS would benefit
from supporting a smooth continuum of models from design to runtime,
and vice versa. In this vision paper, we introduce a vision for supporting
model-based DevOps practices, and we infer the corresponding research
roadmap for the modeling community to address this vision by discussing
a CPS demonstrator.

1   Introduction

We are currently facing a dramatically increasing complexity in the development and operation of systems with the emergence of *Cyber-Physical Systems
(CPS)* [9]. This demands for more comprehensive and systematic views on all
aspects of systems (e.g., mechanics, electronics, software, and network) not only
in the engineering process, but in the operation process as well [2]. Moreover,
flexible approaches are needed to adapt the systems' behavior to ever-changing
requirements and tasks, unexpected conditions, as well as structural transformations [6].

To engineer interdisciplinary systems such as CPS, *modeling* is considered as
the universal technique to understand and simplify reality through abstraction,
and thus, *models* are used throughout interdisciplinary activities within engineering processes which is often referred to Model-Based Systems Engineering
(MBSE) [3]. However, in order to deal with current requirements such as the

© Springer Nature Switzerland AG 2020
J.-M. Bruel et al. (Eds.): DEVOPS 2019, LNCS 12055, pp. 84–94, 2020.
https://doi.org/10.1007/978-3-030-39306-9_6

flexible adaption of CPS to changing requirements, the operation processes of CPS as well as their interplay with the engineering processes and vice versa has to be taken into consideration. This raises the question how model-based DevOps practices for CPS can be achieved. Such practices are currently highly needed to reduce the time between identifying the necessity for a change and putting the appropriate change into production.

This paper discusses a vision for model-based DevOps practices for CPS (Sect. 2) as well as the challenges which have to be tackled in order to realize this vision by the help of a CPS demonstrator (Sect. 3). Finally, we conclude with an outlook on several research lines which may build on the discussed model-based DevOps practices, in the form of a short term research roadmap (Sect. 4) and long term perspectives (Sect. 5).

2   Overall Vision

While current DevOps principles apply to code integration, deployment, delivery and maintenance in the software industry, we envision the application of the very same principles at the model level for the development of CPS. In such a vision, the various domain-specific development models are seamlessly integrated with operations, either via models at runtime (e.g., model-based MAPE-K loop or digital twins) or via a combination of software and hardware components within a given environment.

Initially introduced for the design phases in software development, model-driven engineering (MDE) approaches cover nowadays the entire life cycle. First extended to support the elicitation of the requirements and the expected use cases, models have been then intensively used for automating the development and analysis of complex systems, and more recently to support dynamic recon-figurations of dynamically adaptable systems. As illustrated in Fig. 1, various tool-supported approaches have been explored and developed to cover all these phases. Most of these approaches are nowadays largely used in industry and help engineers to increase the quality and productivity of modern developments [11].

MDE approaches appear particularly useful in the context of systems engineering (a.k.a. MBSE), for the development of complex software-intensive systems, also referred as cyber-physical systems. Such systems involve heterogeneous concerns (including hardware and software). Models provide a uniform level of abstraction to reason over the entire system and support automation for analysis, development, monitoring and evolution.

While most of the added value in CPS comes from the software services built on top of the physical architecture (e.g., IoT, smart systems, flexible production systems, etc.), they face the same evolution than any other software services, including the restricted time to market to meet the final user expectations. Integrating the various approaches and ensuring a model continuum is thus the next level for the adoption of model-based approaches, supporting continuous delivery, monitoring and improvements of the systems.

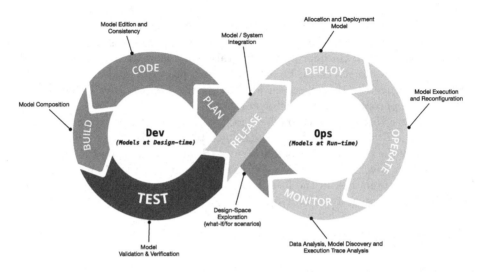

Fig. 1. A model-based DevOps approach

Also, CPS are usually deployed in complex, ever changing, environments. Software services provide the intrinsic required adaptability, that must be validated with regards to heterogeneous hardware. DevOps principles bring monitoring at the first glance, and automate the continuous improvement while guaranteeing this is free of regression.

While it appears obvious that DevOps principles would be beneficial to the development of modern CPS, this requires to promote such principles at the model level. We review in the rest of this paper the challenges raised by such a vision, on the basis of a concrete CPS demonstrator introduced in the following section.

3   A CPS Demonstrator Calling for Model-Based DevOps Practices

In this section, we discuss a CPS demonstrator developed at the Christian Doppler Laboratory for Model-Integrated Smart Production (CDL-MINT).[1] The CPS demonstrator is based on automating, operating, and maintaining a 6-axis robot with the notion of digital twins (cf. Fig. 2) providing different viewpoints such as logical and physical views as well as runtime data–called digital shadow [12]. In the following, we explain the main components of this demonstrator–being software and hardware parts.

For realizing, operating, and maintaining the gripper robot, we follow a model-based methodology which is in line with Fig. 1. The gripper is modeled by using the Systems Modeling Language (SysML). In particular, we employ the block definition diagram and the state machine diagram.

---

[1] https://cdl-mint.se.jku.at.

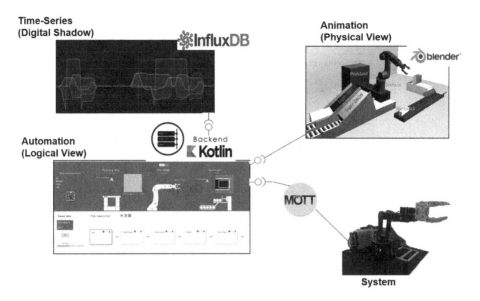

Fig. 2. A CPS demonstrator project.

The block definition diagram is used to define the structure of the gripper including its properties. For instance, we model the BasePosition (BP), Main-ArmPosition (MAP), and GripperPosition (GP) (cf. upper part of Fig. 3) to name just a few properties. These mentioned properties describe the angle positions of the axis of the gripper. These angle positions are set for different realizing different actions (e.g., for driving down, moving left/right, or for picking-up).

The intended behavior of the gripper is described by a state machine, i.e., by detailing the various states and state transitions (cf. middle part of Fig. 3). These states are for instance *DriveDown* and *PickUp*. The states set the variable values specifying the respective angle position to realize in these states.

During operation, the gripper acts as a continuous system and thus, moves in its environment on the basis of a workflow described by the state machine. The particular movements are recorded by axis sensors and returned as continuous sensor value streams. In our excerpt of the system, we show three sensor value streams for the three properties defined in the block definition diagram (cf. lower part of Fig. 3).

The building blocks for the development process as well as for the operation and maintenance processes of the discussed CPS demonstrator are as follows:

- **Logical modeling languages** to define the intended logical structure and behaviour of the system (provided by the SysML language).
- **3D CAD modeling language** for representing the geometry and kinematics of the physical components of the gripper.
- **Code generator** to produce the necessary control code from the logical models for the particular controller platform.

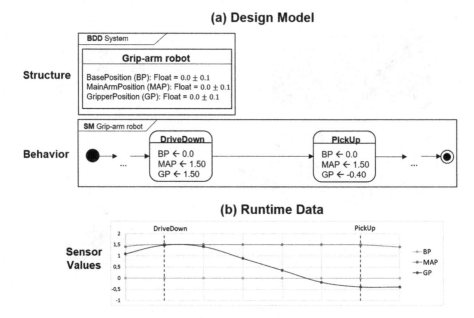

Fig. 3. Design view and runtime view of the CPS demonstrator (Excerpt).

– **Controller**, an extended version of a Raspberry Pi, with connections to the sensors and actuators of the physical device. For the gripper, every axis has a dedicated actuator and sensor which are connected to the controller via GPIO (general-purpose input/output) pins.
– **Physical device**, i.e., the gripper, with sensors and actuators.

In order to move from a classical model-based engineering to a model-based DevOps process as outlined in Fig. 1, dedicated extensions to the previously described setting are required in order to realize an efficient and effective usage of models. In particular, design models have been employed for development in many different settings and domains and allowed for automating the code generation process. In addition, several work also proposed to use runtime models during the operation of a system. However, the transition from development to operation and vice versa has been mostly overlooked. In the following, we shortly summarize the need to take these transitions into account.

– **Moving from Dev-to-Ops**: While most MDE tooling allow for moving from the model level to the code level, further activities in the direction of operations are often not explicitly supported. However, for settings such as described for the CPS demonstrator, we need further support to test the controller combined with the system to automatize before moving to the actual system level as well as to automatically deploy the control code on particular platforms.

– **Moving from Ops-to-Dev**: In addition to the use of runtime models to perform self-configuration and optimization within a particular design, monitoring is important to understand the actual operation of a system to explore new designs. This means, in addition to prescriptive and predictive runtime models, we also need descriptive runtime models which can be linked back to the design to reason about possible re-designs, model improvements such as providing a higher precision or energy minimisation. In summary, we need a way to link the data streams from the systems to our design models to close the loop.

In the following section, we detail these two research dimensions by the concrete challenges we are facing and outline some directions to take.

4   Research Roadmap

In this section, we present our research roadmap (cf. Fig. 4) by discussing a set of important challenges which have to be tackled to realize the aforementioned vision (cf. Fig. 1). We categorize the challenges in two kinds: (i) we present the challenges to continuously move from model-based development to operations, and (ii) the challenges to continuously move from operations to model-based development. We ground the challenges by giving concrete links to the CPS demonstrator introduced in the previous section.

4.1   From Dev to Ops

C1: Integration of MDE Techniques: In the past decade, a plethora of different techniques for validation, verification, evolution, transformation of models have been proposed. However, how these techniques may be bundled into a pipeline for continuously integrating, building, testing, and deploying models into production environments is less explored. The only exception is the work by García and Cabot [4] who married continuous deployment technologies and model-driven technologies.

For the CPS demonstrator, model changes have to trigger code generation scripts, test case generators, deployment scripts for running the code on a virtual representation of the physical gripper, i.e., its digital twin, in the simulation platform. As soon as this virtual level is certified, the code has to be deployed in the production environment to test it on the real physical device. For this process, we require a pipeline which can connect modeling tools, simulation tools, code generators, testing tools, as well as continuous deployment tools. In the best case, these pipeline should allow for incremental techniques to save computation costs and to guarantee an instant re-deployment.

C2: Integration of Heterogeneous Artefacts: While current model-based technologies provide common services for model-based artefacts by following certain meta-modeling standards or other conventions, other artefact kinds such as technical drawings, software components or hardware descriptions cannot be

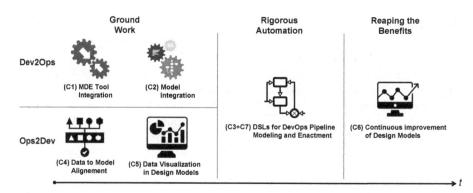

Fig. 4. Summary of the research challenges to support a model-based DevOps for Cyber-Physical systems.

directly integrated with models. However, this would be highly needed in order to allow for a progressive integration starting in the engineering process and going until the deployment process.

For the CPS demonstrator, integration between the logical controller model and the physical models, i.e., the 3D CAD models, is required in order to run virtual simulations before moving to the production site. Currently, these type of tools are often realized on different technologies with different languages (even legacy meta-languages used to define these languages) and simulators.

C3: Languages for Dev-to-Ops Pipelines: Previously a lot of research has been spent on languages for megamodeling, i.e., how different models are connected, and for model transformation chains, i.e., how models are pushed through a network of transformations. However, more specific languages may be needed to describe the pipelines from Dev-to-Ops. Such languages would allow to explicitly model the process instead of scripting these processes in different technologies. We proposed one approach going in this direction in the past by extending Gradle with explicit megamodeling and transformation chain DSL [10].

For the CPS demonstrator, we first require open APIs on all levels: software modeling tool, 3D CAD modeling tool, programming IDEs, simulation platforms, etc. In addition to open tools, a particular language to describe the complex process of moving from the modeling activities to the finally deployed system with necessary interaction points, e.g., a human has to validate the graphical simulation of the virtual gripper models, is required.

4.2 From Ops to Dev

C4: Tracing Operational Data to Design Models: The first challenge in this category is to map back the runtime data (e.g., measures about performance, energy consumption, masses, costs, etc.) into the documentation provided on top of development design models. Existing modeling languages often lack a viewpoint for operations or provide do not provide dedicated guidelines how such information may be represented, e.g., see UML, SysML, and many DSLs. Dedicated extensions to these languages are required to link to operational data or to store summaries of operational data in models.

For the CPS demonstrator, we have to record and represent the realized positions of the gripper to reason about tolerance ranges on the model level and to validate the precision of the final system. In SysML such information is currently not representable. However, there are some dedicated efforts for SysML in the standardization process of SysML v2[2] to provide state histories for components.

C5: Embedded Visualization of Operational Data in Design Models: Operational data is naturally becoming huge in size for complex systems. Even if operational data is already traced to design models, current modeling languages and modeling editors most often fail short in visualization aspects. Additional requirements for visualization of design models occur such as how to visualize the underlying quality of the data such as uncertainties. Integrating sophisticated visualization techniques from the information visualization community [1] seems beneficial in order to provide an understanding of operational data embedded in design models at a glance.

For the CPS demonstrator, dedicated diagrams have to be supported to visualize the runtime data (we refer again to the bottom of Fig. 3). Just showing large runtime data in property windows in current modeling editors is not helpful for modelers to reason on runtime events and values. New diagram types are needed for our current modeling languages and tools to visualize time series information (for instance as different kind of charts[3]) or time series visualization tools have to be integrated in the engineering tools.

C6: Utilizing Operational Data for Continuous Checks and Improvements of Design Models: Runtime models have gained considerable attention in model-driven engineering, mostly in the context of self-* systems. Exploiting runtime models for continuously checking, profiling, enriching and improving design models (possibly through additional predictive models) would allow to reason about the next versions of a system's design [7]. Runtime models are indeed already very helpful here, but currently not all runtime models are in line with the design models. For instance, assume the transform of the runtime models back into traces which can be replayed by simulators for animation, exploration, etc., on the design models.

For the CPS demonstrator, we need the possibility to play in the runtime traces from the physical system, e.g., to reproduce errors which occurred during operation, in the virtual representation (both, physical and logical view)). This may require dedicated transformations of runtime logs of the system to the design model level. These data transformations may be systematically engineered as

---

[2] http://www.omgsysml.org/SysML-2.htm.

[3] For an example, see: https://sparxsystems.com/enterprise_architect_user_guide/ 14.0/model_publishing/define_a_time_series_chart.html.

coupled transformations with respect to the design time model transformations employed to reach the code level.

C7: Languages for Ops-to-Dev Pipelines: Dedicated languages are needed to support the modeling of Ops-to-Dev pipelines. For instance, such languages are required to provide provenance for the extracted runtime models and linked design models, for the specification of indicators, e.g., metrics, KPIs, of interest, as well as the required data exchange between different monitoring, analysis, and design tools.

For the CPS demonstrator, we need dedicated languages to describe properties such as state realizations, request/response times, precision of certain actions, etc. This further requires to have a hybrid query language which is on the one hand powerful on very large data, e.g., time series recorded on the system level and on the other hand is able to produce at the same time model structures to populate runtime models and to compute derived properties which may be attached to the design models, e.g., for a given command for the gripper to move to a particular position, the average realized position may be annotated to the action in the state machine.

4.3 Synopsis

To sum up, the road ahead summarized in Fig. 4 we see as follows. In particular, in stage 1, the challenges C1, C2, C4, and C5 can be considered as ground work which is required to lift MDE to the next level for both phases, design and operation. As soon as these challenges are tackled, a rigorous automation support is required to build and enact DevOps pipeline efficiently. Thus, challenges C3 and C7 have to be tackled in stage 2. Finally, as soon as the foundations are achieved and an appropriate level of automation support is reached, the benefits of realizing a continuous engineering process by continuously improving the design models based on runtime data (cf. challenge C6) may be realized in the final stage.

5 Looking Ahead

Looking ahead the vision presented in this paper, we present in this section different perspectives that would leverage the implementation of the proposed research roadmap.

Business concerns, as presented in the BizDevOps approach [5], require to reason over the global system. Such an approach would benefit from the application of the DevOps principles at the model level as models are closer to the application domain and provide a comprehensive representation of the system, including its environment and possible extra functional properties related to business concerns. For this, an additional integration dimension opens up. In particular, there is the need for aligning enterprise models and design models which is provided by reference enterprise architecture frameworks. Finally, for reporting back the performance of the system on the business level, runtime monitoring of requirements as well as enterprise models seems beneficial.[4]

The smooth combination of the Dev-to-Ops and Ops-to-Dev continuums would provide advanced feature to support live modeling [8]. Live modeling environments would provide continuous and immediate feedback to modelers about the impact of their changes on the execution behavior of a model eliminating any delay between modelers' actions and feedback on their effects. Therewith, they should offer flexibly to explore the design space easing the development of complex software-intensive systems, facilitating learning, and improve quality and efficiency in the development process. In addition to applying operations at the level of the digital twin or the system itself, this would enable the simulation of the operations themselves to explore what if scenarios.

Finally, promoting DevOps principles at the model level enables to push backward its use early in the development process. Hence, DevOps principles would not only apply to the integration, deployment and delivery of the global system, but can also apply at a finer grain for the different concerns addressed during the development process, and across the various abstraction levels. These two dimensions (separation of concerns and levels of abstraction) complement the Dev-Ops dimension, and would possibly lead to powerful development process where automation and continuous feedback is not only available at the level of the global system, but also at the level of the different concerns and across the various levels of abstraction.

Acknowledgments. This work has been partially supported and funded by the Austrian Federal Ministry for Digital and Economic Affairs, the National Foundation for Research, Technology and Development, by the FWF under the grant numbers P28519-N31 and P30525-N31, and the Inria/Safran collaboration GLOSE.

References

1. Aigner, W., Miksch, S., Schumann, H., Tominski, C.: Visualization of Time-Oriented Data. Human-Computer Interaction Series. Springer, London (2011). https://doi.org/10.1007/978-0-85729-079-3
2. Broy, M., Schmidt, A.: Challenges in engineering cyber-physical systems. Computer **47**(2), 70–72 (2014)
3. Estefan, J.: Survey of model-based systems engineering (MBSE) methodologies. INCOSE MBSE Focus Group 1–47 (2007)
4. García, J., Cabot, J.: Stepwise adoption of continuous delivery in model-driven engineering. In: Proceedings of DEVOPS (2018)
5. Gruhn, V., Schäfer, C.: BizDevOps: because DevOps is not the end of the story. In: Fujita, H., Guizzi, G. (eds.) SoMeT 2015. CCIS, vol. 532, pp. 388–398. Springer, Cham (2015). https://doi.org/10.1007/978-3-319-22689-7_30
6. Lee, E.A.: Cyber physical systems: design challenges. In: Proceedings of the 11th IEEE International Symposium on Object-Oriented Real-Time Distributed Computing (ISORC), pp. 363–369 (2008)

---

[4] As an example from industry see: https://www.softwareag.com/info/innovation/enterprise_digital_twin/default.html.

7. Mazak, A., Wimmer, M.: Towards liquid models: an evolutionary modeling approach. In: Proceedings of the 18th IEEE Conference on Business Informatics (CBI), pp. 104–112 (2016). https://doi.org/10.1109/CBI.2016.20
8. Tendeloo, Y.V., Mierlo, S.V., Vangheluwe, H.: A multi-paradigm modelling approach to live modelling. Softw. Syst. Model. **18**(5), 2821–2842 (2019). https://doi.org/10.1007/s10270-018-0700-7
9. Vangheluwe, H., et al.: MPM4CPS: multi-paradigm modelling for cyber-physical systems. In: Proceedings of the Project Showcase @ STAF 2015, pp. 1–10 (2016)
10. Weghofer, S.: Moola - a Groovy-based model operation orchestration language. Master's thesis, TU Wien (2017)
11. Whittle, J., Hutchinson, J., Rouncefield, M.: The state of practice in model-driven engineering. IEEE Software **31**(3), 79–85 (2014)
12. Wolny, S., Mazak, A., Wimmer, M., Konlechner, R., Kappel, G.: Model-driven time-series analytics. Enterp. Model. Inf. Syst. Archit. **13**(Special), 252–261 (2018). https://doi.org/10.18417/emisa.si.hcm.19

A DevOps Perspective for QoS-Aware Adaptive Applications

Martina De Sanctis[1(✉)], Antonio Bucchiarone[2], and Catia Trubiani[1]

[1] Gran Sasso Science Institute, L'Aquila, Italy
{martina.desanctis,catia.trubiani}@gssi.it
[2] Fondazione Bruno Kessler, Trento, Italy
bucchiarone@fbk.eu

Abstract. This paper presents a vision on how to apply the DevOps paradigm in the context of QoS-aware adaptive applications. The goal is to raise awareness on the lack of quantitative approaches that support software designers in understanding the impact of design alternatives at the development and operational stages. To this end, in this paper we: (i) verify the compliance of a design for adaptation approach with the DevOps life-cycle; (ii) perform the runtime monitoring of dynamic IoT systems, through Quality-of-Service (QoS) evaluation of system parameters, to guide a QoS-based adaptation with the goal of fulfilling QoS-based requirements over time.

1 Introduction

DevOps is a novel trend that aims to bridge the gap between software development and operation teams, and round-trip engineering processes become essential in such a context [1]. When applied to adaptive applications, it brings new challenges since it is still unclear when and how it is possible to enable which adaptations, even more, when evaluating the Quality-of-Service (QoS) characteristics of systems (e.g., performance and reliability) [2]. Moreover, applications are required to face the increased *flexibility* and *dynamism* offered by modern pervasive environments. This firmly demand for *adaptive* applications that are able to adapt to their actual environment (i.e., the currently available resources) and to new situations (e.g., missing services, changes in the user requirements and needs). Adaptive applications are a reality, and a key challenge is to provide the capability of dealing with the *continuously changing and complex environments* in which applications operate.

In our recent work [3] we introduced the automated formation of *the most suitable* Emergent Configurations (ECs) [4] in the Internet-of-Things (IoT) domain. In particular, ECs consist of a set of things that connect and cooperate temporarily through their functionalities, to achieve a user goal. To derive optimal ECs in terms of QoS, we make use of a model-based approach that embeds the specification of QoS-related properties of IoT things, and further support the specification of a QoS-based optimization problem returning the

© Springer Nature Switzerland AG 2020
J.-M. Bruel et al. (Eds.): DEVOPS 2019, LNCS 12055, pp. 95–111, 2020.
https://doi.org/10.1007/978-3-030-39306-9_7

most suitable EC. However, one of the main limitations of [3] is that the runtime monitoring of the formed ECs has been neglected. In fact, there are some QoS-related characteristics associated with things that may change over time, e.g., the battery level of devices decreases when they are in use or increases after charging. These aspects of runtime adaptation of things are not handled in [3], where the selection of devices is driven by some preliminary check on their current status only. The goal of this paper is to extend the approach in [3] to enable the runtime monitoring of system parameters and trigger a QoS-based adaptation (e.g., switching among actuators with similar QoS-based characteristics but different battery level) of ECs periodically.

The rest of the paper is organized as follows. Section 2 describes a motivating example in the IoT context. Section 3 provides background information. In Sect. 4 we discussed how to match an adaptation-based approach to the DevOps life-cycle. The QoS-based adaptation of ECs in the IoT provided in this work, together with the conducted experimentation, are illustrated in Sect. 5. Section 6 reports our afterthoughts, while related work and conclusion are presented in Sect. 7.

2   Motivating Example

In this section we present the IoT Smart Light (SL) scenario, where things cooperate to achieve a predefined light level in a lecture room. Consider, for instance, a university campus made by different buildings hosting diverse types of rooms, e.g., libraries, dormitories, classrooms, offices. Each room is equipped with several IoT things, i.e., light sensors, curtains, and lamps. The things, along with their functionalities, are configured to be controllable via a mobile application allowing authorized users to increase/decrease the light level while moving in different rooms, based on their needs. For instance, in a lecture room, the lecturer can decide to decrease the light level when giving a presentation through a projector or, to the contrary, to increase it when using the blackboard. A possible way to achieve such goals is to dynamically identify an EC made, for instance, by the user's smartphone, a light sensor, and available curtain(s) and lamp(s). The selected light sensor measures the current light level in the room, and subsequently the lamps are turned on/off, and the curtains can be opened or closed. In our previous work [3], the scenario has been extended by adding the possibility of fulfilling extra-functional requirements besides the functional goal of the application (e.g., adjusting the light level). For instance, *the committer may want to minimize the power consumption of all the devices installed in the campus, while guaranteeing users' satisfaction.*

However, besides the *static attributes* (e.g., power consumption, sensing accuracy) that are provided by vendors and defined once for each device, other *dynamic attributes* that change over time or are independent from the vendor, must be considered when looking for the proper devices. In fact, it is necessary to take into account the system context evolution and adapt parameters accordingly. Specifically: (i) the selection of a sensor or an actuator leads to a decrease of a certain amount its battery level and activating their charging whether it is no longer available for the application, e.g., the battery level is lower than 50%. The charging status may be interrupted or devices might be constrained to fill their battery up to a certain threshold value (e.g., larger than 90%) before they can be selected again; (ii) devices can be subject to failures, making them no longer available for participating in the EC of devices; (iii) the light level in a room is further affected by environmental characteristics, e.g., the ambient light decreases while the evening comes, thus it might be that the provided light level may no longer meet the user requirement.

3   Background

This work builds upon an existing *design for adaptation* approach [5,6] for adaptive applications. The aim of the approach is twofold: (i) introduce mechanisms enabling adaptation in the life-cycle of applications, both in the *design* and in the *run-time* phases and, (ii) support the continuous development and evolution of adaptive applications operating in dynamic environments. The approach relies on the Domain Objects (DOs) model. More precisely, DOs allow developers to define independent and heterogeneous things/services as well as their dynamic interactions in a uniform way. This way, they do not need to deal with the heterogeneity of things and their communication protocols, but they can work at a more abstract level. At design time, to model things, developers wrap them as DOs. Each DO implements its own behavior, namely the *core process*, which models its capability (e.g., the light sensing capability of a light sensor). Then, for its intended execution, a DO may optionally require capabilities provided by other DOs (e.g., the light sensing and the lamp actuating capabilities are externally required by the SL application). In fact, each DO exposes one or more *fragments* (e.g., the 'sense light level' fragment) describing offered services that can be *dynamically* discovered and used by other DOs. Both core process and fragments are modeled as *dynamically customizable processes*, by means of the Adaptive Pervasive Flows Language (APFL) [6]. We furthermore highlight that the task of wrapping things as DOs is done only *una tantum*, i.e., when a new device type/brand is available.

Since the actual system can vary in different execution contexts, the system realization is performed closer to its execution, that is, when the actual environment is known. This guarantees as much as possible the success of the provided applications (e.g., in terms of their applicability, correct execution, coherent adaptation). The dynamic cooperation among DOs is performed by exploiting different *adaptation mechanisms and strategies* [7] (e.g., refinement mechanism) allowing applications to adapt to different situations (e.g., select the proper services, react to a context change) at runtime. At design time, APFL allows the partial specification of the expected behavior of a DO through *abstract activities*, i.e., activities that the DO does not implement itself; they are defined only in terms of a goal (e.g., sense the light) and they represent open points in DOs' processes and fragments. At runtime, the refinement mechanism allows abstract activities *to be refined* through the (composition of) fragments offered by other DOs, whose execution leads to achieve the abstract activity's goal. This enables a *chain of refinements*, supported by advanced techniques for the dynamic and incremental service composition and re-configuration, based on Artificial Intelligence (AI) planning [8]. To experiment with this approach please refer to [9].

When considering QoS-based characteristics of adaptive applications, further challenges arise, since it is indeed not trivial to evaluate such characteristics (e.g., system response time) of systems subject to run-time variability (such as workload fluctuations, services availability). In this case, adaptation needs have to be extended to target functional goals while meeting QoS-based requirements. To this aim, in our recent work [3] we extended the approach by embedding the specification of QoS-related properties at the level of things. This allows the automated formation of the most suitable ECs relying on the selection of QoS-based optimal devices.

4 Compliance of the Design for Adaptation with the DevOps Life-Cycle

The DevOps paradigm recently emerged [10] to decrease the gap between the design of a software product and its operation. Such paradigm provides a process (i.e., Dev *–plan, code, build, test–*, and Ops *–release and deploy, operate, monitor–*), but it is not constrained to any specific modeling and analysis formalism, or tool. This implies that the life-cycle is based on a set of pillars (e.g., collaborative development and continuous integration [11]), but its implementation is fully decidable by the DevOps team.

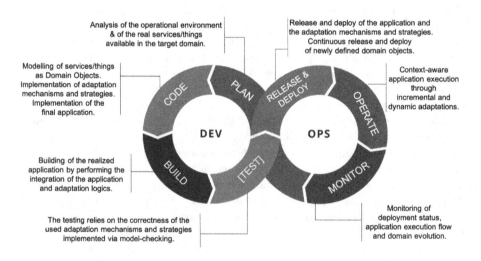

Fig. 1. Detailed mapping between the design for adaptation and DevOps life-cycles.

Similarly, our design for adaptation approach [5,6] has also been defined with the aim of reducing the distance between the design of adaptive applications and their runtime adaptation. Hence, we are interested to investigate at what extent the design for adaptation approach can be considered compliant with the DevOps paradigm.

To this end, we performed a mapping between the two life-cycles, as sketched in Fig. 1. For each DevOps phase, we describe the corresponding activities performed when exploiting the design for adaptation approach.

Plan. Our approach supports the planning of application development, which can be seen as the transition towards the code stage. This is done by defining a domain model that describes the specific operational environment in which the provider wants to instantiate the application to be developed (e.g., the SL application). More precisely, the domain is modeled as a set of domain properties describing specific concepts of the domain (e.g., light sensing, lamp actuating). At the same time, another important task to accomplish during this phase is an accurate analysis of the available devices/services that are part of the targeted domain (e.g., available devices, their functionalities and brands), which will be used in the next stages.

Code. In this phase, three main tasks are performed: (i) the identified devices and services are wrapped as DOs; (ii) the adaptation mechanisms and strategies provided by the approach are enabled (this task does not require any development activity to developers); (iii) the final application, such as SL, is designed as a DO as well. DOs are specified in the xml language while the modeling of DOs behaviors (i.e., core processes and fragments) is performed by using APFL [6]. No further programming languages are needed at this stage. In Fig. 2 we report an example of a light sensor (i.e., the Sensmitter[1]) expressed as a .xml file representing the corresponding light sensor's DO. In particular, it shows the pointers to the DO's constituent parts, such as its domain knowledge (see lines **4–7**), its state (see lines **9–25**), its core process (see line **27**), and its fragment(s) (see line **28**). The DO's state also contains QoS-related attributes (see lines **16–24**), besides state variables. Specifically, regarding the SL scenario, the specification of light sensors is augmented with three metrics such as power consumption, sensing accuracy and battery level[2]. Differently from the other attributes, the battery level is dynamic, i.e., the state of the device' battery can be dynamically updated since it changes over time.

Build. In this phase the application is built by performing the integration between the application and adaptation logic. Indeed, the former represents *what* the application is designed to do (e.g., adjust the light level) and it is specified at design time. The latter specifies *how* to do it (e.g., by combining available light sensors and actuators), and it can vary in different execution contexts, since the availability of things can change dynamically. To deal with this dynamicity, the

---

[1] https://www.senssolutions.se/.

[2] Note that metrics can be expressed in different units for sensors and actuators of different brands, however such units can be converted to a common reference unit in the DO model, thus to avoid misleading comparison.

```
1 <?xml version="1.0" encoding="UTF-8"?>
2 <tns:domainObject name="SensmitterLightSensor" xmlns:tns="http://.../">
3
4     <tns:domainKnowledge>
5         <tns:internalDomainProperty name="domainProperties/LightSensing">
6     </tns:internalDomainProperty>
7     </tns:domainKnowledge>
8     <!-- List of state variables -->
9     <tns:state>
10        <tns:stateVariable name="DeviceID" type="string">
11            <tns2:content type="anyType">Sensmitter_435</tns2:content>
12        </tns:stateVariable>
13        <!-- Other state variables here -->
14
15        <!-- QoS-related attributes -->
16        <tns:QoSAttribute name="PowerConsumption" type="integer">
17            <tns2:content type="anyType">2.5</tns2:content>
18        </tns:QoSAttribute>
19        <tns:QoSAttribute name="SensingAccuracy" type="integer">
20            <tns2:content type="anyType">8</tns2:content>
21        </tns:QoSAttribute>
22        <tns:QoSAttribute name="BatteryLevel" type="integer">
23            <tns2:content type="anyType">100</tns2:content>
24        </tns:QoSAttribute>
25    </tns:state>
26
27    <tns:process name="processes/PROC_SensmitterLightSensor"/>
28    <tns:fragment name="fragments/LS_senseLight"></tns:fragment>
29
30 </tns:domainObject>
```

Fig. 2. Domain object model for the Sensmitter light sensor [3].

application logic includes open points where the adaptation can take place (e.g., dynamic devices selection).

Test. This phase deals with the testing of the final application when the adaptation mechanisms and strategies are in their operational stage. Currently, our approach does not provide a testing environment able to simulate the adaptive applications. However, as demonstrated in [8], the services composition (i.e., a plan) returned by the adaptation planner (implementing the adaptation mechanisms and strategies via model-checking) is correct by construction. In other word, if a plan is found, it is guaranteed that its execution allows the application to reach a situation in which the goal of the adaptation problem is satisfied.

Release and Deploy. After the testing, both the SL application and the adaptation mechanisms and strategies are released and deployed, being ready for the execution. Obviously, the application domain continuously evolves due to new available services and devices (e.g., a new light sensor of a different brand has been installed in the campus). This triggers the application evolution resulting in continuously releasing and deploying newly defined DOs.

Operate. At operational stage, our approach provides enablers for the automatic formation and adaptation of ECs. After the approach extensions made in [3], the devices selection and composition is also driven by QoS-related requirements (e.g., the sensing accuracy of light sensors has to be larger than a threshold). As introduced in Sect. 3, the run-time operation of applications relies on

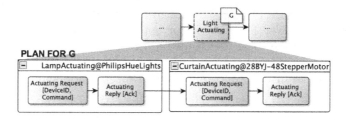

Fig. 3. Excerpt of the Smart Light execution example [3].

different adaptation mechanisms and strategies [7] that handle the dynamicity of the environment in which applications operate. These mechanisms are process-based and, in particular, they rely on the use of APFL and its constructs (i.e., abstract activities, annotations). Figure 3 provides an example of the *abstract activity refinement mechanism* to better understand the adaptation functioning. It represents an excerpt of the SL execution, i.e., the refinement of the *Light Actuating* (goal G in Fig. 3) abstract activity, depicted with a dotted line[3]. The fragments composition returned for this refinement is made by two fragments provided by those actuators in the room whose QoS-related characteristics are compliant with the QoS-based requirements stated in the SL application (e.g., minimize power consumption). Specifically, the fragments *Lamp* and *Curtain Actuating*, respectively provided by the *Philips Hue Lights*[4] and the *Stepper Motor*[5] DOs are selected, composed and injected in place of the abstract activity they refine.

Monitor. The connection point between the Dev and the Ops cycles is a monitoring step that is in charge of enacting changes, triggered by both evolution and adaptation needs. Indeed, in this phase, the deployment status, the application execution flow and the domain evolution are constantly observed. Furthermore, there are some QoS-related characteristics associated to things that may change over time, e.g., the battery level. These aspects of runtime evolution of things have not been handled by our approach in [3] that instead computes some preliminary check on the current status of devices only. In this work, instead, we enable a runtime monitoring to update these changing values and trigger a QoS-based adaptation (e.g., switching among actuators showing similar QoS-based characteristics but with different battery level) of ECs, periodically. In particular, performing a QoS-based adaptation does not lead to a new execution of the whole DevOps life-cycle. As opposite, the detection of application's evolution needs (e.g., availability of new device types in the operational environment) leads to a new execution of the DevOps life-cycle.

Summarizing, the stages described above represent the DevOps-based contributions of the design for adaptation approach. As expected, due to its aim

---

[3] The complete overview of the SL execution can be found in [3].
[4] https://www2.meethue.com/en-us.
[5] https://bit.ly/2VmRegr.

of reducing the distance between the design of adaptive applications and their runtime adaptations, the life-cycle of our approach easily maps with DevOps. Moreover, the approach itself is extended in this paper to deal with the monitoring of QoS-based characteristics of adaptive applications subject to runtime variabilities, thus to further contribute to the DevOps paradigm.

5   QoS-Based Evaluation of Adaptive by Design Applications

In this section we provide an overview of the functioning of QoS-based adaptation of previously formed and enacted ECs, and we report on a concrete example (see Sect. 2) some experimental results demonstrating the usefulness of the approach.

5.1   Overview

The automated formation of ECs based only on purely functional requirements shows the drawback that an optimal usage of resources is not guaranteed, possibly leading to end-users unsatisfaction. To deal with these issues, in [3] we extended our modeling formalism to include the specification of QoS-based properties, and enable a QoS-aware formation of ECs. The specification of QoS-related characteristics, indeed, is performed at the level of DOs, as shown in Fig. 2. In particular, each thing is associated to an arbitrary number of metrics inherited from its producer. Thus, we enhanced the specification of DOs (e.g., those representing real world things in the environment) by adding QoS-related attributes. The default setting of extra-functional requirements (i.e., min, max, threshold value) is enabled by developers in the setting of the SL application, but no assurance can be given. End-users may have different preferences while using the available things, hence they can modify such requirements. This is later translated into the QoS-based optimization problem that guides the formation of the most suitable ECs.

In this paper we are interested to study the usefulness of our approach in terms of QoS-based resilience to changes and their impact on the DevOps life-cycle. To this aim, we enabled the QoS-based adaptation of ECs, by implementing a runtime monitoring, i.e., periodically monitor the dynamic attributes of the devices involved in a running EC. Specifically, instead of considering static attributes only, in the following we focus on dynamic attributes that require adaptation while the system is up and running. The approach we propose in this paper contributes to the DevOps domain since it jointly considers development and operational properties of software systems; more in details it tackles the following three main characteristics:

- **updates of inner system parameters at operational stage**, i.e., there are some system characteristics that change overtime and it is necessary to update their value, e.g., the battery level of mobile devices is consumed when they are in operation and such a parameter requires to be updated accordingly.

- **system failures**, i.e., there are some software and hardware components that do not properly work at operational stage and it is necessary to substitute them, or to foresee recovery techniques that allow their recovery. This last point opens an interesting line of research that we leave as part of our near future research.
- **environment**, i.e., there are some environmental characteristics that may affect the users' perception and contribute to the selection of different design alternatives, e.g., the light of the day may be low, medium, and high, and this contributes to calculating differently the required leftover. For example, in our motivating example (see Sect. 2), if the required light level is equal to ten, but e.g., the environment provides eight already, then lamp actuators are required to fill the remaining two units of lighting.

5.2   Experimentation

Experimental Settings.   Table 1 reports the QoS-related characteristics of employed devices. Specifically, our scenario includes light sensors and lamps acting as actuators. For sensors we have five different instances of a different brand $(LS_1, \ldots, LS_5)$, and their sensing accuracy is specified in the first row of the table. For lamps, we also have five different instances of a different brand $(LA_1, \ldots, LA_5)$, and their light level is specified in the second row of the table. All devices show a battery decrease unit that indicates how much their battery is decreased when they are in operation. Such values are reported in the last row of Table 1. All these values represent an estimation of QoS-related characteristics for arbitrary things, however, further numbers can be considered as well when other specification of things is available.

In the following we discuss three main experiments that have been performed to evaluate different *dynamic* aspects of our motivating example.

Experiment$_1$ - runtime availability of devices conditioned to their battery level. In this experiment we are interested to show that the selection of devices is currently driven by the battery level that is updated and changes over time. This means that when selected for use, the battery of devices is decreased and, when lower than a certain threshold (e.g., 70% in our experimentation), the devices are set to a charging state and not available up to when they are usable again since their battery level goes over a predefined threshold (e.g., 80% in our experimentation).

Experiment$_2$ - runtime availability of devices conditioned to their battery level and failures. In this experiment we aim to demonstrate that software and hardware failures randomly occur and they affect the operational stage of the system. The application needs to take such failures into account. This analysis is also helpful when considering the number of sensors and actuators to put in place, in fact it is obvious that a restricted number of available devices may lead to no alternative options whether all sensors and/or actuators are in a failing state condition.

Experiment$_3$ - runtime availability of devices conditioned to their battery level, failures and conditions of the environment. As mentioned above, there

Table 1. QoS-related characteristics.

	Light Sensors					Lamps				
	LS_1	LS_2	LS_3	LS_4	LS_5	LA_1	LA_2	LA_3	LA_4	LA_5
sensing accuracy	4	7	2	10	8	-	-	-	-	-
light level	-	-	-	-	-	4	8	6	1	3
battery decrease	1	2	3	4	5	2	4	6	8	10

might be some environmental aspects that affect the users' perception. For example, the light is conditioned to the time of the day and available actuators are required to fill the gap between the perceived environment and the application requirements. This means that depending on the time of the day, some actuators may be not valid for the fulfillment of stated system requirements. We considered three main light environment levels (i.e., low, medium, and high) and we investigated the availability of lamps moving among such three settings.

In the remaining of the section we argue on collected experimental results while considering multiple observation runs (i.e., up to 100 in our experimentation) denoting several intervals of time of the same duration when the application is up and running.

Experimental Results. In the following we describe the conducted experiments and collected results, related to the three experiments reported above.

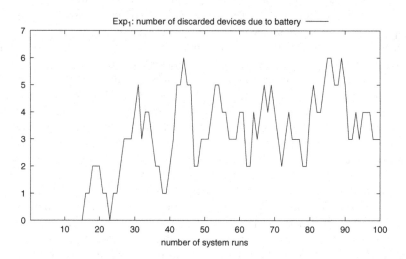

Fig. 4. Exp_1 - runtime availability of devices conditioned to their battery level.

Figure 4 shows the runtime availability of devices conditioned to their battery level. On the x-axis we report the number of system runs, i.e., up to 100 time

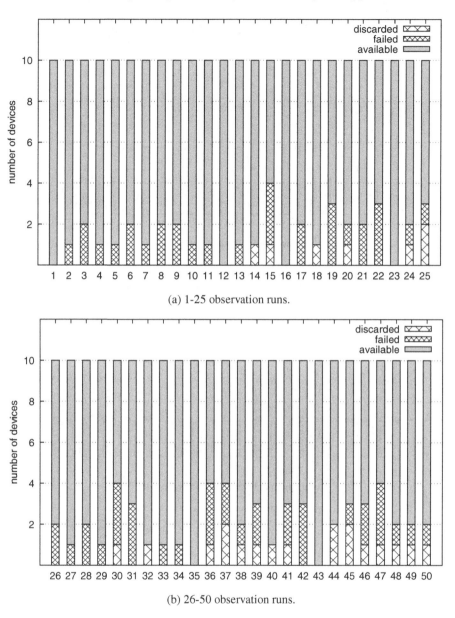

(a) 1-25 observation runs.

(b) 26-50 observation runs.

Fig. 5. Exp_2 - runtime availability of devices conditioned to their battery level and random failures (up to 50 observation runs).

frames. On the y-axis we show the total number of discarded devices, including both sensors and actuators. As expected, initially all devices are up and running, at the 16-th run one of the devices shows a low battery, later on two devices, and so on. These discarded devices are recharged in the subsequent runs, in fact

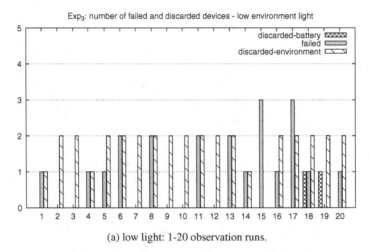

(a) low light: 1-20 observation runs.

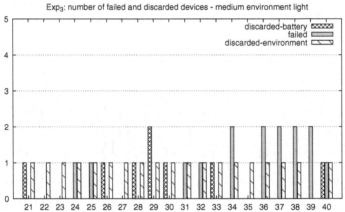

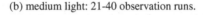

(b) medium light: 21-40 observation runs.

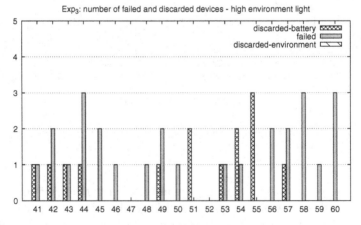

(c) high light: 41-60 observation runs.

Fig. 6. Exp_3 - runtime availability of devices conditioned to their battery, random failures, and different levels of environment light.

at the 23-th run no devices are discarded, their battery is considered enough to accomplish the planned tasks. As expected, we can notice that the availability of devices is fluctuating, and the number of discarded devices varies between one and six, but in average across all runs it turns out to be around three. All these numbers are indicators of the devices availability over time due to their battery characteristics, and these evaluations are helpful to understand the evolution of the application under analysis.

Figure 5 depicts the runtime availability of devices conditioned to their battery level and random failures. For lack of space and readability reasons, we show 1–25 observation runs in Fig. 5(a), and 26–50 observation runs in Fig. 5(b); the remaining runs are omitted but show a similar trend. At the first run all devices are available, but starting from the second run and up to the 11-th run we can notice up to two devices (per run) showing failures. At the 12-th run all the devices are available again, and discarded devices (due to low battery) start to appear at the 14-th run. This is because the battery decrease requires some time to become critical, whereas failures are random and can happen anytime, even in the first run itself. Some runs encounter a mix of failed and discarded devices, e.g., at the 15-th run we have one discarded device and three failed ones. Later on, we can see that few runs show the availability of all devices, but most of them report failures and/or devices with low battery. In average, across all the 100 runs, we found 0.64 discarded devices due to low battery and 1.29 failed devices. Similarly to the previous experiment, all these numbers represent indicators of the devices availability over time due to battery decrease and failures, and our application resulted to be exposed to few unavailable devices on average.

Figure 6 shows the runtime availability of devices conditioned to their battery, random failures, and different levels of environment light. Figure 6(a) focuses on a low environment light level (e.g., early morning), i.e., the sensing reports a light level set from the environment that is estimated to be equal to 2. To achieve the stated requirement (light level larger than 5 units), all the devices contributing with a light level larger than 3 units are sufficient to fulfill the end users need. When moving to the medium scenario (e.g., late morning), see Fig. 6(b), we considered 4 units as the environment light level; for the high scenario (e.g., mid day), see Fig. 6(c), we stick on 5 units that basically indicate the suitability of all devices, no matter of their power since the environment itself is sufficient. As expected, in Fig. 6 we can notice that the number of discarded devices due to the environment progressively decreases while moving across the observation runs, and this is due to an increasing environment light level. In average, across the 60 runs, we found an average of 0.4 discarded devices (due to battery), 1.05 failed devices, and 0.9 discarded devices (due to the environmental conditions). Similarly to previous experiments, all these numbers indicate that our application is marginally affected by battery, failures, and environmental changes.

Summarizing, the presented three experiments aim to demonstrate that QoS-based adaptation is feasible, and our approach allows the quantification of how the design settings (i.e., the intrinsic characteristics of available devices) contribute to some properties of the running application, thus to get further knowledge on its operational stage. Note that the execution time of running 100 runs varies in a narrow interval, and its average is less than 2 s, thus to assess the efficiency of the approach.

6 Discussion

Our approach includes a set of limitations that we discuss in the following.

Flexible Guarantees. It may happen that, when looking for an EC, the application is not able to provide a solution that strictly meets the stated requirements. This problem is exacerbated when QoS-based requirements are also considered, since they further restrict the devices selection space. As future work we plan to introduce techniques that identify the "closest" EC, i.e., the one slightly deviating from requirements, but probably still satisfying the end users. This can be performed by moderately modifying the stated requirements and executing the process as it is.

Recovery Policies. As demonstrated in our experimentation, devices are subject to failures and this implies a lower number of suitable ECs. To address this issue, we plan to extend our approach by minimizing the mean time to repair, so that failed devices are fixed more efficiently and they soon become available again. To this end, a component should be added to trigger recovery policies that automatically provide strategies (e.g., restart, reset to default settings) for some or all sensors/actuators.

Adaptation as a DevOps-Cycle Itself. In this paper we proposed a mapping between the life-cycle of a design for adaptation of adaptive applications on the classical DevOps life-cycle. This means adaptation is an integrated activity in all the DevOps phases within the considered application. As opposite, we can envision a DevOps-cycle focusing on adaptation mechanisms only, so that design, build, test, deliver, operation and evolution are dedicated phases for adaptation concerns. In other words, applications and adaptation mechanisms should be correlated but, at the same time, able to evolve independently of each other, also considering that they might be realized by diverse professionals with different skills and roles.

Centralized vs. Distributed. Our approach is currently centralized, in fact it leverages on an *adaptation engine* and a *process engine*, both operating in a centralized manner. As future work, we plan to decentralize these two engines, so that the execution of applications can run in distributed environments. As consequence, the QoS-based evaluation of adaptive applications must evolve accordingly, in order to manage those QoS characteristics particularly affected by distributed executions, e.g., response time.

Adaptation and Application Testing. As discussed in Sect. 4, currently our approach does not provide a testing environment and, for the correct execution of applications, it relies on the used adaptation mechanisms and strategies that exploit model-checking [8]. As future work, we plan to implement our own testing environment able to verify the built applications (w.r.t. requirements) through the evaluation of (i) applications executions, (ii) services composition, and (iii) (QoS-based) adaptations.

7   Related Work and Conclusion

Evaluating QoS-based characteristics of adaptive systems and applications is not trivial, in fact they are subject to run-time variability (such as workload fluctuations, services availability). As we said, in this case, adaptation needs have to be extended to target functional goals while meeting QoS-based requirements. Our previous work in this direction focused on performance-related issues: in [12] we make use of performance models to analyze the dynamics of performance indices; in [13] performance models are guided by model predictive control techniques to achieve performance guarantees; in [14] we identified the sources of uncertainties (e.g., deployment infrastructure) affecting performance in the DevOps life-cycle.

In [15] the authors introduce ENACT aimed to enable DevOps in trustworthy smart IoT systems. To this end, they propose to evolve DevOps methods and tools to address specific IoT related challenges, as for instance the continuous quality assurance. In our approach, the adaptation takes place at behavioral level, by exploiting a domain-independent approach. In contrast, ENACT, whose focus is mainly on the trustworthiness, supports architectural adaptations at operational time and with a strong focus in the IoT domain. Cito et al. [16] advocate the need to capture feedback from operations data and mapping them on software development life-cycle phases, in order to drive informed decisions. This becomes particularly relevant in the DevOps context that aims on promoting synergies between the development and execution of software systems. As a first attempt in this direction, we enabled the monitoring of dynamic QoS-based characteristics whose changes trigger a new execution of the SL application leading to a new EC of sensors and actuators. As discussed in Sect. 6, other steps are required to enable a feedback-loop between the Dev and Ops cycles. The work in [17] shares with our work the idea that IoT-based applications must be able to automatically adapt to changes in the QoS of their component services. To this aim, the authors exploit a collaborative QoS prediction of candidate services that enables a goal-driven service composition which, in turn, allows a QoS-based adaptation to be performed. In [18] a DevOps environment for design-time modeling and optimization, and runtime control is proposed. Here, the goal is to minimize the execution cost of cloud applications providing QoS guarantees by design. Summarizing, all the discussed approaches represent valid competitors with our DevOps-based design for adaptation, and we plan to further investigate the comparisons in the near future.

In this paper we presented a DevOps perspective for QoS-aware adaptive applications. In particular, we provided a mapping between an approach for adaptive by design applications and the DevOps life-cycle, along with QoS-based adaptation. A motivating example illustrates the feasibility of the approach, and calls for future research. Besides all the directions mentioned in Sect. 6, we are interested to industrial case studies to further investigate the soundness of the proposed methodology.

References

1. Jiménez, M., Castaneda, L., Villegas, N.M., Tamura, G., Müller, H.A., Wigglesworth, J.: DevOps round-trip engineering: traceability from Dev to Ops and back again. In: Bruel, J.-M., Mazzara, M., Meyer, B. (eds.) DEVOPS 2018. LNCS, vol. 11350, pp. 73–88. Springer, Cham (2019). https://doi.org/10.1007/978-3-030-06019-0_6
2. Iftikhar, M.U., Weyns, D.: ActivFORMS: a runtime environment for architecture-based adaptation with guarantees. In: International Conference on Software Architecture - Workshops, pp. 278–281 (2017)
3. De Sanctis, M., Spalazzese, R., Trubiani, C.: QoS-based formation of software architectures in the Internet of Things. In: Bures, T., Duchien, L., Inverardi, P. (eds.) ECSA 2019. LNCS, vol. 11681, pp. 178–194. Springer, Cham (2019). https://doi.org/10.1007/978-3-030-29983-5_12
4. Alkhabbas, F., Spalazzese, R., Davidsson, P.: Architecting emergent configurations in the Internet of Things. In: International Conference on Software Architecture, pp. 221–224 (2017)
5. Bucchiarone, A., De Sanctis, M., Marconi, A., Pistore, M., Traverso, P.: Design for adaptation of distributed service-based systems. In: Barros, A., Grigori, D., Narendra, N.C., Dam, H.K. (eds.) ICSOC 2015. LNCS, vol. 9435, pp. 383–393. Springer, Heidelberg (2015). https://doi.org/10.1007/978-3-662-48616-0_27
6. Bucchiarone, A., De Sanctis, M., Marconi, A., Pistore, M., Traverso, P.: Incremental composition for adaptive by-design service based systems. In: International Conference on Web Services (2016)
7. Bucchiarone, A., Marconi, A., Pistore, M., Raik, H.: A context-aware framework for dynamic composition of process fragments in the internet of services. J. Internet Serv. Appl. 8(1), 6 (2017)
8. Bertoli, P., Pistore, M., Traverso, P.: Automated composition of web services via planning in asynchronous domains. Artif. Intell. 174(3–4), 316–361 (2010)
9. De Sanctis, M., Bucchiarone, A., Marconi, A.: ATLAS: a new way to exploit worldwide mobility services. Softw. Impacts 1, 100005 (2019). http://www.sciencedirect.com/science/article/pii/S2665963819300053
10. Bass, L., Weber, I., Zhu, L.: DevOps: A Software Architect's Perspective. Addison-Wesley Professional, Boston (2015)
11. Humble, J., Farley, D.: Continuous Delivery: Reliable Software Releases Through Build, Test, and Deployment Automation, 1st edn. Addison-Wesley Professional, Boston (2010)
12. Incerto, E., Tribastone, M., Trubiani, C.: A proactive approach for runtime self-adaptation based on queueing network fluid analysis. In: International Workshop on Quality-Aware DevOps, pp. 19–24 (2015)
13. Incerto, E., Tribastone, M., Trubiani, C.: Software performance self-adaptation through efficient model predictive control. In: International Conference on Automated Software Engineering, pp. 485–496 (2017)
14. Trubiani, C., Jamshidi, P., Cito, J., Shang, W., Jiang, Z.M., Borg, M.: Performance issues? Hey DevOps, mind the uncertainty. IEEE Softw. 36(2), 110–117 (2019)

15. Ferry, N., et al.: ENACT: development, operation, and quality assurance of trustworthy smart IoT systems. In: Bruel, J.-M., Mazzara, M., Meyer, B. (eds.) DEVOPS 2018. LNCS, vol. 11350, pp. 112–127. Springer, Cham (2019). https://doi.org/10.1007/978-3-030-06019-0_9
16. Cito, J., Wettinger, J., Lwakatare, L.E., Borg, M., Li, F.: Feedback from operations to software development—a DevOps perspective on runtime metrics and logs. In: Bruel, J.-M., Mazzara, M., Meyer, B. (eds.) DEVOPS 2018. LNCS, vol. 11350, pp. 184–195. Springer, Cham (2019). https://doi.org/10.1007/978-3-030-06019-0_14
17. White, G., Palade, A., Clarke, S.: QoS prediction for reliable service composition in IoT. In: Braubach, L., et al. (eds.) ICSOC 2017. LNCS, vol. 10797, pp. 149–160. Springer, Cham (2018). https://doi.org/10.1007/978-3-319-91764-1_12
18. Guerriero, M., Ciavotta, M., Gibilisco, G.P., Ardagna, D.: A model-driven DevOps framework for QoS-aware cloud applications. In: International Symposium on Symbolic and Numeric Algorithms for Scientific Computing, pp. 345–351 (2015)

Learning Agility from Dancers – Experience and Lesson Learnt

Irina Erofeeva, Vladimir Ivanov$^{(\boxtimes)}$, Sergey Masyagin$^{(\boxtimes)}$,
and Giancarlo Succi$^{(\boxtimes)}$

Innopolis University, Innopolis, Russian Federation
{i.erofeeva,v.ivanov,s.masyagin,g.succi}@innopolis.ru

Abstract. Being on of the youngest field of human endeavours, software development absorbed features of other, older fields, especially engineering, mathematics, and economics. However, being software the product of the creation and being based on a systematic discipline and technical excellence of the participants (the developers), there could be also very interesting interconnections with artistic disciplines. In this paper, we concentrate on the similarities with dance. Dance has a long tradition of instructions and development. The goal of this work is to find interesting points of contact is to identify dancesport methods that could provide the basis for new approaches or practices for software development.

Keywords: Software development · Development methodologies · Dancesport · Ballroom dancing · Comparison

1 Introduction, Motivation and Hypothesis

It is generally accepted that the field of information technology is a product of the technical development of mankind. But what if this sphere has incorporated not only the knowledge of mathematics and physics, but also has sources in more creative areas of human activity? For example, the creation of currently the most popular development methodology, Agile, actually also originated outside the IT sphere.

The firs time it was used by the physicist and statistician Walter Shewhart as the Plan-Do-Study-Act cycles to improve products and processes, then his student, W. Edwards Deming, popularized this method during the reconstruction of Japan after the Second World War and then transferred this method to the industry, which led to the creation of the famous Toyota Production System, the primary source of modern lean manufacturing [15].

Gaining all the experience from both processes of dancesport and software development, a comparative research was conducted to find out intersections and beneficial differences between areas of dancing and computer science and how this connection could be useful, finding out that no one has ever deeply compared software development with such a seemingly distant discipline as dancing to identify possible synergies. Dancesport have been chosen among other disciplines,

© Springer Nature Switzerland AG 2020
J.-M. Bruel et al. (Eds.): DEVOPS 2019, LNCS 12055, pp. 112–120, 2020.
https://doi.org/10.1007/978-3-030-39306-9_8

because it combines both sports and art, that will help us to increase the edge for more broad comparison.

From sport perspective it is possible to gain productivity, motivation and passion, perseverance and ability to overcome fears, to expand barriers. From art perspective also motivation, inspiration and creativity can be considered as a source of innovative ideas for improving software development sphere. Increasing the edge, the opportunity to find more similarities and profitable borrowings grows.

The study was inspired by the notion of Agile methodology and related concepts like the so-called "Heart of Agile" by Cockburn [7]. Because of this all the examples are referring to Agile and Lean concepts. Therefore, the main objective of this research is a contribution to a development methodologies borrowing best practices of dancesport. In order to satisfy this goal the following research questions have to be explored:

- Can a parallel be drawn between dance as a sport and software development?
- Can the IT sphere borrow something from dance sports to improve performance?

2   Background and Related Works

Ballroom dancing is a set of partner dances that are performed both socially and competitively around the world. While dancesport is more narrow and refers to the five International Standard and five International Latin style dances.

In order to discover chosen topic and related studies more journalistic articles had been considered. This can be explained by the definition of the authority: While authority of facts in computer sciences is evidence based and research, the dancing authority is performance based. People who work in dance, and in performance art, understand that authority comes from being able to do the performance [4, 5, 20]. This publications are of great interest for this study, as they illustrate all aspects of the dance sphere that have ever been identified as common with other areas of human activity.

The purpose of this work is to apply the theory of a conceptual blending, that is according to Gilles Fauconnier and Mark Turner a deep cognitive activity that makes new meanings out of old. [13], in comparison of software development and dancing spheres and analyse how techniques coming from dancesport can be used effectively in software development.

The example of this approach is present by Brenda Laurel "Computers as Theatre" [16]. Based on the analysis of the form and structure of the drama of Aristotle the author shows how similar principles can help to understand what people experience when interfacing with computers.

This metaphorical comparison was applied in the fields of dancesport and software development by Lee [17] - also being a dancer in the past and a developer in the present, she drew several abstract parallels between these areas, here are the main points she highlighted as similarities between learning how to code and learning how to dance. She declares, that developers and dancers both focus on the basics, strive to be well-rounded, consider collaboration crucial for improvement.

The author of "Agile dancing. Scrum training. Is it even possible?" (2017) has already drawn a parallelism between dancing and software development. In particular, she has analysed how to apply the Agile methodology to her training process, considering time between competitions as sprints, coach as a product owner, who will know exactly what is the main priority and he will also be able to tell if the sprint is finished with success [3].

One more possible set of parallels were drawn at a seminar at Bilkent University in Turkey [1]. They looked at the methods and processes of software engineering by relating it to the systematic structure of dance. Some common features were highlighted:

- Processes employed in software engineering, such as analysis, design, implementation and testing were associated with the rules of professional dancing
- The Waterfall model examined the steps and the structure that dancers use while preparing a dance performance as if they were a part of engineering.
- Importance of teamwork and professionalism was considered.

Since dance comparing to programming is considered as a simpler and more natural human activity, which children learn from an early age, a large number of courses have been created in which programming concepts are explained through dance. There are courses for K12 students with names like "Coding Choreography" that offer learning programming using dancing. Abstracting to dance, students study concepts such as algorithms, conditionals, functions, loops, patterns, etc. [2].

The course "Dancing computer by Dillon et al. [12] was prepared to teach elementary school students both dance terminology and concepts of coding such as sequencing and conditionals. One of the main goals of this course is to teach children to read code before writing it.

Such courses exist not only for children, but for students, team of students and faculty members from Clemson University also designed a program called VEnvI (Virtual Environment Interactions) [21] that combines basic concepts of computational thinking and basic concepts from dance, so students can dance and pick up key computational skills at the same time. Using VEnvI, students can learn programming concepts like sequencing, looping and conditionals.

The important topic was raised by Rosner [22] - the author states the actual problem of Agile teams - those, that are trying to adopt it or claim following it. Their motivation for using this methodology, such as customer orientation, doing things quicker with less managerial overhead, eliminating planning ahead as it is not useful, turns into real life problems:

- Unclear prioritization of customer requests
- People working on random things

- Managers giving tasks directly to individuals leading to unevenly distributed workloads
- No time estimation possible

The problematic areas are the areas of improvements - which is the goal of the proposed study.

3   Methodology

After analysis and discussion the survey approach was chosen as the most appropriate one for the study. After that the research process was organized within four steps. They include collecting information from professionals, related work, that follows by analysis, based on the gained information:

1. Collect relevant information from dancesport representatives:
   - Review of the relevant literature on dancesport, on its regulations, on the training processes, etc.
   - Interviews with experts to identify aspects not (well) covered in the literature or to clarify uncertain situations.
   - Add personal observation and experience.
2. Conduct interviews among developers from local companies and professional dance athletes to identify the main features of selected disciplines, existing problems and ways to solve them.
3. Analyse answers and define a hypothesis for transferring useful features from dancesport to software development methodologies.
4. Finally, validate results in the field of software through interviews with software managers of software companies.

In order to keep corresponding questionnaires connected the GQM techniques was applied. Initially, Goal Question Metric is a method used by organizations in order to align their business goals with software development strategies and allow measurement-based decision-making [18]. The main goal of this approach is to identify a meaningful metrics for measurement process, but in terms of this study it approach was applied to keep surveys among different professions connected and comparable. Applying this method to the present work, the main goal was determined as identifying the similarities between spheres of dancesport and software development. To make it more precise it was divided into a smaller goals more specific for the each of proposed directions. So that four corresponding goals were identified and expanded with lists of related question:

1. Find out what are the main problems professional have and compare them
2. Identify the most profitable strategies to overcome those difficulties and compare them
3. Understand motivation and self development issues of both professions and compare them
4. Explore and compare the influence of relationship in the team

After two test runs: offline and online, questionnaires were corrected and expand. Online interviews were held among 92 participants, the results were completed with additional comments during further discussion with the part of interviewees, who have shown a special interest in investigation to the topic.

The surveyed are 64 professional dancers and 28 developers from companies in the city of Innopolis. The choice among professional dancers was very diverse: from the lowest professional class (hobby) to the dancers of the most experienced and professional category (M), performing at competitions from the city to the international level. Some had more than 10 years of experience behind their backs, some had already completed their careers and became coaches.

Programmers who participated in the survey also covered a wide range of professions in this field, such as CTO, tester, senior web developer, server developer, team leader, analyst. They all had work experience from 1 to over 10 years. Also, for a deeper understanding of the problems that exist in the field of software development, personal interviews were conducted with the developers of a one-year start-up company.

4   Results and Discussion

In the following section the results of a comparison, based of literature review and interviews with the representatives of both professions, are listed. The section ends with a proposal of improvements of software management components, inspired by beneficial differences between the spheres.

Firstly, dance and programs are similar in their meaning - they both are just algorithms in the beginning, but in terms of dancesport the algorithm depends on rhythm, tempo, style of music, personal experience and experience of the partner, the presence of each of the dancing couples on the floor.

For those who start to dance and want to develop faster there is a chance to practice with more experienced partner. There is a special category called Pro-Am (Professional-Amateur), where the professionals dance with novices or with much less experienced dancers. In this situation both, beginner and professional dancer, gain something useful for their dancesport career: beginner gets a quick start, professional gets a chance to consolidate his knowledge and understand the material deeper during the explanation. In software development it is present as one variation of pair programming, where a beginner and a more experienced developer are working together. Beginner adopts the knowledge, experience and habits of a more experienced specialist, which helps him to learn faster [8,14].

The leading role in the dance pair is always taken by the man, that is, he is responsible for the safety of the pair on the dance floor and for the correct execution of composition. If there is an obstacle in the way of the pair, the partner can change the direction of the movement or dance a more convenient and appropriate movement for this situation, and the girl must follow it. The appointment of a leader in a pair, who chooses strategy in a difficult situation, helps prevent errors on the dance floor. Error prevention in the way of choosing a leader in a team is present in software development in a role of team leader and also project manager.

Pattern is a general, reusable solution to a commonly occurring problem by definition. It has You can start to learn dancing not only with teacher, there are a lot of books [10,13,15] that describe every dance. In these books you will find explanation of every dancing figure step by step and basic routines, that are actually patterns from Christopher Alexander's book [6].

The most common practice in ballroom dancing is recording performances for analyzing the mistakes and revealing the work front for the following workouts. In software development it is called retrospective [23]. Not every team runs retrospective sessions, but every team should, because this is the way to find out what we can do to be better.

The software development methodology called Lean concentrates on minimizing the waste and autonomation of the process and widely used in companies in form of Agile [15]. It's concept of elimination of waste appears in dancesport - after a specific point in sportsman's career, it is obligatory to choose only one program, Standard or Latin, to develop only in one direction. It was noticed, that dancers, who choose two programs are less successful, than those who were concentrated on one goal.

During group practises, where participants have different levels and experience, the coach can mix partners to try different techniques with other partner, this practice help to improve leading and following skills, and identify mistakes that was not obvious with your own partner. In software development is nothing else, then testing piece of software with various inputs.

For now we saw a list of similarities between spheres of dancing and software development, but what are features, that take place in dancing and can be useful in software, but not yet represented? There are also concepts commonly used in the sphere of ballroom dancing, such as warm-up, constant work on basic movements, proper nutrition, proficiency in foundations of the classical dance, that are occasionally was not meant by IT, but they have very crucial influence on athletes performance and success. The preliminary results of comparison is present in Table 1.

Moving along through the proposed plan the study focused on discovering a possibilities of fulfilling the gaps present in software development approaches. On that stage several possible options to fulfill these gaps were proposed and described below.

First gap corresponds to *a daily warm-up activity* to perform better. Dancers do this in order to protect their body from injuries, to eliminate stress of the muscles, also for the better performance using all the potential of their bodies. There is a similar activity present in Agile, which is *daily stand-up meetings* inside the team. This could be regarded as warm-ups, however, the main aim of these meetings is slightly different - every member of a team should share their progress from previous day and plans about upcoming day, while in dancesport warming-up is at first-hand a little repetitions of the main performance. To address this lapse, stand-up meeting could be expanded with *brainstorming about teammate's tasks, where every member of a team will have a chance to provide an ideas of possible solutions for tasks of every participant.*

Table 1. Table of results

Software development	Dancesport
Pair programming	Pro-Am category
Project manager or Team Leader	Man as a leader
Testing with different inputs	Exchanging partners during trainings to find gaps in knowledge
Retrospective sessions	Reviewing competition and practicing videos
Elimination of waste	Choosing and concentrating on one program
Gap	Warm-up before each activity to perform better
Gap	Constant work on basic movements, since they represent the foundation of any composition
Gap	Proper nutrition, so your main instrument - you body works properly
Gap	Proficiency in foundations of the classical dance as the basis for the proper operation of all the muscles of the body

The following gap in IT stands in line with sports diets and proper nutrition. Every professional dancer follows guidelines of healthy nutrition in order to make their body - the main tool for athletes - to be in a perfect shape and condition for the maximum performance rate. A possible parallel with proper nutrition could be *solving working day issues on a more serious level*. By the working day issues the features of a field of programming were meant, namely lack of sleep, especially in start-up project teams, and lack of movement are not just a stereotype, but a lifestyle that decrease a persons cognitive abilities. In parallel with dancesport, this gap should be covered with restricting working hours. While another problem - lack of movement - should be covered with weekly team sport activities.

Constant work on the basic movements and knowledge of the basis of classical dance as the basis for the proper functioning of all the muscles of the body are two remaining features of dancesport that need to be further developed and validated by specialists.

5   Conclusion

The resulting table with the proposed possibilities of adoption of the best practises from dancesport lead to the conclusion, that the research questions stated earlier were successfully answered.

However, the results can be expanded with the help of increasing the number of study participants, expanding the list of questions, as well as more detailed adaptation of the knowledge gained in the field of computer science, also concentrating in specific aspects with more "destructured" organizations, like open source development [11], mobile development [9,24], and internet-based development [19]. In addition, for the further work it is possible to go deeper into biological aspect of the problem - the analysis of the brain reactions during special activities and tasks, related to the profession. According to this comparison it is possible to analyze the brain areas, used to accomplish different tasks. For example, compare impulses during dance classes, perform a learned composition and implement the algorithm just explained. In case of successful experiments, the foundation for a discussion about productivity, attention, etc. can be built.

The remaining part of the study - validation of proposed activities based of dancesport best practices will also improve usability of this study. It can be done with the help of significant amount of software specialists from local Innopolis companies to build reliable statistics. After that the most promising and suitable options should be chosen.

Acknowledgments. We thank Innopolis University for generously funding this research.

References

1. The meeting of software engineering and dancing, January 2012
2. Glowing Coding and Choreography (2013). Accessed 27 June 2018
3. Agile dancing. scrum training. is it even possible?, December 2017. Accessed 28 June 2018
4. Auslander, P.: Liveness: Performance in a mediatized culture (2008)
5. Boyle, M.S.: Play with authority!: radical performance and performative irony. In: Cultural Activism, pp. 199–217 (2011)
6. Christopher Alexander, M.S., Ishikawa, S.: A pattern language (1977)
7. Cockburn, D.A.: Heart of agile
8. Coman, I.D., Sillitti, A., Succi, G.: Investigating the usefulness of pair-programming in a mature agile team. In: Abrahamsson, P., Baskerville, R., Conboy, K., Fitzgerald, B., Morgan, L., Wang, X. (eds.) XP 2008. LNBIP, vol. 9, pp. 127–136. Springer, Heidelberg (2008). https://doi.org/10.1007/978-3-540-68255-4_13
9. Corral, L., Georgiev, A.B., Sillitti, A., Succi, G.: A method for characterizing energy consumption in Android smartphones. In: 2nd International Workshop on Green and Sustainable Software (GREENS 2013), pp. 38–45. IEEE, May 2013
10. Daily, S.B., Leonard, A.E., Jörg, S., Babu, S., Gundersen, K., Parmar, D.: Embodying computational thinking: initial design of an emerging technological learning tool. Technol. Knowl. Learn. **20**(1), 79–84 (2014)
11. Di Bella, E., Sillitti, A., Succi, G.: A multivariate classification of open source developers. Inf. Sci. **221**, 72–83 (2013)
12. Dillon, L.K., Dobbins, A., Owen, C., Evjen, M., Kanouse, D., Sallak, W., Willcuts, B.: Dancing computer (2015). Accessed 28 Oct 2018
13. Fauconnier, G., Turner, M.: The way we think: Conceptual blending and the mind's hidden complexities, May 2003. Accessed 28 June 2018

14. Fronza, I., Sillitti, A., Succi, G.: An interpretation of the results of the analysis of pair programming during novices integration in a team. In: Proceedings of the 2009 3rd International Symposium on Empirical Software Engineering and Measurement, ESEM 2009, pp. 225–235. IEEE Computer Society (2009)
15. Janes, A., Succi, G.: Lean Software Development in Action. Springer, Heidelberg (2014). https://doi.org/10.1007/978-3-642-00503-9
16. Laurel, B.: Computers as theatre, September 2014
17. Lee, C.: Learning to code is just like learning to dance, May 2018. Accessed 28 Oct 2018
18. Mashiko, Y., Basili, V.R.: Using the GQM paradigm to investigate influential factors for software process improvement. J. Syst. Softw. **36**(1), 17–32 (1997)
19. Maurer, F., Succi, G., Holz, H., Kötting, B., Goldmann, S., Dellen, B.: Software process support over the internet. In: Proceedings of the 21st International Conference on Software Engineering, ICSE 1999, pp. 642–645. ACM, May 1999
20. Sedgwick, E.K., Parker, A.: Performativity and Performance. Routledge, London (2013)
21. Ravipati, S.: Students learn computer programming skills through dance, February 2016
22. Rosner, F.: Explain agile like i'm a sports student (2018)
23. Rubin, K.S.: Essential scrum: A practical guide to the most popular agile process (2012). Accessed 27 June 2018
24. Sillitti, A., Janes, A., Succi, G., Vernazza, T.: Measures for mobile users: an architecture. J. Syst. Architect. **50**(7), 393–405 (2004)

Development and Operation of Trustworthy Smart IoT Systems: The ENACT Framework

Nicolas Ferry[1]([✉]), Jacek Dominiak[4], Anne Gallon[3], Elena González[4], Eider Iturbe[6], Stéphane Lavirotte[2], Saturnino Martinez[6], Andreas Metzger[5], Victor Muntés-Mulero[4], Phu H. Nguyen[1], Alexander Palm[5], Angel Rego[6], Erkuden Rios[6], Diego Riviera[7], Arnor Solberg[8], Hui Song[1], Jean-Yves Tigli[2], and Thierry Winter[3]

[1] SINTEF Digital, Oslo, Norway
{nicolas.ferry,phu.nguyen,hui.song}@sintef.no
[2] Université Côte d'Azur, CNRS, I3S, Sophia Antipolis, France
{stephane.lavirotte,jean-yves.tigli}@univ-cotedazur.fr
[3] EVIDIAN, Les Clayes-sous-Bois, France
{anne.gallon,thierry.winter}@evidian.com
[4] Beawre Digital SL, Barcelona, Spain
{jacek.dominiak,elena.gonzalez,victor.muntes-mulero}@beawre.com
[5] Paluno (The Ruhr Institute for Software Technology),
University of Duisburg-Essen, Duisburg, Germany
{andreas.metzger,alexander.palm}@paluno.uni-due.de
[6] Fundación Tecnalia Research & Innovation, Derio, Spain
{eider.iturbe,saturnino.martinez,angel.rego,
erkuden.rios}@tecnalia.com
[7] Montimage, Paris, France
diego.riviera@montimage.com
[8] Tellu IoT AS, Oslo, Norway
arnor.solberg@tellu.no

Abstract. To unleash the full potential of IoT, it is critical to facilitate threation and operation of trustworthy Smart IoT Systems (SIS). Software development and delivery of SIS would greatly benefit from DevOps as devices and IoT services requirements for reliability, quality, security and safety are paramount. However, DevOps practices are far from widely adopted in the IoT, in particular, due to a lack of key enabling tools. In last year paper at DevOps'18, we presented the ENACT research roadmap that identified the critical challenges to enable DevOps in the realm of trustworthy SIS. In this paper, we present the ENACT DevOps Framework as our current realization of these methods and tools.

Keywords: DevOps · Internet-of-Things · Trustworthiness

1 Introduction

To fully realize the potential of the IoT, it is important to facilitate the creation and operation of the next generation IoT systems that we denote as Smart IoT Systems (SIS). SIS typically need to perform distributed processing and coordinated behaviour across IoT, edge and cloud infrastructures, manage the closed loop from sensing to

© Springer Nature Switzerland AG 2020
J.-M. Bruel et al. (Eds.): DEVOPS 2019, LNCS 12055, pp. 121–138, 2020.
https://doi.org/10.1007/978-3-030-39306-9_9

actuation, and cope with vast heterogeneity, scalability and dynamicity of IoT systems and their environments.

Major challenges are to improve the efficiency and the collaboration between operation and development teams for the rapid and agile design and evolution of the system. To address these challenges, the ENACT H2020 project [7] embraces the DevOps approach and principles. DevOps [10] has recently emerged as a software development practice that encourages developers to continuously patch, update, or bring new features to the system under operation without sacrificing quality. Software development and delivery of SIS would greatly benefit from DevOps as devices and IoT services requirements for reliability, quality, security and safety are paramount. However, even if DevOps is not bound to any application domain, many challenges appear when the IoT intersects with DevOps. As a result, DevOps practices are far from widely adopted in the IoT, in particular, due to a lack of key enabling tools [13, 19].

Current DevOps solutions typically lack mechanisms for continuous quality assurance [13], *e.g.*, mechanisms to ensure end-to-end security and privacy as well as mechanisms able to take into consideration open context and actuation conflicts (*e.g.*, allowing continuous testing of IoT systems within emulated and simulated infrastructures). It also remains challenging to perform continuous deployment and evolution of IoT systems across IoT, edge, and cloud spaces [13]. Our recent systematic studies have found a lack of addressing trustworthiness aspects in the current IoT deployment and orchestration approaches [14, 15]. These are key features to provide DevOps for trustworthy SIS.

To address this issue, ENACT will deliver a set of tools for the DevOps of trustworthy SIS. In our former paper [7], we presented the ENACT research roadmap that identified the critical challenges to enable DevOps in the realm of trustworthy SIS. We also introduced the related contribution of the ENACT project and an evolution of the DevOps methods and tools to address these challenges. In this paper, we aim at presenting the ENACT DevOps Framework as our current realization of these methods and tools.

The remainder of this paper is organized as follows. Section 2 presents the overall architecture of the ENACT DevOps Framework, including its architecture and details about the different tools that form this framework. Section 3 exemplifies how they can be used all together to develop and operate trustworthy SIS. Section 4 details how trustworthiness is used as a driver for feedback between Ops and Dev activities. Section 5 summarizes the list of models shared between all the ENACT tools. Finally, Sect. 6 presents related works and Sect. 7 concludes.

2   The ENACT Approach

The ENACT DevOps approach is to evolve DevOps methods and techniques to support the development and operation of smart IoT systems, which *(i)* are distributed, *(ii)* involve sensors and actuators and *(iii)* need to be trustworthy (*i.e.*, trustworthiness refers to the preservation of security, privacy, reliability, resilience, and safety [9]).

2.1   Conceptual Architecture of the ENACT DevOps Framework

ENACT provides an integrated DevOps Framework composed of a set of loosely coupled tools. Still, these tools can be seamlessly combined, and they can easily integrate with existing IoT platform services and enablers. Figure 1 shows the set of tools that forms the ENACT DevOps Framework as well as the relationships between these tools. This conceptual architecture consists of five layers, where each layer denotes a particular level of abstraction, complexity and dynamicity.

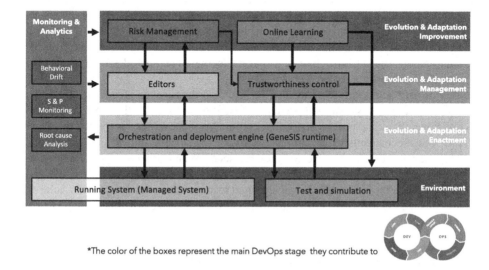

*The color of the boxes represent the main DevOps stage they contribute to

Fig. 1. The ENACT overall architecture

From the most abstract to the most concrete (*i.e.*, from the farthest to the closest to the running system), the layers are described as follows:

1. **Evolution & Adaptation Improvement Layer:** This layer provides the mechanisms to continuously improve and manage the development and operation processes of trustworthy SIS. On the one hand, the Risk Management tool helps organizations to analyze the architecture of their Smart IoT Systems and detecting potential vulnerabilities and the associated risk (in particular related to security and privacy aspects) and propose related mitigation actions. Risk management tools typically relates to the Plan stage in the DevOps process. However, in ENACT we will extend the scope to provide continuous risk management. On the other hand, the Online Learning tool focuses on improving the behaviour of the adaptation engine that will support the operation of trustworthy SIS. This tool typically relates to the Operate stage of the DevOps process. In general, the improvement layer provides feedback and knowledge to all the other DevOps stages with the aim to improve the development and operation of trustworthy SIS. Thus, in this architecture, information from this layer are provided to the evolution and adaptation management layer with the aim to improve it.

2. **Evolution & Adaptation Management Layer:** This layer first embeds a set of editors to specify the behaviours as well as the orchestration and deployment of SIS across IoT, Edge and Cloud infrastructure. These editors integrate with mechanisms to maximize and control the trustworthiness of the system. All together, these components cover activities in both the Dev and Ops parts of a DevOps process and in particular to the code, build and operate stages. The activities performed at this layer are strongly affected by the inputs from the improvement layer.

3. **Evolution & Adaptation Enactment Layer:** This layer bridges the gap between development and operation as its goal is to enact the deployment and adaptation actions decided at the Evolution & Adaptation Management Layer. The mechanisms of this layer monitor and manage the deployment of the running system.

4. **Environment Layer:** This layer consists of the running system together with the environment and infrastructure in which it executes. This includes both production and testing environments.

5. **Monitoring and Analytics Layer:** This layer is orthogonal and feeds the other four. The tools at this layer are supporting the monitoring stage of the DevOps process and typically aim at providing feedback from Ops to Dev. More precisely, this layer provides mechanisms to monitor the status of the system and of its environment. This includes mechanisms to monitor the security and privacy of a SIS. In addition, it performs analytic tasks providing: *(i)* high level notifications with insights on ongoing security issues, *(ii)* diagnostics and recommendations on system's failures, and *(iii)* feedback on the behavioural drift of SIS (*i.e.*, system is functioning but not delivering the expected behaviour).

2.2   Evolution and Adaptation Improvement Layer

The improvement layer consists of two tools: *(i)* the Risk Management tool and *(ii)* the Online Learning tool.

Risk Management: The Risk Management tool provides concepts and tools for the agile, context-aware, and risk-driven decision support and mechanisms for application developers and operators to support the continuous delivery of trustworthy SIS. The approach is an evolution of the MUSA Risks management tool [17] that focused security for cloud-based systems. The extension comes with the ability to define IoT-related risks, both by selecting predefined risks stored in a catalogue or allowing users to define them. It also allows for the assessment of such risks. The Risk Management tool integrates with the DevOps cycle to continuously monitor the risk mitigation status through evidences collectors and, thus, enable continuous risk management. The Risk Management tool consumes as input a catalogue of risk treatments, catalogues of security and privacy controls, and an orchestration and deployment model. It produces as output a risk management plan, which includes a set of risk treatment suggestions, and continuous information about the status of the implementation of the different treatments, as well as the effectiveness of these treatments when this information is available.

Online Learning: The Online Learning tool supports a system in the way it adapts itself. Adaptation helps a system to maintain its quality requirements in the presence of environment changes. To develop an adaptive system, developers need an intricate understanding of the system implementation and its environment, and how adaptation impacts system quality. However, due to design-time uncertainty, anticipating all potential environment changes at design-time is in most cases infeasible. Online learning facilitates addressing design-time uncertainty. By observing the system and its environment at run-time, online learning can automatically refine a system's adaptation capabilities. One of the most widely used online learning techniques is reinforcement learning, which can learn the effectiveness of adaptation actions through interactions with the system's environment. All existing reinforcement learning approaches use value-based reinforcement learning, which are not able to cope with large, continuous environment states (cf. Sect. 6). To address this issue we instead realize our Online Learning tool, we employ policy-based reinforcement learning, a fundamentally different reinforcement learning technique. In a further state the tool should be able to take behavioural drift information as an input to trigger new learning phases. At this state the online learning tool consumes information about the current environment state of the system to adapt, and attributes of the system that can be used to compute a reward to evaluate the current parameter setting. It then produces a new parameter setting which can be applied to the system, so that a new time-step in the underlying sequential decision problem is reached.

2.3   Evolution and Adaptation Management Layer

The evolution and adaptation management layer is composed of two main groups of tools: *(i)* the editors and *(ii)* the trustworthiness controls.

The editors are meant to support DevOps engineers in specifying the behaviour and deployment of SIS. This includes:

ThingML: ThingML [12] is an open source IoT framework that includes a language and a set of generators to support the modelling of system behaviours and their automatic derivation across heterogeneous and distributed devices at the IoT and edge end. The ThingML code generation framework has been used to generate code in different languages, targeting around 10 different target platforms (ranging from tiny 8-bit microcontrollers to servers) and 10 different communication protocols. ThingML models can be platform specific, meaning that they can only be used to generate code for a specific platform (for instance to exploit some specificities of the platform); or they can be platform independent, meaning that they can be used to generate code in different languages. In ENACT, ThingML can be used to specify the behaviour of software components that will be part of a SIS. As part of ENACT, ThingML is extended with mechanisms to monitor and debug the execution flow of a ThingML program. Following the ThingML philosophy, the proposed monitoring mechanism is platform independent, meaning that the concepts monitored at the target program execution are refined as ThingML concepts. The ThingML run-time consumes as input ThingML programs and produces as output an implementation of an application component.

GeneSIS: GeneSIS [6] is a tool to support the continuous orchestration and deployment of SIS, allowing decentralized processing across heterogeneous IoT, edge, and cloud infrastructures. GeneSIS includes: *(i)* a domain-specific modelling language to model the orchestration and deployment of SIS; and *(ii)* an execution engine that supports the orchestration of IoT, edge, and cloud services as well as their automatic deployment across IoT, edge, and cloud infrastructure resources. GeneSIS is being built as part of ENACT and inspires from CloudML [4], a tool for the deployment of multi-cloud systems. GeneSIS will also embed the necessary concepts (both in the language and in the execution engine) to support the deployment of security and privacy controls [5] and monitoring mechanisms as well as for the deployment of actuation conflict managers. Finally, GeneSIS will offer specific mechanisms to support the deployment of ThingML programs. The GeneSIS execution engine consumes as inputs deployable artefacts (*i.e.*, implementation of application components that need to be allocated on host services and infrastructure) and a GeneSIS deployment model. It produces as output a GeneSIS deployment model with run-time information (*e.g.*, IP addresses), notifications about the status of a deployed system, and actually deploys the SIS.

Actuation Conflict Manager: The Actuation Conflict Manager tool supports the identification, analysis and resolution of actuation conflicts. The identification of actuation conflicts is done during development and thus relies on the overall architecture of the SIS. It consists in identifying concurrent accesses to the same actuator or actuators interacting through a shared physical environment. The analysis of the conflicts consists in understanding the flow of data coming to the actuators. This includes understanding where the data originated from as well as the path it followed (*i.e.*, through which components) before reaching the actuator. The conflict resolution will provide DevOps engineers with the ability to either *(i)* select an off-the-shelf actuation conflict manager or *(ii)* design their own actuation conflict manager with safety requirements. Finally, the actuation conflict manager tool will support the integration of the actuation conflict manager into the SIS. The Actuation Conflict Manager consumes, as input, an orchestration and deployment model and produces and provides, as output, an actuation conflict manager together with a new orchestration and deployment model (that includes the actuation conflict manager).

The trustworthiness control tools are meant to ensure the trustworthiness of a SIS. This includes:

Diversifier: At development time, the Diversifier consumes as input a GeneSIS deployment model or a ThingML behaviour specification and produces as output multiple diverse specifications. At the current stage, the architecture diversification is focused on diversifying the composition of reusable blocks, and the code (behaviour) diversifier is focused on the diversification of communication protocols. At run-time, the diversifier aims at managing a large and dynamic number of sub-systems with emerging and injected diversity, in order to achieve the robustness and resilience of the entire system. In short, it monitors and records the diversity among subsystems, managing the lifecycles of these subsystems, and controls the upgrading, deployment and modification of software components on these subsystems.

Security and Privacy controls: Security and Privacy control tool is a set of multiple mechanisms that, in a complementary way, can provide security and/or privacy to different elements of a SIS. It will provide security controls embedded in the IoT platform related to integrity, non-repudiation and access control. Moreover, the communications sent through the IoT platform can be stopped based on specific pre-defined rules related to the behaviour of the SIS. The tool will be further enhanced with a Security and Privacy Control Manager that can enable, disable and configure the controls provided within the Security and Privacy control tool.

Context-Aware Access Control: The Context-Aware Access Control tool is a solution for dynamic authorization based on context for both IT and OT (operational technologies) domains. In particular, this tool provides Context-aware risk and trust-based dynamic authorization mechanisms ensuring *(i)* that an authenticated IoT node accesses only what it is authorized to and *(ii)* that an IoT node can only be accessed by authorized software components. Access authorizations will be adapted according to contextual information. Context may be for instance the date and time an access authorization is requested, the geolocation of this request, or it can be dynamic attributes coming from other external sources (sensors, other applications, etc.). The Context-Aware Access Control tool consumes as inputs rules for contextual adaptation and access control policies.

2.4   Evolution and Adaptation Enactment Layer

The adaptation enactment layer basically consists of the GeneSIS execution environment. From a deployment model specified using the GENESIS Modelling language, the GENESIS execution environment is responsible for: *(i)* deploying the software components, *(ii)* ensuring communication between them, *(iii)* provisioning cloud resources, and *(iv)* monitoring the status of the deployment. The GENESIS deployment engine implements the Models@Run-time pattern [2] to support the dynamic adaptation of a deployment with minimal impact on the running system. It provides the other tools with interface to dynamically adapt the orchestration and deployment of a SIS.

2.5   System Layer

In addition to the running system, this layer encompasses the test and simulation tool.

Test and simulation: Test and simulation tool provides concepts and tools for running application scenarios against the set of programmed circumstances. The tool-set is aiming to provide a baseline for performance, resilience testing as well as risk management testing. It does replicate the behaviour of previously observed devices and is able to play back the sensors data against the programmed scenarios. The tool consumes the treatments from the risk management group and produces the report for the outputs of the scenarios.

2.6   Monitoring and Analytics Layer

The monitoring and analytics layer is composed of three tools: *(i)* the Security and Privacy Monitoring tool, *(ii)* the Root Cause Analysis tool, and *(iii)* the Behavioural Drift Analysis tool.

Security and Privacy Monitoring: The Security and Privacy Monitoring tool allows the IoT application operator to monitor the security and privacy status of the IoT system at different layers. The tool will capture and analyse data from multiple and heterogeneous sources such as raw data from network, system and application layers, as well as events from security monitoring components such as intrusion prevention and intrusion detection systems (IPS/IDS). All the data will be processed and displayed in a common dashboard, which includes processed information in the form of alerts, statistics and graphs. This information will be further enhanced with a standardized classification of security events (such as MITRE ATT&CK) and candidate security controls that can mitigate the detected potential threat.

Root Cause Analysis: The main objective of the Root Cause Analysis (RCA) module is to provide the ENACT platform with a reliable tool capable of detecting the origin of failures on the system. This engine relies on both instrumentation of the software (logs generation or specific instrumentation software) and monitoring of the devices and network. The RCA tool will use these data as the principal input to generate a graph of the system, which will be used to identify the scope of the detected anomalies. Later, the graph that represents the potential impact of the anomalies will be matched against a previously-assessed anomalies database, whose Root Cause is already known. This process will be further enhanced with feedback from the system administrator, who will be able to decide which is the best match for the anomaly detected. The feedback received from the user (the correct and erroneous matches) will be used by the RCA module to adjust its calculation and learn from the context of the system.

Behavioural Drift Analysis: The objective of the Behavioural Drift Analysis tool is to detect whenever a SIS derives (during operation) from its expected behaviour (at development time) and to provide the DevOps engineer with comprehensible representations and models of the drifting behaviour. The drift is measured via a set of probes and sensors that monitors the behaviour of the SIS and by comparing what is observed to the behaviour modelled during development. The DevOps engineer has thus access to a dashboard with representations that aim at facilitating drifts diagnostic by displaying metrics and drifting behaviour models. The Behavioural Drift Analysis tool consumes, as input, a behavioural model of the SIS as well as implementations of the monitoring probes. It produces, as output, measurements describing behavioural drifts as well as a behavioural model updated based on run-time observations.

3   An Example of the ENACT Workflow

Figure 2 depicts an example of workflow between the ENACT development tools.

First, a DevOps engineer can use GeneSIS (aka., the orchestration and deployment tool) to specify the overall architecture of a SIS (①). This model can thus serve as input for the Risk Management tool, which will help conducting a risk analysis and assessment and may result in a set of mitigation actions, for instance advocating the use of a specific set of security mechanisms (②). As a result, the DevOps engineer may update the model describing the architecture of the SIS before its refinement into a

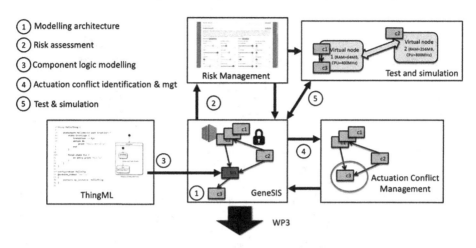

Fig. 2. The ENACT development toolkit

proper deployment model. The DevOps engineer might also use ThingML to implement some of the software components that should be deployed as part of the SIS (③). At this stage, the Actuation Conflict Manager enabler can be used to identify actuation conflicts – *e.g.*, concurrent accesses to an actuator (④). This enabler will support the DevOps engineer in either selecting or designing an actuation conflict manager to be deployed as part of the SIS (typically as a proxy managing the accesses to the actuator). Finally, the SIS can be simulated and tested, in particular against security threats and scalability issues (⑤) before being sent to GeneSIS for deployment.

As depicted in Fig. 3, before deployment, the DevOps engineer may use the Diversifier to increase the overall robustness of the system (⑥). This tool can generate different variants, but still functionally equivalent, of the components of the SIS (*e.g.*, different versions of the software components are deployed making the overall SIS more robust to security and privacy attacks). After diversification, the SIS can be deployed using GeneSIS. Once the SIS in operation, a set of ENACT tools are responsible for its run-time monitoring and control. Monitoring tools are depicted on the right part of Fig. 3 (⑦). First, the Behavioural Drift Analysis tool can be used to understand to which extent a SIS behaves (in the real world) as expected (during development). This is important as a SIS typically operates in the midst of the unpredictable physical world and thus all the situations it may face at run-time may not have been fully understood or anticipated during development. Second, the Security and Privacy monitoring tool can be used to identify security and privacy breaches. Third, in case of failure, the Root Cause Analysis tool provides DevOps teams with insights on the origin of that failure. Control tools are depicted on the left part of Fig. 3. First, the Context-aware Access Control tool can be used to manage accesses from services to sensors and actuators and the other way around (⑧). Accesses can be granted or removed based on context information. Finally, the Online Learning enabler uses reinforcement learning techniques to enhance the adaptation logic embedded into a SIS (⑨).

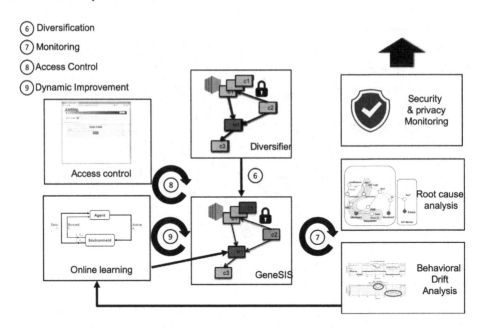

Fig. 3. The ENACT operation toolkit

4   Trustworthiness as a Driver for Feedback Between Ops and Dev

One of the core values of DevOps is to improve synergies and communications between development and operation activities. When software is in production it often produces a plethora of data that ranges from logs to high level indicators (*e.g.*, performance indicators, context monitoring). All these data gathered at run-time can serve as valuable feedback [3] from operation to development and, in particular, it can serve to evolve and improve the SIS by triggering a new development cycle. Some of the challenges are thus to properly integrate development and operation tools and to seamlessly integrate feedbacks from run-time into development tools. In this section, we illustrate how we address this challenge in the project.

In the context of ENACT, one of the main drivers for triggering a new development cycle of a SIS on the basis of observations from operation is to improve its trustworthiness, and in particular its security, privacy, resilience, reliability and safety. In the following (see Fig. 4) we illustrate how security and privacy run-time information can be used to continuously assess risk and can, in turn, lead to an evolution of a SIS.

First, a DevOps engineer can use GeneSIS (aka., the orchestration and deployment tool) to specify the overall architecture of a SIS. The resulting deployment model can be sent to the Risk Management enabler. The latter is thus used to perform a risk assessment that will result in a set of risk treatment suggestions. A risk treatment can be a procedure to follow in order to mitigate a risk or simply a recommendation to use a specific software solution or mechanism (*e.g.*, a security control solution such as the Context-Aware Access Control). It is worth noting that a procedure can also include

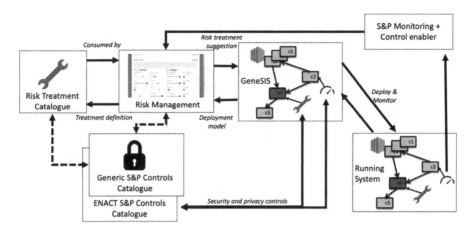

Fig. 4. Continuous risk management

a recommendation for using a specific software solution or mechanism. These recommendations are typically linked to concrete implementations of the solution or mechanisms. In particular, it can leverage a generic security and privacy controls catalogue that includes state of the art security and privacy solutions or the ENACT security and privacy controls catalogue (*i.e.*, the controls implemented in ENACT). It is worth noting that by security and privacy controls we not only refer to mechanisms to implement security or privacy measures but also to mechanisms to monitor security and privacy. The Risk Management enabler embeds a catalogue of risk treatments and can be used to specify and add new ones into the catalogue. From the risk treatment suggestions, the DevOps engineer may decide to evolve its deployment model specifying that specific security and privacy controls (whose implementation is indicated in the suggestion and depicted in Fig. 4 as the green icons) should be deployed together with the SIS. After deployment, GeneSIS monitors the status of the deployment whilst the Security and Privacy controls enablers gather security and privacy data from the probes deployed together with the systems. Both tools send some of the gathered metrics to the Risk Management enablers. These metrics are associated to the risk models and used to continuously assess risk.

In the following (see Fig. 5), we illustrate how run-time information from the root cause analysis and behavioural drift analysis enablers can be used to improve the resilience, reliability and safety of a SIS.

The Behavioural drift analysis tool aims at observing the actual behaviour of a SIS at run-time and at comparing it with the behaviour that was expected at development time. One result of the comparison is a value called: behavioural drift metric. A behavioural drift may result from a problem in the conception of the SIS, an indirect actuation conflict (*e.g.*, applications are properly design but their actions on the physical environment are somehow conflicting) or an unexpected reaction of the surrounding physical environment. Because it is difficult for a DevOps engineer to understand and take actions simply on the basis of a behavioural drift metric, the tool performs an analysis of this

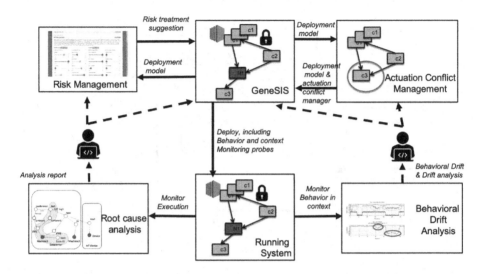

Fig. 5. Continuous improvement of resilience, reliability, and safety

drift, which consists in comparing the model of the expected system's behaviour and the observed one on the basis of what is actually happening at run-time (*e.g.*, the behaviour model is no more deterministic, some probabilities of transitions between states can increase from zero and others can decrease from one). In case a behavioural drift is observed, the tool will provide the DevOps engineer with the analysis, the latter can in turn adapt the SIS via GeneSIS.

The Root cause analysis tool will observe the execution of the system and, in case of failures, report on its origin. Such report will be provided to the DevOps engineer, who can in turn adapt the SIS via GeneSIS or perform a new risk assessment.

5   Shared Models and Artefacts

The ENACT Framework tools manipulate and exchange different types of models and software artefacts as illustrated in Fig. 6. Models are represented as rectangles whilst software artefacts (*i.e.*, binaries, scripts, etc. which are generated from or are part of a tool, and used or managed by another) are depicted by circles. A model is embedded in a tool when it is directly used in the internal of the tool.

It is worth noting that the GeneSIS and ThingML models are the most reused amongst the tools. This is because they are the key models specifying the architecture and behavior of a SIS whilst the other are mainly used to manage trustworthiness aspects of the SIS. In the following we shortly describe each model:

- **GeneSIS deployment Model:** is written in a domain-specific modelling language to specify deployment model – *i.e.*, the orchestration and deployment of SIS across the IoT, edge, and cloud spaces.
- **ThingML Model:** is written in a domain specific modelling language to specify the behavior of distributed software components.

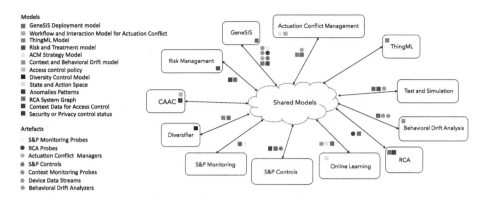

Fig. 6. Models manipulated and exchanged in the ENACT framework

- **Workflow and Interaction Model for Actuation Conflict Model:** describes the interactions between the software components that form a SIS and their relationship with actuators, thus, supporting the identification of both direct and indirect actuation conflict.
- **Risk and Treatment Model:** describes risk and treatment suggestions.
- **ACM Strategy:** takes the form of a set of extended ECA rules describing the behavior of a custom actuation conflict manager.
- **Context and Behavioural Drift:** can be used to describe the SIS operational context and to describe its observed behavior (compared to the expected one).
- **Access Control Policy:** is a set of rules that define whether a user or device must be permitted or denied accessing to a resource.
- **Context Data for Access Control:** provides contextual data on a user and his devices. These data are dynamic attributes and come from other external sources.
- **Diversity Control Model:** a model maintained at run-time that reflects the status in term of deployment, software version and health of a fleet of IoT systems or subsystems.
- **State and Action Space:** for the online learning tool, the state space represents different environment situations, while the action space represents the different actions the online learning tool may execute to improve the adaptation logic of the Smart IoT system.
- **Anomalies Pattern:** is used to describe a set of patterns, which will be the baselines for the RCA enabler to check the existence of anomalies and maps them to their Root Cause.
- **RCA System Graph:** is a snapshot of the current status (*e.g.*, network activity, system logs, detected anomalies) of the monitored system.
- **Security and Privacy Control Status:** provides information about the status of the security and privacy mechanisms used in the SIS. It is used to understand the current status of the risk but also the progression of the treatment.

In the following we shortly describes each software artefact:

- **Security and Privacy Monitoring Probes:** are deployed together with the SIS with the aim to monitor the status of specific security and privacy aspects. There are probes at the network, application, and system levels.
- **Root Cause Analysis Probes:** retrieve information from the logs generated by the devices on the IoT System, but they will also be able to interact with hardware-based probes (such as the MMT-IoT Sniffer) and software-based solutions (such as Snort and Suricata).
- **Actuation Conflict Managers:** are deployed together with the SIS and are responsible for managing the accesses to conflicting actuators (direct or indirect). All accesses to the actuators should go via the actuation conflict manager. Actuation conflict managers are either provided off-the-shelf or can be designed for a specific type of conflict.
- **Security and Privacy Controls:** are implementations of security and privacy mechanisms to be deployed together with the SIS.
- **Context Monitoring Probes:** are monitoring the context of a SIS. They are deployed together with the SIS and are, in particular, used by the behavioral drift analyzers.
- **Device Data Streams:** are records of devices outputs and inputs used by the test and simulation tool to replay devices behavior.
- **Behavioral Drift Analyzers:** are software components generated by the Behavioral drift analysis tool. They are responsible for analysing a specific behavior of a SIS. Multiple Behavioral Drift Analyzers can be deployed together with the SIS.

6   Related Work

For some years now, multiple tools and solutions have emerged to support the DevOps of software systems and in particular to automate their testing, build, deployment and monitoring. However, to the best of our knowledge, there is no DevOps support tailored for smart IoT systems today [13, 19]. According to [19] a key reason is: "the extremely dynamic nature of IoT systems poses additional challenges, for instance, continuous debugging and testing of IoT systems can be very challenging because of the large number of devices, dynamic topologies, unreliable connectivity, and heterogeneous and sometimes invisible nature of the devices". In the following we discuss related work for both the development and operation of SIS.

Continuous Development of SIS: The survey in [14] illustrates a lack of approaches and tools specifically designed for supporting the continuous deployment of software systems over IoT, edge, and cloud infrastructure. For example, several solutions are available on the market for the deployment of cloud-based systems such as CloudMF [4], OpenTOSCA [18], Cloudify[1], and Brooklyn[2]. Those are tailored to provision and manage virtual machines or PaaS solutions. In addition, similar tools focus on the

---

[1] http://cloudify.co/.
[2] https://brooklyn.apache.org.

management and orchestration of containers, *e.g.*, Docker Compose[3], Kubernetes[4]. Opposed to hypervisor virtual machines, containers such as Docker containers leverage lightweight virtualization technology, which executes directly on the operating system of the host. As a result, Docker shares and exploits a lot of the resources offered by the operating system thus reducing containers' footprint. Thanks to these characteristics, container technologies are not only relevant for cloud infrastructure but can also be used on edge devices. On the other side, few tools such as Resin.io and ioFog are specifically designed for the IoT. In particular, Resin.io provides mechanisms for *(i)* the automated deployment of code on devices, *(ii)* the management of a fleet of devices, and *(iii)* the monitoring of the status of these devices. Resin.io supports the following continuous deployment process. Once the code for the software component to be deployed is pushed to the Git server of the Resin.io cloud, it is built in an environment that matches the targeted hosting device(s) (*e.g.*, ARMv6 for a Raspberry Pi) and a Docker image is created before being deployed on the target hosting device(s). However, Resin.io offers limited support for the deployment and management of software components on tiny devices that cannot host containers. The same applies to Microsoft IoT Hub[5].

In addition, the survey in [14] also highlights that very few primary IoT deployment studies address *(i)* security and privacy aspects, and *(ii)* the management of actuators (and actuation conflict). Even if no DevOps solutions for IoT systems embed specific mechanisms for the management of actuation conflicts, the core of this challenge relates to the generic problem of managing features interactions. Indeed, when a global functionality is obtained from a set of shared features, there is a risk for unintended and undesirable interactions between the features. However, because current work on this topic do not focus on the IoT application domain, they encompass the following weaknesses. They give a low degree of importance to *(i)* the modelling of the physical environment as part of the conflicts identification process, and *(ii)* to reusability, scalability and dynamicity as part of the resolution process.

Similarly, there is a lack of risk analysis methodologies that are adapted to agile contexts but still achieve the level of analysis and detail provided by traditional risk assessment and mitigation techniques, in particular related to NFRs. Fitzgerald *et al.* [8] illustrate how Lean Thinking [20] can be applied to continuous software engineering. Authors even go beyond software development and consider issues such as continuous use, continuous trust, etc., coining the term "Continuous" (Continuous Star). However, they do not explicitly tackle challenges related to continuous risk management.

Continuous Operation of SIS: By observing the system and its environment at runtime, online learning can automatically refine a system's adaptation capabilities. One of the most widely used online learning techniques is reinforcement learning, which can learn the effectiveness of adaptation actions through interactions with the system's environment. However, so far, all existing reinforcement learning approaches use value-based reinforcement learning and thus face two key limitations. First, they face the exploration/exploitation dilemma, which requires developers to fine-tune the amount

---

[3] https://docs.docker.com/compose/.

[4] https://kubernetes.io.

[5] https://azure.microsoft.com/fr-fr/services/iot-hub/.

of exploration to ensure convergence of the learning process. Second, most approaches store the learned knowledge in a lookup table, which requires developers to manually quantify environment states to facilitate scalability. To realize the Inline Learning too, we thus automate both these manual activities by employing policy-based reinforcement learning, a fundamentally different reinforcement learning technique. Thereby, our Online Learning tool is able to cope with large, continuous environment states. In a further state the tool should be able to take behavioural drift information as an input to trigger new learning phases.

Online learning is meant to be performed at run-time, considering observations about the physical environment, the state of the system, and so the context. Context-awareness is key to collect sensor data, to understand it and to provide valuable information to reasoning engines. Since the first definition of context [1] a lot of middleware and software frameworks have emerged. Already in 2014, [16] finds 50 context-aware solutions in the scientific literature and today lot of well-known approaches are available [11] to collect sensors and probes data leveraged for modelling various contextual concerns (location, situation, social environment, etc.). However, SIS pose new challenges. Indeed, as far as physical things are concerned, no guaranty can be made on their availability on the long run. The underlying infrastructure of SIS can thus be volatile. Moreover, the purpose of some of these systems can only be achieved from interactions with the physical environment through actuators (*e.g.*, Heating, Ventilation and Air-Conditioning controllers). In this context, these systems can possibly be affected by unanticipated physical processes over which they have no control, leading their behaviour to potentially drift over time in the best case or to malfunction in the worst case. As said, many platforms include context awareness and monitoring mechanisms (*e.g.*, SOFIA2[6], FIWARE[7] with the Orion Context Broker for instance). However, these platforms do not consider behavioural drift monitoring as an awareness criterion. This is what is addressed by our behavioral drift analysis tool.

7   Conclusion

We presented the ENACT DevOps Framework which offers a set of novel solutions to address challenges related to the development, operation, and quality assurance of trustworthy smart IoT systems that need to be distributed across IoT, edge and cloud infrastructures and involve both sensors and actuators. These enablers are under development as part of the ENACT H2020 project and will be delivered as open source artefacts.

Acknowledgement. The research leading to these results has received funding from the European Commission's H2020 Programme under grant agreement numbers 780351 (ENACT).

---

[6] https://sofia2.com.
[7] https://www.fiware.org.

References

1. Abowd, G.D., Dey, A.K., Brown, P.J., Davies, N., Smith, M., Steggles, P.: Towards a better understanding of context and context-awareness. In: Gellersen, H.-W. (ed.) HUC 1999. LNCS, vol. 1707, pp. 304–307. Springer, Heidelberg (1999). https://doi.org/10.1007/3-540-48157-5_29

2. Blair, G., Bencomo, N., France, R.: Models@run.time. IEEE Comput. **42**(10), 22–27 (2009). https://doi.org/10.1109/MC.2009.326

3. Cito, J., Wettinger, J., Lwakatare, L.E., Borg, M., Li, F.: Feedback from operations to software development—a devops perspective on runtime metrics and logs. In: Bruel, J.-M., Mazzara, M., Meyer, B. (eds.) DEVOPS 2018. LNCS, vol. 11350, pp. 184–195. Springer, Cham (2019). https://doi.org/10.1007/978-3-030-06019-0_14

4. Ferry, N., Chauvel, F., Song, H., Rossini, A., Lushpenko, M., Solberg, A.: CloudMF: model-driven management of multi-cloud applications. ACM Trans. Internet Technol. (TOIT) **18**(2), 16 (2018)

5. Ferry, N., Nguyen, P.H.: Towards model-based continuous deployment of secure IoT systems. In: 1st International Workshop on DevOps@MODELS (2019)

6. Ferry, N., et al.: Genesis: continuous orchestration and deployment of smart IoT systems. In: 2019 IEEE 43rd Annual Computer Software and Applications Conference (COMPSAC), vol. 1, pp. 870–875 (2019). https://doi.org/10.1109/COMPSAC.2019.00127

7. Ferry, N., et al.: ENACT: development, operation, and quality assurance of trustworthy smart IoT systems. In: Bruel, J.-M., Mazzara, M., Meyer, B. (eds.) DEVOPS 2018. LNCS, vol. 11350, pp. 112–127. Springer, Cham (2019). https://doi.org/10.1007/978-3-030-06019-0_9

8. Fitzgerald, B., Stol, K., O'Sullivan, R., O'Brien, D.: Scaling agile methods to regulated environments: an industry case study. In: International Conference on Software Engineering, ICSE 2013, pp. 863–872. IEEE Press (2013). http://dl.acm.org/citation.cfm?id=2486788.2486906

9. Griffor, E.R., Greer, C., Wollman, D.A., Burns, M.J.: Framework for cyber-physical systems: volume 1, overview. Technical report (2017)

10. Humble, J., Farley, D.: Continuous Delivery: Reliable Software Releases Through Build, Test, and Deployment Automation. Addison-Wesley Professional, Boston (2010)

11. Künzler, F., Kramer, J.N., Kowatsch, T.: Efficacy of mobile context-aware notification management systems: a systematic literature review and meta-analysis. In: 2017 IEEE 13th International Conference on Wireless and Mobile Computing, Networking and Communications (WiMob), pp. 131–138. IEEE (2017)

12. Morin, B., Fleurey, F., Husa, K.E., Barais, O.: A generative middleware for heterogeneous and distributed services. In: 19th International ACM SIGSOFT Symposium on Component-Based Software Engineering (CBSE), pp. 107–116. IEEE (2016)

13. NESSI: Software continuum: Recommendations for ICT Work Programme 2018+. Nessi report (2016)

14. Nguyen, P.H., et al.: Advances in deployment and orchestration approaches for IoT - a systematic review. In: 2019 IEEE International Congress on Internet of Things (ICIOT), pp. 53–60, July 2019. https://doi.org/10.1109/ICIOT.2019.00021

15. Nguyen, P.H., et al.: The preliminary results of a mapping study of deployment and orchestration for IoT. In: Proceedings of the 34th ACM/SIGAPP Symposium on Applied Computing, SAC 2019, pp. 2040–2043. ACM, New York (2019). https://doi.org/10.1145/3297280.3297617. http://doi.acm.org/10.1145/3297280.3297617

16. Perera, C., Zaslavsky, A., Christen, P., Georgakopoulos, D.: Context aware computing for the internet of things: a survey. IEEE Commun. Surv. Tutor. **16**(1), 414–454 (2013)

17. Rios, E., et al.: Service level agreement-based GDPR compliance and security assurance in (multi) cloud-based systems. IET Software (2019)
18. da Silva, A.C.F., Breitenbücher, U., Képes, K., Kopp, O., Leymann, F.: OpenTOSCA for IoT: automating the deployment of IoT applications based on the mosquitto message broker. In: Proceedings of the 6th International Conference on the Internet of Things, pp. 181–182. ACM (2016)
19. Taivalsaari, A., Mikkonen, T.: A roadmap to the programmable world: software challenges in the IoT era. IEEE Softw. **34**(1), 72–80 (2017)
20. Womack, J., Jones, D.: Lean Thinking: Banish Waste and Create Wealth in Your Corporation, Revised and Updated. Free Press (2003). https://books.google.co.uk/books?id=l8hWAAAAYAAJ

Towards Modeling Framework for DevOps: Requirements Derived from Industry Use Case

Francis Bordeleau[1(✉)], Jordi Cabot[2], Juergen Dingel[3], Bassem S. Rabil[4], and Patrick Renaud[4]

[1] École de technologie supérieure (ETS), Université du Québec, Quebec City, Montréal, Canada
`francis.bordeleau@etsmtl.ca`
[2] ICREA – Open University of Catalonia (OUC), Barcelona, Spain
`jordi.cabot@icrea.cat`
[3] Queen's University, Kingston, Canada
`dingel@cs.queensu.ca`
[4] Kaloom, Quebec, Montréal, Canada
`{Bassem.Guendy,pare}@kaloom.com`

Abstract. To succeed with the development, deployment, and operation of the new generation of complex systems, organizations need the agility to adapt to constantly evolving environments. In this context, DevOps has emerged as an evolution of the agile approaches. It focuses on optimizing the flow of activities involved in the creation of end-user value, from idea to deployed functionality and operating systems. However, in spite of its popularity, DevOps still lacks proper engineering frameworks to support continuous improvement. One of our key objectives is to contribute to the development of a DevOps engineering framework composed of process, methods, and tools. A core part of this framework relates to the modeling of the different aspects of the DevOps system. To better understand the requirements of modeling in a DevOps context, we focus on a Product Build use case provided by an industry partner.

Keywords: DevOps · Modeling · Process

1 Introduction

The complexity of the new generation of systems developed in the context of digital transformation, cloud, smart technologies, IoT, and 5G brings a set of important new challenges, both from a technical and a business perspective. To succeed with the development, deployment, and operation of these systems, organizations must have the agility to adapt to constantly evolving environments to deliver solutions faster and solutions that can be adapted to the needs and environments of the users.

© Springer Nature Switzerland AG 2020
J.-M. Bruel et al. (Eds.): DEVOPS 2019, LNCS 12055, pp. 139–151, 2020.
https://doi.org/10.1007/978-3-030-39306-9_10

In this new generation of systems, software has replaced hardware as the main asset and product differentiator. This comes with important new challenges. Among other things, the success of an organization is now determined by its agility (business and technical) to provide new software capabilities. The success of a company directly dependents on its ability to beat its competitors at the software level, i.e. to develop, deploy, and operate new software capabilities faster and with better quality than its competitors. To achieve this goal, organizations need to maximize the efficiency of their software development process, increase operations efficiency, automate as much as possible, reduce time required to deploy new software, ensure software quality, allow for the integration of new technologies both at the process and product level, support product customization, and enable innovations.

In response to the increasing complexity of developing and managing software products, DevOps[1] has emerged in the last decade as an evolution of the agile approaches. It focuses on optimizing the flows of activities involved in the creation of end user value, from idea to deployed functionality. It extends agile approaches by integrating aspects like System Operation, Customer Support, together with Development to enable a more frequent and reliable releases, and aims at using systematic analysis and automation to improve productivity, predictability and quality.

1.1 Problem

The overall problem we address in our research program is the lack of engineering support for organizations to put DevOps into practice in a scalable and sustainable manner to achieve continuous improvement. Our main goal is to establish an engineering framework, based on methods, process and tools, to support the implementation and evolution of DevOps.

The first problem we address in the development of the DevOps engineering framework is the lack of modeling techniques and framework that can be used to capture the different aspects of a DevOps system (see Sect. 2.2 for definition of DevOps System). Without proper models that can be used to understand and analyse the system in a systematic and scientific manner, continuous improvement becomes an ad hoc journey, and as a result, DevOps and "agility" much too often means "improvisation". Thus, to achieve the DevOps vision and enable continuous improvement, we must first capture the different aspects of the DevOps system in a set of actionable models that allow understanding, analyzing, simulating, and automating the DevOps process and its flows.

---

[1] The term "DevOps" was coined by Patrick Debois in 2009 in Belgium by naming a conference "devopsdays" held in Gent, Belgium. DevOps is at the intersection of development and operations, and it needs to include both.

1.2 Proposed Approach

In this context, a main research questions is: what type of modeling techniques and framework do we need to support the continuous improvement of the DevOps process?

Before we can start investigating and analyzing different modeling techniques, languages, and methods, we first need to define the set of requirements that must satisfied. Our approach consists in iteratively building the set of requirements through the analysis of industrial use cases.

In this paper, we focus on an industrial use case provided by Kaloom[2], an industry partner of our research program. This use case describes different aspects of DevOps currently used at Kaloom, including the product build process, the system architecture, the product planning process, and the product test process.

1.3 Outline of the Paper

The paper is structured as follows: Sect. 2 provides a discussion on related work, Sect. 3 describes DevOps at Kaloom, Sect. 4 defines the set of requirements for the development of the modeling framework, Sect. 5 discusses the future research work, and Sect. 6 provides a conclusion.

2 Related Work

2.1 Background

DevOps is not a destination; it doesn't have an end goal. It is a journey, or an odyssey, that aims at continuous improvement. The three ways of DevOps are defined in [16] as:

- Flow
- Feedback
- Continuous experimentation and learning

Before starting to do anything, it is essential to see the whole DevOps system that is happening between development (Dev) and operations (Ops). The term *DevOps System* is used in our research context to include the product, the people involved in the different phases of its development and operations, the process used to develop and operate the product, and the tools used to support the different phases of the process.

The DevOps vision requires adopting a holistic approach in which these different constituents (product, people, and process) are considered altogether, as opposed to looking at them separately in silos. Global improvements can only be obtained by considering the whole DevOps system, which includes all of its

---

[2] www.kaloom.com.

parts. Otherwise, an improvement in one part may be outweighed by a negative impact on another part. For example, an improvement at the development level may result in an unacceptable cost increase at the operations level, and vice-versa.

Once we have the view of the DevOps system, then we need to focus on the flows to identify the constraint that need to be eliminated to get things moving faster to production and deployment. At this stage, as soon as we start changing things, it is necessary to recognize the feedback loops so that we can evaluate the impact of the changes we are making in the DevOps system (to resolve issues). We need to be able to identify both positive and negative impacts as early and often as possible so that we can take actions based on the feedback. Finally, we need to foster continuous experimentation and learning to enable continuous improvement as the DevOps system is evolving.

2.2   Current Works on DevOps Modeling

While we believe (also supported by some empirical evidence [21]) that modeling and model-driven techniques [6] are crucial in the DevOps broad vision sketched above, modeling support for DevOps is still in its infancy. In fact, we just held the first International DevOps workshop at Models[3].

To the best of our knowledge, there is no standard (or widely accepted) DSLs or metamodels specific for managing DevOps processes. So far, most attempts have attempted to reuse Cloud Modeling Languages [5]. In particular, TOSCA (OASIS Topology and Orchestration Specification for Cloud Applications), as done, for instance, in [24] or [1]. This can work well for web/cloud applications but it not easily generalizable to more complex software development processes.

Such a DevOps metamodel should also reuse many of the concepts already present in the domain of runtime models [4]. As part of this initiative, a large number of performance, monitoring and deployment (meta)models have been proposed. An overview of such models and the potential relationships between them was provided [23].

Some partial proposals to apply modeling to specific parts of the DevOps process or to specific types of systems could also be useful as inspiration for our approach. Among them a research roadmap was proposed for enabling DevOPs in Smart IoT Systems by Ferry et al. [9], where Smart IoT Systems typically operate in a changing and often unpredictable environment. The ability of these systems to continuously evolve and adapt to their new environment is decisive to ensure and increase their trustworthiness, quality and user experience. Garcia-Diaz et al. [11] proposed a prototype to combine continuous integration practice and the model-driven engineering approach. A quantitative evaluation was carried out for different types of development strategies. Garcia and Cabot [10] proposed a stepwise adoption of continuous delivery tools in model-based processes where the modeling tools and its artefacts would be fully integrated

---

[3] https://ace-design.github.io/devops-at-models/.

in the build systems. [3] enables the modeling of the trade-offs of alternative deployment options.

However, as we will discuss in the next sections, just modeling specific aspects of the DevOps process is not enough. We need modeling support to evaluate, simulate and explore the potential alternatives by relying on a more unified, holistic and global perspective of the full DevOps process.

3   Description of DevOps at Kaloom

Kaloom is an emerging company developing a fully automated, programmable data center networking software solution that will disrupt how cloud and data center networks are built, managed and operated for enterprises, cloud providers, gaming companies, data center operators and 5G wireless providers. Kaloom comprises technology veterans with proven track records of delivering large-scale networking, analytics and AI-based solutions for the world's largest networks. Since its foundation, Kaloom has been working on different aspects of DevOps challenges for Software Defined Systems, including the current use case focused on the improvement and reduction of the product build time.

The time required to make a new product build, including microservices build and packaging, is a critical part of overall product development process. Currently Kaloom is working on bringing down the product build time using available tooling and technologies, like build artifact caching, restructuring microservices build, and migrate to more modern go dependency management. Kaloom's objective is to reduce product build down to 3 min. Applying state-of-the-art build tools helped significantly reducing product build time, to about 11 min (from 90 min at the end of 2018), but it is not sufficient for Kaloom's objective. Kaloom is seeking continuous DevOps improvement to remove bottlenecks by researching different tooling and refining the process for better evolution of Kaloom product.

3.1   Product Build and Test Process

Figure 1 illustrates the current Kaloom Continuous Integration/Continuous Deployment (CICD) pipeline based on microservices architecture, where the product build phase consists of microservices builds and overall product packaging. The developer starts by coding and pushing the Git commit as a Merge Request (MR) in GitLab[TM] [12] towards master branch of the concerned microservice code. The commit push triggers a build on Jenkins[TM] [14] to compile the change and vote back on the MR; the compilation includes running unit tests. Then after compilation of the Git commit, static code analysis using SonarQube[TM] [20] scans the change and points out issues, and vote on the MR. The final stage of the development pipeline consists in running tests of the microservice both on a simulated environment and a hardware test environment, and votes back on the MR with test results. Any failure on these stages would mark the MR to be non-mergeable to master branch until the cause of the failure

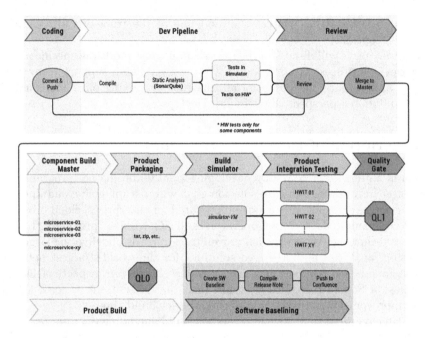

Fig. 1. Product Build within the Continuous Integration/Continuous Deployment (CICD) Pipeline

is addressed. Once all development pipeline stages pass, the MR moves to the review stage where the code is reviewed by peer(s).

After all review comments have been addressed (may require several iterations), the Git commit is merged to microservice master branch and triggers a build of the product, which includes all microservices. At this stage, every microservice is mapped to Git sub-module of the super project which constitutes the product. Then, the product is packaged together, with a new build number assigned, and an initial Quality Level (QL) is set for this product build. Quality level for product build indicates the testing levels that the build passed. The higher the quality level for a product build, the more expensive and longer testing the build passes.

To promote a product build to first Quality Level (QL1), it goes through integration testing for the overall product on both simulated environment and multiple types of hardware. The test framework is based on GoDog and Cucumber [13] and test reporting is done using TestRail ™ [22]. In parallel with integration testing the product is baselined and tagged in source code for this product build number. Release notes are compiled based on the Git commits included in the product build and then release notes are pushed to Confluence [8].

Product builds that pass QL1 integration testing are fed into stress and stability tests which takes up to several weeks to promote the build to higher

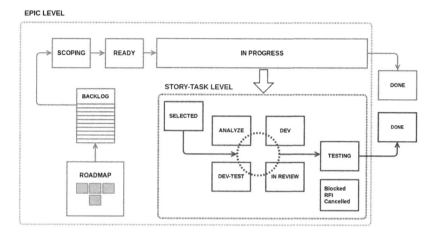

Fig. 2. DevOps Agile Epics/Stories/Tasks workflow

quality levels. The quality levels are set as labels/properties of the build in Artifactory ^{TM} [2] where the binaries are stored. A release build is expected to have sufficient QL before the product is released.

3.2 Product Planning Process

Jira ^{TM} [15] is used for tracking Agile DevOps workflow and product planning. Figure 2 shows the workflow to breakdown product roadmap features into product releases. Figure 3 illustrates the release cycle, where each release is divided into four sprints and each sprint duration is 3 weeks. In these sprints both development and System Integration Verification/Validation (SIV&V) are working towards the target release. An SIV&V team is responsible for developing automated test framework and integration test cases, while development team is responsible for developing both unit tests and microservice feature tests. CICD

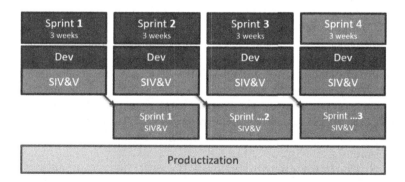

Fig. 3. Agile release cycles

Pipeline and tools are maintained and developed by CICD team. Each team has peer code review within the team by subject expert.

4   Requirements for Process Modeling Languages for DevOps

In this section, we define a set DevOps modeling framework requirements based on the different Kaloom DevOps aspects described in Sect. 3. It is expected that this set of requirements will evolve/grow as we continue to work on other aspects of DevOps at Kaloom, start investigating similar use cases with other industry partners, and broaden the scope to additional use cases.

In this paper, we focus on three requirement categories: general requirements, description requirements, and analysis/simulation requirements.

4.1   General Requirements

As a starting point, the DevOps modeling framework must satisfy a set of general requirements that are associated with the modeling of complex systems. Some of these requirements are common to the modeling needs of any complex environment (e.g. support for modeling at different abstraction levels, definition of mapping relationships between the partial models, etc.), but we would like to emphasize the following requirements that are key for the development of an industrial DevOps-specific modeling framework.

- **RG1- Support for the modeling of different aspects** – As described in the Kaloom use case, the overall DevOps system includes many different aspects, e.g. product build, system architecture (in this case, a microservice architecture), product planning process, and product test process. To support the different aspects, the DevOps modeling framework must allow for the use of a set of modeling techniques. This set of modeling techniques provides the basis for the analysis, simulation, and automation of the different aspects of the DevOps systems.
- **RG2- Support for model integration** – To ensure consistency and coherence between the different models, the DevOps framework must provide support for the integration of different types of models and modeling techniques. Because the semantics of the models can be quite different, their integration will require the definition of a common DevOps metamodel.
- **RG3- Support for tool integration** – Because the set of models used in the DevOps modeling framework require the use of different tools, the modeling framework must also support the integration of different tools. In the context of DevOps, lightweight integrations, often realized using scripts, will be used to increase the agility to modify the workflows and enable fast turnaround.
- **RG4- Support for customization** – Because different organizations have different needs and way-of-working, it is essential that the DevOps modeling framework, and the set of modeling techniques used in the framework,

provides support for customization. This way, organizations can define their own DevOps modeling environment based the DevOps modeling framework.

- **RG5- Support for different viewpoints and perspectives** – People involved in a DevOps systems come from different backgrounds and have interests related to different aspects. For this reason, the DevOps modeling framework must support the definition of different viewpoints to enable the use and presentation of information from different perspectives and for different user profiles. A set of predefined model views [7] for DevOps would be very useful here.

4.2 Description Requirements

From a description perspective, the modeling framework is composed of set of modeling techniques that must support the following requirements.

- **RD1- Use of appropriate modeling techniques** – To support the modeling of different aspects (see RD1 in previous section), we need to select an appropriate modeling technique for each of the different aspects. Based on the Kallom context, the set of modeling techniques that will be investigated includes BPMN [18] for process modeling, UML [17] and SysML [19] for architecture modeling, and Kanban and Scrum process modeling techniques for the project management aspect.
- **RD2- Description of the flows** – One specific aspect that needs to be supported is the description of the flows associated with the different processes, together with a description of the different steps and transitions that compose them. In the context of Kaloom, these flows are currently described using informal diagrams like the ones used for the product CICD Pipeline description shown in Fig. 1 and the DevOps Agile Epics/Stories/Tasks Workflow shown in Fig. 2. Similar descriptions also exist for other aspects/flows. While these diagrams might be appropriate for documentation and communication purposes, their informal nature doesn't allow for analysis and transformation. The DevOps framework must provide proper modeling techniques to replace the current diagrams by actionable models.
- **RD3- Specification of real-time properties** – To enable performance analysis of the different processes/flows, the DevOps modeling framework must support the specification of time and timing constraints of the different elements of the flow models. In the context of the Kaloom, this includes the actual execution time of the different tasks and the improvement targets.
- **RD4- Specification of people (roles), methods and tools** – Since the execution of the flows is realized by a combination of people (roles), methods and tools, the DevOps framework must capture this information in the different elements (steps and transitions) of the flow models. This information constitutes the basis for the analysis and simulation of current flows and potential flow improvements.

4.3   Analysis and Simulation Requirements

A main purpose of the DevOps modeling framework is to support continuous improvement. For this purpose, the modeling framework must not only support the description of the different aspects of the DevOps system, but must also support the analysis and simulation of the models.

From an analysis and simulation perspective, the framework must support the following requirements.

– **RA1- Identification of constraints** – To improve a flow in a DevOps process, we first need to identify the constraint that is preventing faster progress. For this purpose, the DevOps modeling framework needs to provide support for maintaining up-to-date information regarding the time spent in the different elements of the flow, and for analyzing the information to identify the constraint.
– **RA2- Configurability of constraint analysis** – The identification of the constraint depends on the aspect that we are focusing on improving. For example, different constraints would be identified depending if we are focusing on the product build process, the testing process, or the overall feature delivery process. Also, we might want to identify constraints regarding different quality attributes, like the time required to deliver feature, or the cost associated with the development and operations of a given feature. For this reason, the DevOps modeling framework must support the identification of constraints based on different user-defined global priorities.
– **RA3- Open to the addition of new analysis and simulation techniques** – The identification of global constraints becomes increasing difficult as we improve the DevOps system, and further improvements require the use of more sophisticated techniques. As an example, in the Kaloom context, to improve the product build process from 90 min to 11 min at Kaloom, the identification of the constraints was rather simple. However, it becomes much more complex as we work on further improvements towards the 3 min target. In this context, the DevOps modeling framework must be developed to enable the addition of new analysis techniques as needed.
– **RA4- Support for time-based analysis and simulation** – In the Kaloom context, most of the current improvement objectives are related to the notion of time. For example, reducing the time required for product build, reducing the time required to deliver new features, etc. For this reason, it is essential that the DevOps modeling framework provide first-class support for time-based analysis and simulation. One of our short-term objectives is to evaluate different techniques and tools that can be integrated in the modeling framework.
– **RA5- Investigation and evaluation of different alternatives** – Once we have identified the constraint, the DevOps modeling framework needs to provide support for the analysis of different alternatives to improve the flow. In particular, we need to be able to properly analyze the impact of potential modifications on the overall system to avoid cases where an improvement in one part of the system is outweighed by a negative impact on other parts.

Also, we need to be able to identify both positive and negative impacts of modifications at the analysis level so that we can take actions based on the feedback early in the process. For this purpose, different analysis and simulation techniques need to be evaluated and integrated in the DevOps modeling framework.

- **RA6- Support for tool and technology migration analysis** – Tools and technologies are constantly evolving. The quest for continuous improvement requires that we don't only focus on improving our DevOps processes, but also that we stay on top of the evolution of tools and technologies, and evaluate the potential use of new tools and technologies to improve our overall DevOps system. Such changes require going through migrations that might affect many different aspects of the DevOps system. The impact of a tool (or technology) migration can greatly vary depending on the nature and role of the tool (or technology). It is crucial to properly evaluate the impact of the migration before starting the migration. For this reason, the DevOps modeling framework must provide support for analyzing the impact of potential tool and technology migrations, in terms of costs, risks, and potential gains.

5   Future Work

The plan of this research project is to engage both the modeling and DevOps communities to develop a DevOps modeling framework based on the list of requirements defined in the previous section. In the mid/long-term we hope to have a kind of Digital Twin approach for DevOps that can leverage the telemetry of the DevOps system to feed a model-based replicate of the deployed DevOps infrastructure of a company in order to simulate, evaluate and improve it.

The next phase is planned to further formalize the requirements described in this paper, and add new requirements coming from both the implementation of similar product build use cases in other companies (industry partners) and the extension of the approach to include other aspects of DevOps, e.g. product deployment, software upgrade flow, and product planning.

In the Kaloom context, the scope of the use case presented in this paper will need to be expanded to include other phases, like the review phase. However, in this case, we will need to consider a broader range of factors, including non-automatable and human-based ones, like the review task that requires the involvement of engineers who are involved in other competing activities. Putting top priority on reviews would have a direct impact on other flows. Therefore, a broader perspective must be considered to avoid focusing on local improvements that would have a negative impact at the global organization level.

We are also planning to explore the use of Machine Learning (ML) and Artificial Intelligence (AI)-based techniques to maximize the potential of the runtime DevOps models. This can help to provide additional optimizations, early prediction of potential problems, and trade-off analysis of possible technology alternatives based on simulation of future scenarios derived from the current monitoring data.

Finally, the modeling infrastructure to be developed can be regarded as a complex software artifact in itself. As such, we would like to explore the potential benefits of applying a DevOps approach to complex modeling artifacts to continue the preliminary efforts in [10].

6   Conclusion

The research work described in the paper is part of a larger project that aims at developing an engineering framework, based on methods, process and tools, to support the implementation and evolution of DevOps. This research project involves close relationship with the industry to define the different aspects of the DevOps engineering framework based on concrete industry use cases. The first problem we are addressing is the lack modeling techniques and framework that can be used to capture the different aspects of a DevOps system.

In this paper, we first described different aspects of the DevOps system at Kaloom, one of our industry partners. Then, we defined a set of requirements for the definition of a DevOps modeling framework based on the Kaloom use case. This modeling framework is a core component of the overall DevOps engineering framework that will provide the basis for the analysis, simulation, and automating the DevOps process and its flows. Finally, we provided a discussion on future work.

In conclusion, this paper reflects on the interplay between modeling and DevOps. In particular, the set of requirements defined in Sect. 4 highlights the need to propose a complete modeling framework for DevOps. Just focusing on a DSL or metamodel would not be enough to respond to the industrial needs we have detected in our use case.

References

1. Artač, M., Borovšak, T., Di Nitto, E., Guerriero, M., Tamburri, D.A.: Model-driven continuous deployment for quality devOps. In: Proceedings of the 2nd International Workshop on Quality-Aware DevOps, QUDOS 2016, pp. 40–41. ACM, New York (2016). https://doi.org/10.1145/2945408.2945417
2. Artifactory. https://jfrog.com/artifactory
3. Babar, Z., Lapouchnian, A., Yu, E.: Modeling DevOps deployment choices using process architecture design dimensions. In: Ralyté, J., España, S., Pastor, Ó. (eds.) PoEM 2015. LNBIP, vol. 235, pp. 322–337. Springer, Cham (2015). https://doi.org/10.1007/978-3-319-25897-3_21
4. Bencomo, N., Götz, S., Song, H.: Models@run.time: a guided tour of the state of the art and research challenges. Softw. Syst. Model. 18(5), 3049–3082 (2019). https://doi.org/10.1007/s10270-018-00712-x
5. Bergmayr, A., et al.: A systematic review of cloud modeling languages. ACM Comput. Surv. 51(1), 22:1–22:38 (2018). https://doi.org/10.1145/3150227
6. Brambilla, M., Cabot, J., Wimmer, M.: Model-Driven Software Engineering in Practice, Second Edition. Synthesis Lectures on Software Engineering. Morgan & Claypool Publishers (2017). https://doi.org/10.2200/S00751ED2V01Y201701SWE004

7. Bruneliere, H., Burger, E., Cabot, J., et al.: A feature-based survey of model view approaches. Softw. Syst. Model. **18**, 1931–1952 (2019). https://doi.org/10.1007/s10270-017-0622-9
8. Confluence. https://www.atlassian.com/software/confluence
9. Ferry, N., et al.: ENACT: development, operation, and quality assurance of trustworthy smart IoT systems. In: Software Engineering Aspects of Continuous Development and New Paradigms of Software Production and Deployment - First International Workshop, DEVOPS 2018, Chateau de Villebrumier, France, March 5–6, 2018, Revised Selected Papers, pp. 112–127 (2018). https://doi.org/10.1007/978-3-030-06019-0_9
10. Garcia, J., Cabot, J.: Stepwise adoption of continuous delivery in model-driven engineering. In: Bruel, J.-M., Mazzara, M., Meyer, B. (eds.) DEVOPS 2018. LNCS, vol. 11350, pp. 19–32. Springer, Cham (2019). https://doi.org/10.1007/978-3-030-06019-0_2
11. García-Díaz, V., Espada, J.P., Núñez-Valdéz, E.R., García-Bustelo, B.C.P., Lovelle, J.M.C.: Combining the continuous integration practice and the model-driven engineering approach. Comput. Inform. **35**, 299–337 (2016)
12. Gitlab. https://about.gitlab.com/
13. Godog. https://github.com/DATA-DOG/godog
14. Jenkins. https://jenkins.io
15. Jira. https://www.atlassian.com/software/jira
16. Kim, G., Debois, P., Willis, J., Humble, J.: The DevOps Handbook: How to Create World-Class Agility, Reliability, and Security in Technology Organizations. IT Revolution Press, Portland (2016)
17. Object Management Group (OMG): Unified modeling language (UML) version 2.0. Standard, Object Management Group (OMG), July 2005. https://www.omg.org/spec/UML/2.0
18. Object Management Group (OMG): Business process model and notation version 2.0. Standard, Object Management Group (OMG), December 2011. https://www.omg.org/spec/BPMN/2.0/
19. Object Management Group (OMG): Omg system modeling language version 1.4. Standard, Object Management Group (OMG), August 2015. https://www.omg.org/spec/SysML/1.4
20. Sonarqube. https://www.sonarqube.org
21. Ståhl, D., Bosch, J.: Industry application of continuous integration modeling: a multiple-case study. In: 2016 IEEE/ACM 38th International Conference on Software Engineering Companion (ICSE-C), pp. 270–279, May 2016
22. Testrail. https://www.gurock.com/testrail
23. Vogel, T., Seibel, A., Giese, H.: The role of models and megamodels at runtime. In: Dingel, J., Solberg, A. (eds.) MODELS 2010. LNCS, vol. 6627, pp. 224–238. Springer, Heidelberg (2011). https://doi.org/10.1007/978-3-642-21210-9_22
24. Wettinger, J., Breitenbücher, U., Kopp, O., Leymann, F.: Streamlining devops automation for cloud applications using TOSCA as standardized metamodel. Future Gener. Comput. Syst. **56**, 317–332 (2016). https://doi.org/10.1016/j.future.2015.07.017

Towards Designing Smart Learning Environments with IoT

Mohamad Kassab[1] and Manuel Mazzara[2(✉)]

[1] Pennsylvania State University, Malvern, PA, USA
muk36@psu.edu
[2] Innopolis University, Innopolis, Russia
m.mazzara@innopolis.ru

Abstract. Internet of Things is a rapidly growing network of a variety of different connected objects. Now, because of their ubiquitous nature, educational institutions are looking to incorporate IoTs technologies in teaching and learning activities. This paper contributes to the ongoing discussion on the benefits and challenges of incorporating IoTs in education. More precisely, it provides (i) a summary that reports on results of a systematic literature review we conducted on IoT in education along with a framework for describing and classifying scenarios that involve IoTs for education, (ii) a demonstration of a tool we developed to provide an adaptive learning experience in response to a remote learner's emotions, and (iii) a discussion on three domain-related quality requirements to consider when designing IoTs applications for education; namely, security, scalability and humanization.

Keywords: Internet of Things · Education · Learning · Teaching · IoT · Network of Things

1 Introduction

The IEEE Internet of Thing (IoT) Community defines the IoT as: "...a self-configuring and adaptive system consisting of networks of sensors and smart objects whose purpose is to interconnect "all" things, including every day and industrial objects, in such a way as to make them intelligent, programmable and more capable of interacting with humans" [1]. The term "Internet of Things" was coined by Kevin Ashton in 1999 to refer to uniquely identifiable objects/things and their virtual representations in an Internet-like structure [2]. Currently, there are more than 6.4 billion devices connected to the Internet excluding computers, cellphones, and tablets [3]. This number is projected to reach 20.8 billion devices by 2020, with some estimates even foreseeing as many as 100+ billion connected devices by that time. Regardless of the exact number of devices, spending in this market is expected to increase substantially, with the International Data Corporation (IDC) calculating that the worldwide market for IoT solutions will reach $7.1 trillion in four years [4].

© Springer Nature Switzerland AG 2020
J.-M. Bruel et al. (Eds.): DEVOPS 2019, LNCS 12055, pp. 152–166, 2020.
https://doi.org/10.1007/978-3-030-39306-9_11

Because of its continuous growth, it is useful to discuss a purpose built system within the IoT, referred to as a Network of Things (NoT) [5]. A NoT can be described by five primitives proposed by Voas [5]:

1. Sensor is "an electronic utility (e.g. cameras and microphones) that measures physical properties such as sound, weight, humidity, temperature, acceleration". Properties of a sensor could be the transmission of data (e.g. RFID), Internet access, and/or be able to output data based on specific events.
2. A communication channel is "a medium by which data is transmitted (e.g., physical via Universal Serial Bus (USB), wireless, wired, verbal, etc.)".
3. Aggregator is "a software implementation based on mathematical function(s) that transforms groups of raw data into intermediate, aggregated data. Raw data can come from any source". Aggregators have two actors for consolidating large volumes of data into lesser amounts:
   (a) Cluster is "an abstract grouping of sensors (along with the data they output) that can appear and disappear instantaneously".
   (b) Weight is "the degree to which a particular sensor's data will impact an aggregator's computation".
4. Decision trigger "creates the final result(s) needed to satisfy the purpose, specification and requirements of a specific NoT". A decision trigger is a conditional expression that triggers an action and abstractly defines the end-purpose of a NoT. A decision trigger's outputs can control actuators and transactions.
5. External utility (eUtility) is "a hardware product, software or service which executes processes or feeds data into the overall data flow of the NoT".

Applications for the IoT are already being leveraged in diverse sectors such as medical services field, environmental monitoring, smart homes, industrial internet and smart retail. Now, because of their ubiquitous nature, educational institutions are looking to join the trend and to incorporate IoTs technologies in the teaching and learning activities.

A systematic literature review (SLR) that we conducted on the advantages and challenges of IoTs in education revealed that IoT applications are being proposed to address a diverse range of modes, objectives, subjects, and perceptions in education sector. For example, Gligoric et al. [6] addressed the potential of using IoT technology to build a smart classroom: "Combining the IoT technology with social and behavioral analysis, an ordinary classroom can be transformed into a smart classroom that actively listens and analyzes voices, conversations, movements, behavior, etc. in order to reach a conclusion about the lecturer's presentation and listener's satisfaction". Uzelac et al. propose another example of a smart classroom equipped with a set of sensors able to monitor parameters of the physical environment (for example CO_2, temperature, humidity, noise) and a Blue tooth headset used to capture lecturer's voice with the target to identify parameters of the physical environment in a classroom and evaluate their influence on students' focus [7], this model uses voice and visual sensors. Several studies also propose incorporating IoT technologies to monitor students' attendance and in-class activities (e.g. [8,9]). Studies proposing the incorporation of IoTs in on-line education and on-line laboratories also exist [10–13]. The potential of using IoTs for supporting Ubiquitous Learning (UL) is also reflected; according to many studies (e.g. [8,14,15]) in increasing access to information sharing and enabling students to have personalized access to educational resources.

On the other hand, the nature of education field and the physical and computational constraints poses a number of challenges to systems' developers and designers. These include concerns related to ethical constraints (e.g. student's privacy), technical constraints (e.g. Big data captured from a wide range of heterogeneous sources), economical constraints (e.g. the added cost of technology on education) and physical constraints (e.g. available technology, available communication channels).

This paper contributes to the ongoing discussion on the benefits and challenges of incorporating IoTs in education. More precisely, it provides (i) a summary that reports on results of a systematic literature review we conducted on IoT in education along with a framework for describing and classifying scenarios that involve IoTs for education, (ii) a demonstration of a tool we developed to provide an adaptive learning experience in response to a remote learner's emotions, and (iii) a discussion on three domain-related quality requirements to consider when designing IoTs applications for education; namely, security, scalability, and humanization.

The framework to describe the scenarios is based on Voas's primitives [5] and a proposed classification scheme for potential scenarios for IoTs in education settings.

The remaining of this paper is organized as follows: Sect. 2 reports on the results of the SLR we conducted and discuss a classification scheme of the collected scenarios. Section 3 presents the tool we developed to monitor the learning state for an on-line learner and to provide a personalized course content. Section 4 provides a discussion on domain-related quality attributes. Finally Sect. 5 concludes the paper.

2   Related Work

We conducted a systematic literature review on the topic of incorporating IoT technologies in education. The main goal of this review was to develop an understanding of the scenarios that involve deploying IoT in education, the benefits that arise from this incorporation and the challenges in such a context. While the details of the review process and the corresponding statistics from the results are not the focus of this paper, One of the goals of the conducted SLR was to identify the benefits of applying IoT in education on the basis of the existing scenarios in the selected studies. The results show that we identified a significant variety of positive contributions for IoT technologies on education. In particular, we identified three dimensions to classify emerging scenarios of IoT in education and to discuss the benefits: delivery mode, perception and learning principles (Fig. 1).

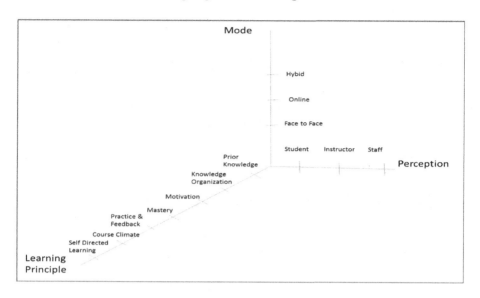

Fig. 1. The three dimensional scheme for IoT in Education.

Perception: The extracted scenarios from the selected studies suggest that IoT technologies will actively complement and enhance certain pedagogical activities with relevance to three perceptions: instructor, student, and staff.

As for the instructor, IoT can help to manage attendance of a class and availability of required equipment/devices for each student [8,9,16,17]. "Installing RFID reader at the entrance of school gate, library, cafeteria, dormitory and teaching building, and other places to identify students' RFID electronic tags, it can obtain the students' activities trajectory" [9]. In addition, with IoT an instructor may initiate and manage class session with voice/facial/gesture commands [18,19], communicate with remote students at different locations and/or collect immediate feedback from students in terms of interests in an activity or lesson and sensor data. Analytics could also be run on the sensor data to evaluate behavior, performance, interest, and participation of each student and provide a summary to the instructor [20,21]. IoTs can help the instructor to confirm the identity for students [22]; it can also help the instructor to identify and help students with special needs [23].

From a student perspective, IoT will help to communicate with classmates (local or remote) [10], share project data, discuss and annotate learning materials in a real-time [11], and access the learning resources remotely (e.g. remote labs) [11–13]. In addition, IoT could also provide support to students with adapted learning resources by integrating content that is based on location, time, date, student-to-student interaction, knowledge level, etc. [15,24].

From a staff perspective, IoT will play designated role in elements such as tracking students. For example, an IoT scenario is reported in [25] on monitoring and maintaining psychological health for students. Another reported contribution is the potential assistance for staff members in managing and tracking fixed and portable academic resources [26,27]. "Using a noise sensor, one classroom can communicate automatically to a neighbor classroom and inform them if the noise level exceeds a certain level. A warning message could be displayed on the LCD screen in the noisy room" [27]. For the public portable equipment (e.g. portable projectors, lab equipment, sports equipment), these can be marked with a tag to be tracked by the RFID technology. The collected data from tracking portable equipment can be further utilized to automatically calculate patterns and trends, and find inefficiencies. IoT can also assist staff members in managing events (e.g. registration events [28], sports events [29]) and in managing the general safety and security [27]. In addition, it can also play a role in institutional energy management [27].

Learning Principle: In [30], the authors listed seven principles that underlie effective learning: (1) student prior knowledge, (2) knowledge organization, (3) motivation, (4) mastery, (5) practice and feedback, (6) course climate and (7) the self-directed learning. These principles are distilled from research from a variety of disciplines [31]. Our findings indicate that IoT technologies will make a positive impact on each of these seven principles.

For example, in [32] the authors propose a smart assistive environment system that uses a Heuristic Diagnostic Teaching (HDT) process where the intention is to identify each student's learning abilities in math as well as their creativity traits. Their proposed system uses a computer, sensors, RFID tag reader and a SmartBox device in order support learning for students with ASD by providing a personalized "practice and feedback" on a case by case basis. Other studies that discuss utilizing IoT to provide personalized learning experience include [15,33].

In [34], Improving student's "motivation" principle is addressed through a proposed scenario aiming at bridging the communication between teachers and students using IoT. In [20], the authors proposed an innovative system based on IoT to analyze the impact of several parameters of the physical environment in a classroom on students' focus, where the term "focus" refers to the students' subjective feeling of their ability to concentrate on a lecture at a given moment. The primary goal was to identify those parameters that significantly affect students' focus in the course climate. Studies with a similar goal include [7] and [35].

In [36] The Story of Things (SoT) system is proposed to enable children to learn the story behind every object they touch in a typical day. Inspired by Living Media and the IoT, "the goal is to change children's awareness through hands-on interaction with the world they live in. A back-of-the-hand display is activated by stick-on finger sensors when a child touches an object. They can tap the display to select from a number of stories stored in a crowd sourced database about that object (e.g. the materials it was made from; the processes used to make it; how it impacts their body; how it will be disposed of; environmental or social rights challenges associated with the object; and how they can take positive action)". This information is overlaid on the world through an augmented-reality contact lens to enhance the "knowledge organization". Another example of utilizing IoT for "knowledge organization" principle is reported in [37] in which the authors discuss a project utilizing project utilizing IoT to improve a child's attitude toward food via learning about food consumption and production and ways to reduce waste on a long term basis.

Delivery Mode: Education can be delivered in one of three broad-based modes: face-to-face, remote or hybrid. The selected studies from the SLR we conducted were almost equally distributed between the face-to-face setting and the on-line setting.

Taking the dimensions of learning mode, perception and learning principles yields general $3 * 3 * 7 = 42$ possible general classes to classify related IoT, providing a general framework for constructing use cases in education. These classes are not mutually exclusive. In addition, each scenario can be specified further with the five primitives proposed by Voas. To demonstrate how the general framework helps to describe IoT for education applications, we present in the next section a tool that we developed to monitor the learning state of an on-line learner (**mode:** on-line, **perception:** (instructor, student), **learning principles:** (motivation, course climate, practice and feedback)).

3   Monitoring Emotional State of On-line Learner: A Tool

There are no adequate empirically proven strategies to address the presence of emotions in education [38, 39].

Incorporating IoTs technologies combined with the power of Big Data analytics to support the detection of (and reacting) to the learner's emotional state during on-line learning experience can positively improve the learners' motivation and satisfaction with the course climate, which may decrease the drop-out rate in an on-line program. The captured data could also lead to insights which can be made functional for the wellbeing of the students and improve the provided "feedback". For example, a simple web cam combined with an already existing emotion detection API can be utilized for an affordable and non-intrusive emotional-based e-learning to detect the facial expressions of the remote learner. The web cam can also be used to capture the learners eye tracking (detecting a learner's gaze location). Companies that provide web cam eye tracking services include GazeHawk and EyeTrackShop. Fitness monitoring devices, such as Fitbit, can also be utilized to take the input of the heartbeat.

With this background in mind, we developed a Learning Management System (LMS) that supports capturing and reacting to remote learner's emotions in real time. The LMS was developed using Python 3.7. The system uses for client APIs: JQuery, material for page UI and Websocket for communicating with web server. The system utilizes for Server APIs: Tornado framework for web service, OpenCV, Keras CNN model, and TensorFlow API for real-time face detection and emotion/gender classification. The integrated system captures user's expressions based on the gender against the on-line content and time stamp. It detects seven emotion expressions: angry, disgust, fear, happy, sad, surprise, neutral.

Once a learner logs into the website, the system triggers a pop up message notifying that the web cam will be turned on. After acknowledging the message and while navigating through the on-line materials (Fig. 2), the system captures facial expressions of a learner. The tool captures user's web cam frame data with websocket addressed once in every 100 ms.

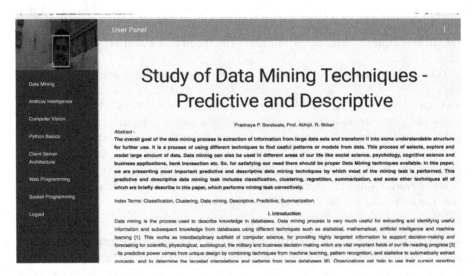

Fig. 2. A screen-shot from the tool at run-time while a remote learner navigates through on-line content

The system evaluates the expressions once every 10 s as per customized parameters which can be modified by a course administrator. The system detects whether user's expressions match with the customized parameters while navigating particular content (e.g. a percentage of emotional expressions (sad, happy, etc.) within any 10 s time frame). If there is a match then the system prompts a learner with the option of supplemental learning materials customized according to learner's state and the particular content (Fig. 3).

In addition, an "aggregator" component sends periodically an aggregated data on the learner's profile and the entire on-line class state to the course instructor. The captured data can serve for the wellbeing of the individual student and for the entire class.

While the initial phase of project successfully integrated a facial emotional expressions API, we are currently working on the next phase of the tool to integrate eye-gaze tracking and heart beats monitoring APIs. These two additional types of detentions will allow us to position more precisely the state of a remote learner simultaneously while reading the course content, participating in the on-line designated discussions forums or writing the course assignments.

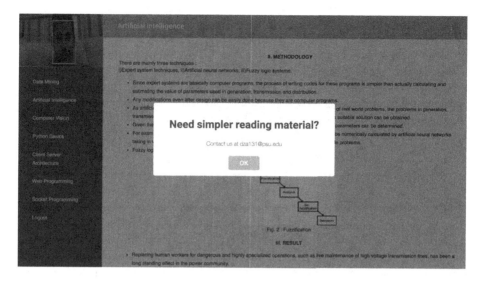

Fig. 3. A screen-shot from the tool at run-time: The tool detects particular % of emotional expressions and prompts the learner with supplemental learning materials corresponding the content

A simple construct for monitoring the on-line learner state use-case scenarios using an IoT as described in this section is shown in Table 1.

Table 1. Online learner's state use-case construct

Model element	Realization
1. Sensor	Webcam, fitbit
2. Snapshot (time)	Once in every 100 ms
3. Cluster	Set of (2) proximity sensors per online learner
4. Aggregator	Determine learning state of the learner
5. Weight	Room layout dependent
6.Communication channel	Compliant network of sensors or clusters or aggregator, wired (Internet) to eUtility
7. eUtility	Remote monitoring software
8. Decision	Personalized content

The initial assessment of the tool was conducted through a workshop session in which students and faculty members from Penn State Engineering Division were invited. The tool was presented and the attendees had the opportunity to run an exploratory testing session with the tool. Each attendee completed a questionnaire by the end of the session. While reporting on the assessment of the tool is beyond the scope of this paper, most of the attendees answered in favor that the capabilities of the tool are likely to improve the overall online learning experience. In spite of the positive impact, comments also pointed out some challenges when incorporating the IoT in this scenario. For example, personalization shouldn't hinder the learner's privacy. The cost of sensors should be reasonable enough not to increase the learning expenses. In addition, there is a need to harmonize heterogeneous data arriving from different sources by different manufacturers. Common challenges related to IoT in education are discussed in the next section.

4   Challenges of Incorporating IoT in Education

When specifying the functionality for IoT education applications, attention is often focused on concerns such as fitness of purpose, big data, interoperability, and so on. Conventional requirements elicitations techniques such as Quality Function Deployment (QFD), Joint Application Development (JAD) and domain analysis among others [40] are usually adequate for these types of requirements. But in IoT applications for education some quality requirements are probably of greater concern.

Based on the SLR we conducted and the initial assessment of the tool, we identified three major qualities that may pose a challenge for IoT in education: Security, scalability, and Humanization. We explore these three qualities further in this section.

Security. Security requirements have always been a crucial aspect of education. Given the increased communication and complexity of IoT technology there is an increase in security-related concerns [41]. Out of the selected studies in the SLR we conducted, 20% of the papers (or 18 papers) discussed security/privacy concerns, making it the most discussed quality. Two of these studies; namely [42,43] discussed particularly the challenge of child privacy when using IoT for education.

It has become increasingly clear that educational systems are vulnerable to cyber-attacks, and the number of attacks are predicted to increase [44]. Students can easily stage cyber-attacks on their institutions; or schools/universities could be prevented from functioning as intended. "Cascade failures may appear, caused by the interconnectivity of a large number of devices, difficult to be simultaneously protected over the air transmission, with all the related problems" [41].

In fact, education, and particularly higher education, is often identified as having a large number of reported data breaches, and at first look, the Privacy Rights Clearinghouse (PRC) database appears to confirm this view. In the United States, there were 727 reported breaches in educational institutions between the years 2005–2014 [45]. This number is the second highest among seven sectors that were investigated (the first is healthcare). About 7% of all academic institutions in U.S. have had a least one breach. From 2005 to 2014, 66% of academic institutions listed in the PRC experienced only one reported breach. However, about one-third of institutions with breaches have had more than one. Six percent of the listed institutions have experienced five or more reported breaches.

Hacking/malware where an outside party accessed records via direct entry, malware, or spyware was the largest proportion of the reported breaches at 36%.

"Many of the devices used in a provisioned, specialized IoT will collect various data whether that surveillance is known or not" [46]. But why are these data being collected? Who owns the data? And where does the data go? These are questions that need to be answered by the legal profession, government entities that oversee education and educational standards groups.

For example, in July 2000, the Higher Education Information Security Council (HEISC) was established. The HEISC provides coordination and support about information security governance, compliance, and data protection and privacy to higher education institutions. To help a better understanding the nuance of information security issues in higher education, members of the HEISC drilled down into the topic of information security and identified their top three strategic information security issues for 2016 [47]. "Planning for and implementing next-generation security technologies" with increasing concerns of the IoT is one of the three strategic issues.

Scalability. By embedding sensors into front field environments as well as terminal devices, an IoT network is able to collect rich sensor data that reflect the real-time environment conditions of the front field and the events/activities that are going on. Advanced data mining technologies can be applied to explore in-depth business insights from these data. Since the data is collected in the granularity of elementary event level in a 7×24 mode, the data volume is very high and the data access pattern also differs considerably from traditional business data. This has motivated a new generation of data management solution, e.g., NoSql database, map-reduce distributed computing framework, etc. [48].

The IoT in education domain is not an exception. Incorporating IoT in education will generate a large volume of data. Hence, the need for analyzing and treating these data in order to capture information and trends emerges. The scalability concern is addressed in seven papers out of the selected primary studies. In [49] the authors address the issue of scalability in the context of providing personalized content to the students based on analyzing a large volume of collected student data and activity. They propose a design for a "social recommender" system that is based on Hadoop and its parallel computing platform. In [50], the authors discuss the scalability concern when designing a learning management system.

With scalability, concerns regarding the discussion on cost of the IoT technology in education becomes also significant. The main question that may arise is whether in the long run IoT devices and Big Data analysis will increase the already existing divide into a two-class learning system: those who can disburse these technologies and those who cannot! At the same time, if going to school should be affordable for everyone, how will schools be able to buy and service these devices? The financial concern of IoT in education is discussed in four selected articles: [41, 42].

Humanization. There are questions on the moral role that IoT may play in human lives, particularly in respect to personal control. Applications in the IoT involve more than computers interacting with other computers.

Fundamentally, the success of the IoT will depend less on how far the technologies are connected and more on the humanization of the technologies that are connected [51]. IoT technology may reduce people's autonomy, shift them towards particular habits and then shifting power to corporations focused on financial gain. For the education system, this effectively means that the controlling agents are the organizations that control the tools used by the academic professionals but not the academic professionals themselves [52].

Dehumanization of humans in interacting with machines is a valid concern and it is discussed in two selected papers: [23, 43]. Many studies indicate that face-to-face interaction between students will not only benefit a child's social skills, but also positively contributes towards the character building. The issue that may arise from increased IoT technologies in education is the partial loss of the social aspect of going to school.

Conversely, using IoT in virtual learning environments can be of a special support to students of special needs (e.g. dyslexic and dyscalculic needs, for example [23]). IoT can offer students with special needs the opportunity to randomly often repeat experiments without major damage to property or cost. Thus, the students with special needs could feel reduced levels of frustration and feel less self-conscience since they could have more time to repeat an experiment. In addition, a prejudice free performance evaluation may be possible the anonymization [23]. For dyslexic and dyscalculic students; for example, it is likely that anonymization will be advantageous for them as possible functions because of IoT (e.g. auto-correct) will improve any bias with a student's score because teachers will not know if they are assessing students with a learning challenge or not [23].

5   Conclusions

The advances in sensors, nano-electronics, smart objects, cloud computing, Big Data and communication on wide scale will make innovation continuous in IoT and it will clout a great number of domains. The education domain is not an exception. While IoT-Education is a new conceptual paradigm and it is still in its starting phase, IoT is set to transform the education domain in many ways in the near future. This paper presents a brief results on a SLR we conducted on current scenarios, advantages and challenges of IoT in education domain. It also demonstrates through a tool we developed one potential for IoT in remote education.

The SLR was conducted by following available guidelines for conducting SLRs [53] to search and categorize all existing and available literature on IoT in education. Our findings from the extracted scenarios in this review were categorized using a classification scheme with three dimensions related to education mode, perception and learning principle. We also argued that the potential of IoT to improve educational outcomes, needs to be moderated with attention to the important challenges uncovered in this literature review. That is; security issues, scalability, and humanization of the delivery system. New learning management systems need to address these challenges while delivering an optimal experience for students, teachers and other stakeholders.

Our work reinforced our belief that in planning IoT education applications, there is strong need for domain expertise and deep inter-professional collaboration (in this case educators and engineers). The US National Institute of Standards and Technologies (NIST) Special Publication SP 800-183, "Networks of Things," provides some guidance in this regard. SP 800-183 defines the underlying science for the IoT describes five primitives (sensor, aggregator, communications channel, external entity, decision trigger) [5]. These five primitives form the basic building blocks of IoTs and a framework for developing IoT scenarios for education domain as we demonstrated in the paper.

References

1. IEEE: IEEE Internet of Things. http://iot.ieee.org/about.html
2. Internet of Things (IoT) history. https://www.postscapes.com/internet-of-things-history/
3. Garthner technical research, Internet of Things. http://www.gartner.com/technology/research/internet-of-things/
4. Asseo, I., Johnson, M., Nilsson, B., Chalapathy, N., Costello, T.: The Internet of Things: riding the wave in higher education. Educause Rev. **51**, 11–31 (2016)
5. Voas, J.: Networks of things. NIST Special Publication, vol. 800, p. 183 (2016)
6. Gligorić, N., Uzelac, A., Krco, S.: Smart classroom: real-time feedback on lecture quality. In: 2012 IEEE International Conference on Pervasive Computing and Communications Workshops (PERCOM Workshops), pp. 391–394. IEEE (2012)
7. Uzelac, A., Gligoric, N., Krco, S.: A comprehensive study of parameters in physical environment that impact students' focus during lecture using Internet of Things. Comput. Hum. Behav. **53**, 427–434 (2015)
8. Alotaibi, S.J.: Attendance system based on the Internet of Things for supporting blended learning. In: World Congress on Internet Security (WorldCIS), pp. 78–78. IEEE (2015)
9. Jiang, Z.: Analysis of student activities trajectory and design of attendance management based on Internet of Things. In: International Conference on Audio, Language and Image Processing (ICALIP), pp. 600–603. IEEE (2016)
10. Yin, C., Dong, Y., Tabata, Y., Ogata, H.: Recommendation of helpers based on personal connections in mobile learning. In: IEEE Seventh International Conference on Wireless, Mobile and Ubiquitous Technology in Education (WMUTE), pp. 137–141. IEEE (2012)
11. Bin, H.: The design and implementation of laboratory equipments management system in university based on Internet of Things. In: International Conference on Industrial Control and Electronics Engineering (ICICEE), pp. 1565–1567. IEEE (2012)
12. Srivastava, A., Yammiyavar, P.: Augmenting tutoring of students using tangible smart learning objects: an IoT based approach to assist student learning in laboratories. In: International Conference on Internet of Things and Applications (IOTA), pp. 424–426. IEEE (2016)

13. Shi, Y., Qin, W., Suo, Y., Xiao, X.: Smart classroom: bringing pervasive computing into distance learning. In: Nakashima, H., Aghajan, H., Augusto, J.C. (eds.) Handbook of Ambient Intelligence and Smart Environments, pp. 881–910. Springer, Boston (2010). https://doi.org/10.1007/978-0-387-93808-0_33

14. Zhiqiang, H., Junming, Z.: The application of Internet of Things in education and its trend of development. Mod. Distance Educ. Res. **2** (2011)

15. Möller, D.P., Haas, R., Vakilzadian, H.: Ubiquitous learning: teaching modeling and simulation with technology. In: Proceedings of the 2013 Grand Challenges on Modeling and Simulation Conference, p. 24 (2013)

16. Borges, V., Sawant, R., Zarapkar, A., Azgaonkar, S.: Wireless automated monitoring system for an educational institute using learning management system (MOODLE). In: International Conference of Soft Computing and Pattern Recognition (SoCPaR), pp. 231–236. IEEE (2011)

17. Gul, S., Asif, M., Ahmad, S., Yasir, M., Majid, M., Arshad, M.S.: A survey on role of Internet of Things in education. IJCSNS **17**(5), 159 (2017)

18. Fuse, M., Ozawa, S., Miura, S.: Role of the internet for risk management at school. In: International Conference on Information Technology Based Higher Education and Training (ITHET), pp. 1–6. IEEE (2012)

19. He, B.-X., Zhuang, K.-J.: Research on the intelligent information system for the multimedia teaching equipment management. In: International Conference on Information System and Artificial Intelligence (ISAI), pp. 129–132. IEEE (2016)

20. Elyamany, H.F., AlKhairi, A.H.: IoT-academia architecture: a profound approach. In: 16th IEEE/ACIS International Conference on Software Engineering, Artificial Intelligence, Networking and Parallel/Distributed Computing (SNPD), pp. 1–5. IEEE (2015)

21. Haiyan, H., Chang, S.: The design and implementation of ISIC-CDIO learning evaluation system based on Internet of Things. In: World Automation Congress (WAC), pp. 1–4. IEEE (2012)

22. Wang, J.: The design of teaching management system in universities based on biometrics identification and the Internet of Things technology. In: 10th International Conference on Computer Science and Education (ICCSE), pp. 979–982. IEEE (2015)

23. Lenz, L., Pomp, A., Meisen, T., Jeschke, S.: How will the Internet of Things and big data analytics impact the education of learning-disabled students? A concept paper. In: 3rd MEC International Conference on Big Data and Smart City (ICBDSC), pp. 1–7. IEEE (2016)

24. Sula, A., Spaho, E., Matsuo, K., Barolli, L., Miho, R., Xhafa, F.: An IoT-based system for supporting children with autism spectrum disorder. In: 2013 Eighth International Conference on Broadband and Wireless Computing, Communication and Applications (BWCCA), pp. 282–289. IEEE (2013)

25. Wang, Y.: The construction of the psychological health education platform based on Internet of Things. Appl. Mech. Mater. **556**, 6711–6715 (2014)

26. Han, W.: Research of intelligent campus system based on IoT. In: Jin, D., Lin, S. (eds.) Advances in Multimedia, Software Engineering and Computing, vol. 1, pp. 165–169. Springer, Heidelberg (2011). https://doi.org/10.1007/978-3-642-25989-0_29

27. Cață, M.: Smart university, a new concept in the Internet of Things. In: 14th RoEduNet International Conference-Networking in Education and Research (RoEduNet NER), pp. 195–197. IEEE (2015)

28. Tan, W., Chen, S., Li, J., Li, L., Wang, T., Hu, X.: A trust evaluation model for e-learning systems. Syst. Res. Behav. Sci. **31**(3), 353–365 (2014)

29. Yueguang, M.G.L.: Application of IoT in information teaching of ethnic colleges. In: Proceedings of the 2013 International Conference on Information, Business and Education Technology (2013)
30. Ambrose, S.A., Bridges, M.W., DiPietro, M., Lovett, M.C., Norman, M.K.: How Learning Works: Seven Research-Based Principles for Smart Teaching. Wiley, Hoboken (2010)
31. Carnegie Mellon University, Eberly Center, principles of learning. https://www.cmu.edu/teaching/principles/learning.html
32. Sula, A., Spaho, E., Matsuo, K., Barolli, L., Miho, R., Xhafa, F.: A smart environment and heuristic diagnostic teaching principle-based system for supporting children with autism during learning. In: 28th International Conference on Advanced Information Networking and Applications Workshops (WAINA), pp. 31–36. IEEE (2014)
33. Peña-Ríos, A., Callaghan, V., Gardner, M., Alhaddad, M.J.: Remote mixed reality collaborative laboratory activities: Learning activities within the InterReality portal. In: Proceedings of the 2012 IEEE/WIC/ACM International Joint Conferences on Web Intelligence and Intelligent Agent Technology, vol. 03, pp. 362–366. IEEE Computer Society (2012)
34. Wan, R.: Network interactive platform ideological and political education based on internet technology. In: Proceedings of the 2016 International Conference on Economy, Management and Education Technology (2016)
35. Ueda, T., Ikeda, Y.: Stimulation methods for students' studies using wearables technology. In: IEEE Region 10 Conference (TENCON), pp. 1043–1047. IEEE (2016)
36. Antle, A.N., Matkin, B., Warren, J.: The story of things. In: Proceedings of the The 15th International Conference on Interaction Design and Children, pp. 745–750 (2016)
37. Gómez, J., Huete, J.F., Hoyos, O., Perez, L., Grigori, D.: Interaction system based on Internet of Things as support for education. Procedia Comput. Sci. **21**, 132–139 (2013)
38. Ha, I., Kim, C.: The research trends and the effectiveness of smart learning. Int. J. Distrib. Sens. Netw. **10**(5), 537346 (2014)
39. Feidakis, M., Daradoumis, T., Caballé, S.: Emotion measurement in intelligent tutoring systems: what, when and how to measure. In: Third International Conference on Intelligent Networking and Collaborative Systems (INCoS), pp. 807–812. IEEE (2011)
40. Laplante, P.A.: Requirements Engineering for Software and Systems. Auerbach Publications, Boca Raton (2017)
41. Georgescu, M., Popescu, D.: How could Internet of Things change the e-learning environment. In: The International Scientific Conference eLearning and Software for Education, Carol I National Defence University, vol. 1, p. 68 (2015)
42. Putjorn, P., Ang, C.S., Farzin, D.: Learning IoT without the i-educational Internet of Things in a developing context. In: Proceedings of the 2015 Workshop on Do-it-yourself Networking: An Interdisciplinary Approach, pp. 11–13. ACM (2015)
43. Murphy, F.E., et al.: i4toys: video technology in toys for improved access to play, entertainment, and education. In: IEEE International Symposium on Technology and Society (ISTAS), pp. 1–6. IEEE (2015)
44. Weber, R.H.: Internet of Things-new security and privacy challenges. Comput. Law Secur. Rev. **26**(1), 23–30 (2010)
45. Grama, J.: Just in time research: data breaches in higher education. EDUCAUSE (2014)

46. Laplante, P., Laplante, N., Voas, J.: Considerations for healthcare applications in the Internet of Things. Reliab. Dig. **61**(4), 8–9 (2015)
47. Grama, J., Vogel, V.: The 2016 top 3 strategic information security issues
48. Zhang, N.: A campus big-data platform architecture for data mining and business intelligence in education institutes. In: 6th International Conference on Machinery, Materials, Environment, Biotechnology and Computer. Atlantis Press (2016)
49. Jagtap, A., Bodkhe, B., Gaikwad, B., Kalyana, S.: Homogenizing social networking with smart education by means of machine learning and Hadoop: a case study. In: International Conference on Internet of Things and Applications (IOTA), pp. 85–90. IEEE (2016)
50. Mehmood, R., Alam, F., Albogami, N.N., Katib, I., Albeshri, A., Altowaijri, S.M.: UTiLearn: a personalised ubiquitous teaching and learning system for smart societies. IEEE Access **5**, 2615–2635 (2017)
51. E. Tech, Internet of Things and the humanization of health care technology
52. Gubbi, J., Buyya, R., Marusic, S., Palaniswami, M.: Internet of Things (IoT): a vision, architectural elements, and future directions. Future Gener. Comput. Syst. **29**(7), 1645–1660 (2013)
53. Budgen, D., Brereton, P.: Performing systematic literature reviews in software engineering. In: Proceedings of the 28th International Conference on Software Engineering, pp. 1051–1052. ACM (2006)

Opunit: Sanity Checks for Computing Environments

Samim Mirhosseini[✉] and Chris Parnin[✉]

North Carolina State University, Raleigh, NC 27695, USA
{smirhos,cjparnin}@ncsu.edu

Abstract. Computing environments, including virtual machines and containers, are essential components of modern software engineering infrastructure. Despite emerging tools that support the creation and configuration of computing environments, they are limited in testing and validating the construction of these environments. Furthermore, professionals and students new to these concepts, lack feedback on their construction efforts. In this paper, we argue that the design of environment testing tools should fundamentally support asserting essential properties, such as reachability and availability, in order to maximize usability and utility. We present OPUNIT, an environment testing tool that supports assertion of these properties. We describe properties students failed to check when testing computing environments, which guided the design of OPUNIT. Finally, we share our early experiences with using OPUNIT in the classroom to support education and training in configuration of computing environments.

Keywords: Configuration management · Environment verification · Testing · DevOps training

1 Introduction

Software developers no longer simply build software in isolation: They now are expected to continuously deploy fixes and experimental features to production environments serving millions of customers. Making such ultra-fast and automatic changes to production means that testing and verifying the design and implementation of computing environments is increasingly important. However, based on the 2018 State of DevOps Report [6], only 36% of participants have capacity for dedicated testing of computing environments in their companies, making environment construction easy to get wrong. For example, GitLab lost 300 GB of customer data after accidentally deleting their production database [5]. Even worse, they could not restore the data because they discovered their backup procedure had been failing due to a mismatch in versions between the dump utility (`pg_dump 9.2`) and their database (`PostgreSQL 9.6`).

Unfortunately, the skills required to construct and test these computing environments supporting continuous deployment requires expertise and training that

© Springer Nature Switzerland AG 2020
J.-M. Bruel et al. (Eds.): DEVOPS 2019, LNCS 12055, pp. 167–180, 2020.
https://doi.org/10.1007/978-3-030-39306-9_12

is even more rare and highly sought than data science skills.[1] For example, Mozilla's Kim Moir says she "recently looked at the undergrad classes required to graduate with a computer science degree from a major university, and [she] was struck by [a lack of] practice on deploying code. In most computer science programs, there is little emphasis on infrastructure" [3]. Similarly, Google's Boris Debic claims that "Release engineering is not taught; it's often not even mentioned in courses where it should be mentioned" [3]. For this reason, Facebook's Chuck Rossi considers hiring release engineers "is like finding unicorns."

In this study, we used our experiences and observations from five years of teaching over 400 students the concepts and tools related to continuous deployment in a university course [1]. Consider one assignment, where students were installing and configuring an open-source chat server called Mattermost[2], which works much like Slack[3]. The computing environment requires several components: a database, system dependencies, the Mattermost server itself, and several configuration files (`systemd` services, `mysql.cnf`, and `config.json` for Mattermost). In configuring this environment, many things could go wrong. For example, a simple typo or malformed JSON in a configuration file could result in an non-functioning environment, but with little hints as to why. To diagnose this problem, students might need to check a variety of system components using a myriad of tools and shell utilities in which they have little experience, such as `mysql` shell, `systemctl`, `journalctl`, `cat`, `grep`, and `jq`. In response, we would have to ask a series of questions: *"did you check your mysql credentials,"* *"did you check your connection string is correct,"* *"did you run jsonlint on your configuration file."* Other times, strange behaviors would result from incidental factors, which we would only resolve after asking, *"did you check dns,"* *"did you check your VM's memory size."* Overall, this experience of asking students to perform various sanity checks eventually helped, but resulted in a frustrating and problematic learning environment for students.

To make matters worse, no single tool can support this process meaning students must simultaneously learn many. For example, `ps`, `top`, `ss`, `cURL`, `netcat`, `free`, `lsof`, `who`, `last`, `dmsg`, `history`, `vmstat`, `dstat`, `iostat`, `htop`, `find` and more. In this paper, we argue for two ways to help with the mentioned shortcomings: (1) Train software engineers to be able to recognize desirable properties of a computing environment, (2) Provide them a simple means for evaluating these properties. To this end, we formalized these checks in a simple environment verification tool, OPUNIT. We categorized common student mistakes and issues into violations of properties that computing environments should have. These properties can be verified to easily point out the cause of common issues related to environment setup. Categories of the properties which we include are *availability*, *reachability*, *identifiable*, and *capability*. They respectively indicate whether an environment provides expected services, can access specified resources, has certain items (files, software, etc.), and supports required operations.

---

[1] http://stackoverflow.com/insights/survey/2017#salary.

[2] https://mattermost.com/.

[3] https://slack.com/.

Finally, we share our early experiences with OPUNIT as a training aid in a DevOps course. First, we used OPUNIT to verify the student's initial local computing environments to ensure they contained appropriate tools and capabilities for the course. Next, we used OPUNIT in workshops and homework assignments to provide formative feedback on their progress (Fig. 1). Then, we administered a usability and feedback survey. Students indicated OPUNIT has increased their confidence about their work because they could ensure they have completed tasks correctly by running the tests. They also showed continued interest in using the tool for other courses and future assignments.

To summarize, our contributions are:

- Environment properties that are root causes for the most common issues students experience.
- OPUNIT, a tool for environment verification, inspired by the common properties in student issues.
- A survey about OPUNIT to suggest its effectiveness as a training tool.

2   Properties

Based on our experience with students in software engineering courses and a specialized DevOps course, we categorized common student mistakes. Then we identified four main properties of a computing environment which can be checked to point out these mistakes. In this section we explain the properties that we identified, an example of student issues related to those properties as well as a verification method that can help point out the issue, and finally application of those properties.

2.1   Availability

Environment functionality depends on availability of services that were set up in previous steps of environment construction. One common issue that students face occurs when they write a whole configuration script without intermediate testing. As a result, they often experience errors which they incorrectly ascribe to the last step they worked on. In reality, the errors often lie in one of the earlier steps. By supporting the ability to check *availability* of services, students can better test their configuration scripts incrementally, allowing them to establish stepping stones of progress.

Example Problem. *Expected services are not available in the environment, because they have not been started:* The goal is to run automated GUI tests for a web application using `Selenium`[4]. Students run the tests, but the server was not able to start successfully before the tests executed. As a result, all of the GUI tests fail as none of web application pages can be served. They often think

---

[4] https://docs.seleniumhq.org/.

Fig. 1. OPUNIT's verify command to test pipelines workshop

this is because of not running `Selenium` tests correctly, or the tests are really failing. More careful inspection of logs is required to find the reason for the test failures.

The failed server start up can have many different causes. For example, a `bind exeception` could occurs if there is another server running on the same port and often happens due to other instances of the same application still running in the

```
{                           {                           {
    "a": "b",                   "a": "b",                   "a": "e"
    "c": "d"                    "c": "e",                   "c": "d"
}                           }                           }
```

Fig. 2. Examples of students' broken JSON files shown in red color (Color figure online)

background. Another cause can be a broken formatting in configuration files, like an extra "," at the end of a JSON configuration file. This was a common failure because students used string replacements instead of using a utility like jq, and created a broken JSON format as shown in Fig. 2 in red color.

Example Verification. If the configuration management scripts was tested incrementally, student would have been able to send a simple HTTP request using cURL utility to test if the server is started and can respond to requests.

Application. This property helps with ensuring availability of services before running a task. For example, it can be implemented as a simple HTTP request to a web server, to see if it is available. This idea has been implemented in Google Borg's tasks [7]. Each task implemented an internal health check end-point, and this allowed Borg to send an HTTP request to this end-point to do a health check on each task. Automating the steps for checking availability property allows the user to do a quick health check without having to learn cURL utility or other more complicated tools.

2.2 Reachability

Another common issue among students is unexpected software failures as a result of an *unreachable* resource. We might not be able to access a resource because of various reasons such as a missing/wrong configuration file, wrong file permissions, and bad firewall rules. Checking reachability of these resources can help find the reason for the failures. In other words, after discovering an *unavailable* service, checking *reachability* of its related resources can help find the root cause for this unavailability.

Example Problem. *Database is not reachable in the environment because credentials has not been updated in a configuration file:* The goal is to start a web application that requires database access. This application uses a configuration file to store database credentials. Forgetting to update and correctly ensure appropriate access rights to configuration files is a common mistake among students. The application may start without explicit errors, and the UI pages may even be rendered, but the pages will be missing information. Finding the problem will require more careful inspection of the logs from this web application.

Example Verification. Existence of database configuration file should be checked using `ls -l <config_file>`, and this file's permissions should be accessible by the application. So students need to at least understand Unix file permissions and know what parameters they need to use with `ls`. While the check itself may be relatively simple, students may not be well-attuned to pay attention to details such as mismatches in group permissions of a file. Automating these steps will also require experience with tools such as `grep`. And finally, if the permission needs to be changed, students also need to understand how to use the `chmod` command.

Application. Reachability issues in industry, especially in microservices, is even more crucial: *"Reachability is definitely an important thing, security group changes that make downstreams unreachable in a microservice architecture can be dangerous."*[5] Automated verification of reachability of the resources will prevent reachability issues. It can be implemented as a series of requests to all the needed resources, and triggered after each change to know when reachability is affected.

2.3   Identifiable

Another common property that causes confusion for students is related to the version of installed software, wrong content in configuration files, and such *identifiable* properties or items in the environment. We called these types of properties identifiable because of their relation to one of the core components in traditional configuration management, "identification".

Example Problem. *Unexpected behavior when wrong version of a dependency is installed:* One of the most common observed issues with setting up an environment for running a specific software occurs when incompatible versions of dependencies are installed. For example, if the software required MySQL v5.7, it may not work as expected if version v8 is installed. *GitHub does not link commit authors to their profile on GitHub:* Another example of *identifiable* property is when students forget to create git configuration file, `.gitconfig`, and as a result their git commits are not linked to any GitHub account.

Example Verification. Most utilities use a `-v or --version` option to print their current version; this can be used to check if the installed version is the same as the expected version. Also, the content of the configuration files can be checked by opening the files and manually checking for expected changes. Manually checking these properties may not seem very difficult, but automating the steps for checking them will require experience with Unix utilities such as `cat`, `grep`, `awk`, and more.

---

[5] Personal correspondence from industry.

Application. One of primary objectives in real-world configuration management is to install tools and systems, and fine-grain details. Many of these details can be categorized as *identifiable* properties. As we explained earlier, a serious case of not testing this property happened at GitLab in 2017. GitLab's version of dump utility (`pg_dump 9.2`) was not compatible with the version of their database (`PostgreSQL 9.6`) which resulted in failure in the backup process and unrecoverable loss of 300 GB of customer data. A simple verification of the versions could prevent such incidents. Automating the steps needed for checking the mentioned *identifiable* properties of environment will enable the user have more confident about their environment setup without having to learn how to write a testing script.

2.4   Capability

Capability property is about ensuring that the system has sufficient resources to support required operations. *Capability* of the environment is typically related to the hardware, which is another important property that can effect how applications run. A few examples of this property are number of CPU cores, amount of RAM, free disk space, and virtualization support.

Example Problem. One of the workshops in our software engineering and DevOps courses focuses on provisioning virtual machines. 64-bit virtual machines require having a CPU which supports virtualization (VT-x on Intel and AMD-V on AMD CPUs). Most modern CPUs and laptops support virtualization but many manufacturers disable this feature by default. So, when students try to create a virtual machine, they receive a complicated error messages which is hard for them to understand.

Example Verification. On Windows, virtualization status can be checked in Windows Task Manager. On Linux virtualization support can be checked by inspecting CPU flags and looking for **vmx** and **svm** flags. Modern Apple computers (macOS) have virtualization enabled by default.

Application. One of the most common issues with setting up a system for building java programs, such as a Jenkins[6] executor, was memory limitations. Students would provision instances with 1 GB of RAM, and would experience a variety exotic errors, none of which made it clear insufficient memory was the root cause. By introducing a capability check for RAM, we can reduce the likelihood that students experience these issues.

---

[6] https://jenkins.io/.

3   Opunit

Inspired by the properties that we identified, we developed an environment testing automation tool, OPUNIT. Figure 1 shows an example of the test results on a DevOps workshop which was about constructing a delivery pipeline using git hooks. This workshop was completed inside a virtual machine. In this study, we are specially concerned with the needed verification in the initial phase of environment creation, rather than monitoring the application for changes.

The goal of OPUNIT is to be a simple tool for verifying the construction of a computing environment by asserting the properties we introduced. Often, multiple properties must be verified and checked in order to understand the cause of a misconfiguration.

3.1   Using Opunit

OPUNIT uses a YAML configuration file, `opunit.yml`, to define the verification steps. Listing 1 shows an example `opunit.yml` file. The verification steps are defined under `checks` property. In this example, OPUNIT will be using `node --version` command to verify version of `node` is in semver[7] range `^10.x.x`. OPUNIT tests can be started with `opunit verify` command. OPUNIT searches the default paths for an `opunit.yml` file and runs the provided checks against the target environment.

```
1   - group:
2       description: "Check node.js support"
3       checks:
4       - version:
5           cmd: node --version
6           range: ^10.x.x
```

Listing 1: An example `opunit.yml` file with a simple check for having the appropriate version of nodejs installed.

3.2   Checks

OPUNIT uses automated scripts, *checks*, to implement how each property needs to be checked. To verify the Availability property, OPUNIT uses a check called "availability" which runs a command on target environment followed by a HTTP request to do a health check. A simple example of `version` check is shown in Listing 1. This check has two parameters, the command that needs to be executed to get the version, and a semver range that the version should be in. OPUNIT has *checks* to verify all the mentioned properties in Sect. 2 and each require different parameters which are explained in more details in OPUNIT documentation[8].

---

[7] https://semver.org/.

[8] https://github.com/ottomatica/opunit.

In summary the supported checks are `availability` to check if a service can be started successfully, `reachability` to check reachability of specified resources, `contains` to check content of specified files, `version` to check version of the specified tool and comparing it with the provided semver range, `service` to check status of installed Linux services, `timezone` to check timezone of the environment, `cores` to check number of available CPU cores, `virt` to check if virtualization is supported, and `disk` and `memory` to check the memory size available disk space.

3.3   Environments

The target Environment that OPUNIT verifies can be the local machine, a remote server, a virtual machine or a container. OPUNIT also supports all three common operating systems, macOS, Windows, and Linux. Supporting various types of environments and operating systems allowed us to use OPUNIT in classroom.

The environment type in some cases can be automatically inferred based on the existence of other configuration files in the project, or the arguments passed to the `verify` command. For example if there is a `Vagrantfile` in the project, OPUNIT will try to connect to that Vagrant virtual machine. Or, if OPUNIT is executed with `opunit verify root@example.com:2222` command, then OPUNIT will use ssh to connect to the target environment. OPUNIT has a few more advanced inference rules in the tool's documentation which we don't discuss in this paper.

3.4   Report

After OPUNIT verification checks are executed, the results are printed in the terminal window. Figure 1 shows an example of this report. The green check ($\checkmark$) indicates that a check was passed, while the red x ($\times$) indicates that a check failed. The report is very verbose and includes both expected and actual values for each check. Each check can also include a description defined in `opunit.yml` file. The descriptions for the *checks* proved very useful for learning in workshops as we discuss in the next sections.

4   Experiences

To better understand the impact of using OPUNIT in the classroom, we integrated the tool in our DevOps course. In this section we discuss the experiences of students using OPUNIT, as well as feedback we received from them.

4.1   Supporting Initial Course Setup

In the first week, students are required to prepare their local development environment for the rest of semester. `opunit profile CSC-DevOps/profile:519.yml`[9]

---

[9] https://github.com/CSC-DevOps/profile/blob/master/519.yml.

verifys their development environment's configuration. `profile` is an `opunit.yml` file hosted in a GitHub repository.

The resulting output is shown in Fig. 3. Notice that one of the checks under "Editor Support", fails to validate. This check looks for syntax highlighting being enabled for `vim`. This check fails because the `.vimrc` file is not present on the machine.

Fig. 3. Result of running an OPUNIT profile

4.2   Using Opunit for Workshops

We added OPUNIT checks in a workshop about pipelines by providing students an opunit.yml file. In this workshop students learn how to use git hooks to run static analysis checks before committing their code and then triggering deployment of an application on git push. We provided them an interactive way of knowing what they need to complete for the workshop. Each OPUNIT check had a description that help with understanding the corresponding task. When students start the workshop, all the OPUNIT checks fail and as they complete the workshop, they see OPUNIT checks start passing.

YAML snippet in Listing 2 shows the opunit.yml file used in the workshop. In this snippet three types of checks are shown, contains check, reachable check and version check. contains check verifies that students have updated the pre-commit hook to run npm test command, reachable check verifies students created needed directories, and version check verifies they installed a version of pm2 package in the range ^3.2.4.

```
 1   - group:
 2       description: "Pre-commit setup"
 3       checks:
 4         - contains:
 5             comment: App is a submodule, its hooks are located in
              ↪   `.git/modules/App/hooks`.
 6             string: npm test
 7             file: .git/modules/App/hooks/pre-commit
 8
 9   - group:
10       description: "Deploy directory setup"
11       checks:
12         - reachable:
13             - deploy
14             - deploy/production-www
15             - deploy/production.git
16         - version:
17             comment: Install with `npm install pm2 -g`
18             cmd: pm2 --version
19             range: ^3.2.4
```

Listing 2: Part of the opunit.yml file used in the pipelines workshop

4.3   Student Feedback

After students used OPUNIT for supporting their development environment setup and for completing a workshop, we sent them a feedback form with open-ended responses and an usability survey [2] to collect data about their experience with the tool. We used this feedback to find possible issues and determine if OPUNIT was effective in supporting students.

Feedback. In the feedback form, we asked students to explain how their experience with OPUNIT was comparing to the other assignments that they completed without using OPUNIT. The responses showed that using OPUNIT made it very easy for the students to know if they completed all the necessary tasks or they missed something. In many instances students explained how OPUNIT saved them a lot of time by showing them descriptive errors about what mistakes they made in doing a task. Students explained that they had higher level of confidence when they completed the workshop that took advantage of OPUNIT. Finally, students also showed interest in using OPUNIT in their future assignments and even in other courses.

Usability. On the usability survey, we asked students ten multiple choice questions as shown in the Likert chart in Table 1. Summary of the survey responses confirms the findings of our general feedback form, about *higher level of confidence* and *interest in using the tool in the furure*. Additionally, student responses showed OPUNIT was easy to learn without spending too much time. Most of the students also think they are likely to be able to use OPUNIT in their future projects, without needing assistant from us.

OPUNIT has been effective in classroom and provided good support for training configuration of computing environments. Very few students had difficulty in running the tool. They mostly liked seeing the green check marks after completing each task and indicated this increased their confidence. Students even showed interest in using OPUNIT in future assignments and other courses. We think this is the right direction for OPUNIT, however there are limitations which we try to resolve, and improvements which we plan to add. We discuss these limitations and future directions in next sections in more details.

Based on our observation, we believe one of the reasons for why students are often confused and have a hard time when debugging environments is that they fail to **read** and **understand** the error messages. In many cases that students asked us for help in debugging, we noticed the errors explicitly and clearly indicates the problem. However, students either did not carefully read the error messages, or the did not understand it. An example of such error message is "`Permission 0644 for /Users/ubuntu/id_rsa are too open.`" which makes SSH ignore a key. As mentioned by an StackExchange user who asked a similar question[10], a reason for not reading the error messages and logs can be frustration.

I failed to read the output due to a combination of frustration, disillusionment and pessimism

As mentioned by students in our general survey, OPUNIT improved students' confidence. If the written `opunit.yml` file includes description for the possible causes of the failures, it can especially be helpful for student who missed the error message details as we mentioned earlier.

It's all about confidence and I think that opunit gives me such confidence.

---

[10] https://superuser.com/questions/1159790/chocolatey-python-am-i-doing-it-wrong?rq=1#comment1672782_1159793.

Table 1. Follow-up survey responses

		Likert Responses[1]						Distribution[2]		
	% Agree	SD	D	N	A	SA		50%	0%	50%
I thought opunit was easy to use.	92%	0	0	2	15	11				
I think that I would like to use opunit in my future projects.	89%	0	1	2	11	14				
I found the various features in opunit were well integrated.	88%	0	0	3	19	4				
I would imaging that most people would learn to use opunit very quickly.	85%	0	1	3	11	13				
I felt very confident using opunit.	64%	0	2	8	9	9				
I needed to learn many things before I could get going with opunit sanity checks.	28%	6	10	4	6	2				
I think that I would need assistance using opunit in my future projects.	14%	7	9	8	3	1				
I thought there were too much inconsistency in the opunit tool.	3%	8	13	6	1	0				
I found opunit very cumbersome/awkward to use.	3%	15	10	2	1	0				
I found opunit unnecessarily complex.	0%	12	15	1	0	0				

[1] Likert responses: Strongly Disagree (SD), Disagree (D), Neutral (N), Agree (A), Strongly Agree (SA).   [2] Net stacked distribution removes the Neutral option and shows the skew between positive (more useful) and negative (less useful) responses. ■ Strongly Disagree, ▨ Disagree, ▨ Agree; ■ Strongly Agree.

5   Future Directions

OPUNIT is a new tool and it's important to realize its limitations. One limitation is the type of checks that OPUNIT supports. Although OPUNIT checks cover many common properties that we identified, there could be more properties which we have not considered. Furthermore, current OPUNIT checks can be extended to support more fine-grain verification. To address this, we accept pull requests and feature requests for the tool, and we are actively adding more checks as we find the need for them.

After seeing promising effectiveness in the current version of OPUNIT, we think adding a CI system integration is an appropriate next step. Using OPUNIT in a CI system will allow developers and students automatically get feedback about the changes they make on every git commit. Another possible future direction for OPUNIT are adding monitoring capabilities and combining our idea of checks with chaos engineering principles [4]. This will allow developers easily measure resilience of the environment and configuration in turbulent conditions.

Additionally we plan to extend our interviews with the professionals to find other properties that are checked in industry and improve the list of supported checks in OPUNIT. The new OPUNIT checks that we have identified and plan to implement are integration with different services. For example, support for verifying write access of a GitHub token, or verifying needed rules in AWS[11] EC2 security groups. Finally, as we mentioned earlier, the currently supported checks still can be improved by better fine-grain verification.

6   Conclusion

This paper describes the design of an environment testing tool, OPUNIT, guided by experiences and observations obtained after five years of teaching the concepts and tools related to continuous deployment. Our experience in a DevOps course showed that our tool was effective and this could be a step in the right direction, however there is more work to be done.

Acknowledgement. This material is based in part upon work supported by the National Science Foundation under grant number 1814798.

References

1. DevOps 519. https://github.com/CSC-DevOps/Course/#devops-csc-519
2. Opunit Survey. https://forms.gle/uhBYmtftdsfj5TxP8
3. Adams, B., Bellomo, S., Bird, C., Marshall-Keim, T., Khomh, F., Moir, K.: The practice and future of release engineering: a roundtable with three release engineers. IEEE Softw. **32**(2), 42–49 (2015). https://doi.org/10.1109/MS.2015.52
4. Basiri, A., Jones, N., Blohowiak, A., Hochstein, L., Rosenthal, C.: Chaos Engineering. O'Reilly Media, Inc., Newton (2017)
5. GitLab: Postmortem of database outage of January 31. https://about.gitlab.com/2017/02/10/postmortem-of-database-outage-of-january-31/
6. Puppet: 2018 state of DevOps report. https://puppet.com/resources/whitepaper/state-of-devops-report/
7. Verma, A., Pedrosa, L., Korupolu, M.R., Oppenheimer, D., Tune, E., Wilkes, J.: Large-scale cluster management at Google with Borg. In: Proceedings of the European Conference on Computer Systems (EuroSys), Bordeaux, France, p. 18 (2015)

---

[11] https://aws.amazon.com/.

Towards Bridging the Value Gap
in DevOps

Gail C. Murphy[1]([⊠])[iD] and Mik Kersten[2]

[1] Department of Computer Science, University of British Columbia,
Vancouver, Canada
`murphy@cs.ubc.ca`
[2] Tasktop Technologies Inc., Vancouver, Canada
`mik.kersten@tasktop.com`

Abstract. The DevOps movement, which combines software development with information technology operations, enables the more frequent delivery of changes to a software system. Adopting DevOps practices is seen as enabling the ability to deliver more. But is the more that is getting done actually of value to the end user or to the producing organization? In this paper, we describe how the ideas of value streams are being applied to software development and how more systematic handling of features is key to enabling an increased focus on the delivery of value.

Keywords: Software requirements · Value stream maps · Software development productivity

1 Introduction

The ability of software to transform how we work and live is immense. As we realize these opportunities, there is an ever increasing need for software. This realization is not new: for the last 50 years, since the 1968 NATO Software Engineering conference, there have been discussions about the many issues involved in producing operational software that meets desired needs on time and on budget [9]. Over the last fifty years, there have been many advances to address this need. Whereas it used to take months or years to develop new functionality—a feature—for a software system, by the early 2000s, the adoption of agile practices and principles, alongside other improvements, dropped the time to develop new features to the order of weeks [10].

Although the time required to develop a new feature decreased, organizations in the early 2000s still faced challenges getting newly developed features deployed into use. Often, the release of the software required shipping the software on physical media, which might only occur once per year. In the second decade of the 21st century, DevOps—short for Development and Operations—ideas, which consider how to integrate development, delivery and operations of the software, helped further accelerate the ability to develop and deliver features quickly [4],

© Springer Nature Switzerland AG 2020
J.-M. Bruel et al. (Eds.): DEVOPS 2019, LNCS 12055, pp. 181–190, 2020.
https://doi.org/10.1007/978-3-030-39306-9_13

with some organizations now able to deliver new features and fixes hundreds of times per day [15].

The primary focus of DevOps practices has been on the back-end of the software development life-cycle. This focus can be seen through the tools that support DevOps, which focus on the build environment, continuous integration, continuous delivery and monitoring of the performance of the software in use [3]. The metrics used to track the adoption of DevOps practices reinforce this emphasis on the back-end of development. For instance, the DORA State of the DevOps Report that gathers data from tens of thousands of technology professionals focuses on such metrics as lead time, which is defined as "how long it takes to go from code commit to code successfully running in production" [12, p. 14].

This focus on the back-end of the software development life-cycle leaves open the question of whether the increase in code changes deployed to operations are seen as meaningful changes to the end users receiving the changes. The focus on the back-end places an assumption that many features can be built quickly such that the tracking of use of features can help weed out which carry value for the user.

In this paper, we argue that leaving the notion of 'value' implicit and unrefined in this way limits the ability of software developers to efficiently deliver flows of value consistently to users. We demonstrate the implicit nature of value by reporting on the range of meanings of what a feature is across a number of popular open source systems. We briefly outline areas of future research that might help provide a more consistent meaning for value through features, thus enabling a focus on value flow in the context of DevOps. Such a focus could allow software development teams to more consistently match their effort and work to producing value to their end users.

We begin with a short review of previous approaches that consider the notion of value in the software development lifecycle (Sect. 2). We then discuss how a software development lifecycle helps organize and frame the steps, methods and tools used in software development (Sect. 3) and introduce how the concept of value streams from manufacturing can be systematically applied to software development (Sect. 4). We then show that there is a need to systematize how we consider value in the form of features to enable a more meaningful application of value stream concepts to software development (Sect. 5). We outline the value gap (Sect. 6) and briefly suggest research that might help to bridge this gap (Sect. 7).

2   Value in Software Engineering

The term "value" has two common English definitions.

One way in which the term "value" is used and defined is to describe the worth or use of something. Boehm has used this meaning of the term to argue that too many of the software development approaches and practices in use are value-neutral, which is no longer appropriate given the need to increasingly consider software as part of the system, such as part of a business process, in which the software is embedded [2]. Boehm argues that it is time to take a "value-based" approach to software engineering in which value considerations are taken into account as part of the many decisions made in software development. He outlines a value-based software engineering agenda that is needed to help the research and industrial communities consider value as an integral part of the software development life-cycle.

In this paper, we use the term "value" in the same way as Boehm to indicate the worth or usefulness of what is being produced as part of software development. The directions we describe are one step towards the challenges in tracking value through the lifecycle. In considering how value might be connected in the front-end of software development to a back-end DevOps platform, this paper is complementary to the growing body of work in identifying value at the requirements stage of development (e.g., [13]).

The second way in which the term "value" is used is to describe principles or standards of behaviour, particularly in relation to a judgement of what is important. Consideration of human values in software is a growing area of interest in software engineering. For example, Mougouei and colleagues lay out a research roadmap for defining human values related to software development, integrating those values into design and then measuring whether the values are realized [8].

The two concepts of value—as something of worth and as something describing principles—are interlinked. We leave the exploration of the linkage of ideas in this paper with the concept of values as principles to future work.

3   Framing the Software Development LifeCycle

To discuss the production of value, we need a frame for the production cycle. The concept of the lifecycle of software development provides such a frame.

There is no single lifecycle model used for all software development. The methods and tools and how they are organized and used to develop software differ depending on the kind of software being built. For example, building the software for a cyber-physical system, such as rover to explore the planet of Mars, likely requires approaches that place a heavier emphasis on the use of formal requirements approaches as there will be limited ability to alter the software once deployed. The software development lifecycle employed in such a case may more closely resemble a waterfall lifecycle with more up-front work placed on the requirements of the overall system [14]. On the other hand, the methods and tools used to build a cloud-based business system, such as a system to support human resources at an organization, are likely to place more emphasis on the quick development and experimentation of features, with less emphasis on the specification of the features. The software development lifecycle employed in such a case may be more iterative [7].

In this paper, we consider a software development lifecycle in which the front-end is based on agile practices where specifications (requirements) consist of epics, user stories and defects [16]. The back-end of development in this life-cycle uses DevOps practices, including continuous builds, continuous integration and continuous delivery and deployment [4]. Figure 1 presents an abstract version of one iteration of this flow for illustration. While we consider that focus is placed on decreasing the time from user story definition to deployment, it is not uncommon that steps in this process are repeated for a given user story, such as multiple iterations through continuous build and integration, before deployment.

Fig. 1. An abstract depiction of a software development lifecycle.

A key intent in adoption of such a software development lifecycle is the faster flow of new functionality—features—to an end user. As stated in the State of DevOps report in 2017, this approach "helps teams ship features that customers actually want more frequently [and] [t]his faster delivery cycle lets teams experiment, creating a feedback loop with customers" [11, p. 7].

4   Value Streams

Simply increasing the ability to produce more software through a faster flow of feature delivery does not necessarily mean that what is produced is of value to the end user. An analysis of six Finnish software companies showed that while software product features are seen as the core of value creation for an end user, "focusing on features and launching them as fast as possible can cause problems from the perspective of customer value" [5, p. 277].

To help determine which features have value, DevOps practices advocate the gathering of feedback on feature use, such as tracking the amount of use of a feature by end users [4]. This form of tracking provides only one aspect of value late in the software development life-cycle. It does not enable a software development organization to optimize its production of value through upfront analysis and tracking of the delivery of value through various stages of the software development life-cycle. To better understand how to improve software development life-cycles, software development managers can apply techniques from lean production, such as value stream mapping. Poppendieck and Poppendieck popularized the use of value stream mapping to identify waste in a software development process [10]. When a manager maps a value stream of software development, they consider all processing steps needed to go from customer request for new functionality to delivery of that functionality. Surfacing these steps enables analysis to consider how to eliminate waste and optimize effort in the production of value in software. Early applications of value stream mapping to software focused on the flow of artifacts. More recent applications also consider communication or information flows involved in the production of software [1]. However, these approaches still focus on the steps and information coordination of software development and do not enable a modelling or tracking of the end-value of the items moving through the value stream map. As a result, an organization using these approaches must focus on an analysis of process making significant assumptions about the value of the software resulting from the process. This implicit notion of value makes it difficult for an organization to optimize their software development practices towards value.

Kersten has introduced a framework, called The Flow Framework^{TM}[1], that enables a correlation between the artifacts flowing through a value stream of a software development process to business outcomes [6]. This framework enables the tracking of flow items for a value stream associated with the development of a software product. Kersten defines flow items as features, defects, risks and technical debt. Many organizations can map these concepts to particular constructs in the tools that they use, such as mapping user stories stored in an agile tool to features. The Flow Framework^{TM} can be enacted for various chains of tools used in a software development process to allow the tracking of value stream metrics defined by Kersten. For example, an organization can track flow velocity, which an organization might define as the number of features completed over a given time for a product value stream, or flow time, which can be defined as the time taken from when a feature enters the value stream until it is done. These metrics can then be tracked against business outcomes such as the value of the product in revenue or the quality of the product.

5   Exploring Features in Open Source

The Flow Framework^{TM} provides a means to relate flow items to business outcomes and a means to operationalize the tracking of flow items through a software product value stream. Applying The Flow Framework^{TM} to better track, manage and optimize value produced through a software product value stream requires a determination of how to associate value with flow items flowing through the stream and to then correlate that value to business outcomes. For instance, assume value for the end-user is added to a software product by the delivery of software features. To enable management and optimization, an organization will either need to break desired functionality into features of similar value or will need to normalize the value associated with features. To investigate whether there might already be defined approaches to features and value occurring in practice, we consider how features are defined in three popular open source projects: Kubernetes, Moodle and Firefox. These three projects were chosen as they represent different kinds of software systems with different kinds of end-users:

---

[1] The Flow Framework^{TM} was created by Mik Kersten and is a trademark owned by Tasktop Technologies.

- Kubernetes supports the deployment, scaling and management of container-ized applications and is largely systems software with little interface to the user;[2]
- Moodle is an open source learning platform with significant capabilities for both authoring content to appear on the platform and for interacting with users in different roles, such as teacher or student;[3] and
- Firefox is an open source web browser, which must work across different operating systems for users with a wide variance of computer expertise.[4]

We consider how features are defined and managed for each of these systems in turn.

5.1   Kubernetes

The Kubernetes open source project involves over 1700 contributors who have contributed over 68,000 commits with 415 releases. Kubernetes is hosted on github.com and uses the github.com issue tracker as a means of tracking functionality desired by users and developers.

To gain a sense of how features are tracked through the github.com issue tracker for Kubernetes we analyzed the open issues for version v1.12. We found that the Kubernetes team uses github.com labels as a means of classifying the issues being tracked. 188 labels were in use for v1.12. Issues are tagged with multiple labels. For example, as Fig. 2 shows an issue may carry tags indicating it is a feature, its stage of development and so on. This approach to classifying work tracked as issues is manual, relying on the developers to apply the appropriate subset of the 188 available labels. There is no obvious identification in an issue of the amount of value defined for a feature. Table 1 shows the number of closed issues for three of the earlier releases of Kubernetes. As can be seen from the table, there is no consistency in the number of different kinds of items per release, calling into question how value might be associated with issues tagged as a feature.

Table 1. Work tags for closed flow items in three versions of Kubernetes

Version	v1.8	v1.9	v1.10
Bug	118	41	104
Feature	24	6	17
Technical debt	5	1	0
Area/security	6	6	3

---

[2] github.com/kubernetes/kubernetes.
[3] moodlee.org.
[4] www.mozilla.org.

5.2   Moodle

The Moodle open source project has over 450 contributors who have created over 90,000 commits with over 300 releases. Moodle uses an agile tracking tool, JIRA, to track work to be performed. As Fig. 3 shows, developers are able to tag work according to agile software development concepts, such as epics, stories and new features. At the time we analyzed the Moodle JIRA, there were over 1000 open new features. However, there was no obvious consistent linkage of the different work items; for instance, features were not obviously related to epics. While there is more structure to work related to features in the Moodle development, there appear to be multiple approaches being taken to prioritize work, such as a user association for which users can pay to prioritize features. As with Kubernetes, the value of a given feature is still implicit.

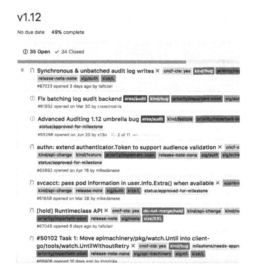

Fig. 2. Tagged work items in Kubernetes.

5.3   Firefox

Earlier, we described that a suggested DevOps practice is to gather feedback from usage to help gauge the value of a delivered feature. FireFox uses this approach in its TestPilot program. One capability developed through TestPilot was SnoozeTabs which enables pausing browser tabs to be brought back at a later user-specified time. The development of SnoozeTabs involved feedback collected over 400,000 sessions by over 58,000 users. Although data is provided in terms of feedback, the Firefox development does not obviously track how different features that are part of the delivered capability of SnoozeTabs are used. As with the other developments, the value of features is implicit.

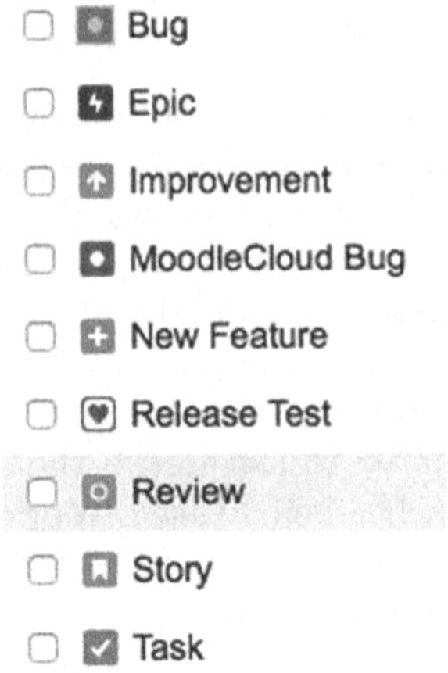

☐ ⚙ Bug

☐ ⚡ Epic

☐ ⬆ Improvement

☐ ◆ MoodleCloud Bug

☐ ➕ New Feature

☐ ♥ Release Test

☐ ◎ Review

☐ 🔖 Story

☐ ☑ Task

Fig. 3. Work item structure in Moodle

6   The Value Gap

Table 2 shows a comparison between the different ways features are defined and tracked in each of the open source systems considered and the challenges with relating those features to value. This table shows that, at least in a sample of open source projects in the wild, there are very different approaches to defining and tracking features. Without consistency in how features are defined and how features relate to end user value, it is challenging, if not impossible, to manage and optimize the development life-cycle. For instance, if the relative value of two features is not known, how does an organization determine how to prioritize the features against each other? An approach that simply delivers both features and determines later if there is value creates significant work that may later be discarded and also may cost the organization in lost opportunity to use that effort to create a different feature of value.

7   Bridging the Gap

How do we bridge the gap between the front-end of the software development life-cycle where value is largely implicit and inconsistent and the DevOps practices that are enabling more to be delivered faster to users? We believe the gap can be bridged through an enhanced focus on modelling and measuring the front-end of the software development lifecycle. In particular, there needs to be an enhanced focus on how features to be delivered are defined and in the linking of those features to delivered value.

One direction that could be investigated is to be able to systematize the work being performed for a system. For example, without substantial change to existing processes, machine learning techniques might be applied to a system's issue tracking system to automatically learn how to categorize new issues as they

Table 2. Summary of feature identification in three open source systems

	Feature designation	Challenges
Kubernetes	Labelling	Largely manual; Value implicit and inconsistent
Moodle	Issue structure and prioritization	Multiple approaches; Value implicit and inconsistent
Firefox	(Testpilot) Unclear how relates to feature tracking	Multiple approaches; Value implicit and inconsistent

are entered appropriately (e.g., as a feature or technical debt). Tool support that could help produce a well-categorized set of issues from which to learn could help improve the learning process. The advantage of creating such an approach would be to help ensure the items flowing into a value stream are more consistently defined.

The consistent descriptions of work being performed through well-categorized issues could then be connected to value through telemetry approaches or focus groups. An area to explore is the development of rules or patterns to tag defined work with likely value quanta. Over time, feedback could be used to refine the tagging of likely value up-front to allow organizations to manage and optimize their value stream. If likely value could be tagged against defined work, it might also allow negotiation of value to be delivered with potential customers.

An enhanced early ability to consistently define features and estimate their value, coupled with an ability to track features across the value stream of a product, such as provided by the Flow Framework^{TM}, would enable a full lifecycle approach to delivering the features of true use and value to end users faster.

Acknowledgements. Support provided by NSERC RGPIN-2016-03758 is gratefully acknowledged. The authors would also like to thank the anonymous reviewers for their helpful comments in revising this work.

References

1. Ali, N.B., Petersen, K., Schneider, K.: Flow-assisted value stream mapping in the early phases of large-scale software development. J. Syst. Softw. **111**, 213–227 (2016)
2. Boehm, B.W.: Value-based software engineering. ACM SIGSOFT Softw. Eng. Notes **28**(2), 4 (2003)
3. Ebert, C., Gallardo, G., Hernantes, J., Serrano, N.: DevOps. IEEE Software **33**(3), 94–100 (2016)
4. Gene Kim, G.S., Behr, K.: The Phoenix Project. IT Revolution Press (2013)
5. Kauppinen, M., Savolainen, J., Lehtola, L., Komssi, M., Töhönen, H., Davis, A.M.: From feature development to customer value creation. In: 17th IEEE International Requirements Engineering Conference, RE 2009, Atlanta, Georgia, USA, 31 August–4 September 2009, pp. 275–280 (2009)

6. Kersten, M.: Project to Product. IT Revolution Press (2018)
7. Larman, C., Basili, V.R.: Iterative and incremental development: a brief history. IEEE Comput. **36**, 47–56 (2003)
8. Mougouei, D., Perera, H., Hussain, W., Shams, R.A., Whittle, J.: Operationalizing human values in software: a research roadmap. In: Proceedings of the 2018 ACM Joint Meeting on European Software Engineering Conference and Symposium on the Foundations of Software Engineering, pp. 780–784 (2018)
9. Software engineering: Report on a conference sponsored by the NATO science committee (1968). http://homepages.cs.ncl.ac.uk/brian.randell/NATO/nato1968.PDF
10. Poppendieck, M., Poppendieck, T.: Lean Software Development: An Agile Toolkit. Addison-Wesley, Boston (2003)
11. Research, D.: Assessment: 2017 state of DevOps (2017). http://services.google.com/fh/files/misc/state-of-devops-2017.pdf
12. Research, D.: Assessment: Accelerate: State of DevOps: Strategies for a new economy (2018). http://services.google.com/fh/files/misc/state-of-devops-2018.pdf
13. Rodríguez, P., Mendes, E., Turhan, B.: Key stakeholders' value propositions for feature selection in software-intensive products: an industrial case study. IEEE Trans. Softw. Eng. (2018)
14. Royce, W.: Managing the development of large software systems. Proc. IEEE WESCON **26**, 1–9 (1970)
15. Savor, T., Douglas, M., Gentili, M., Williams, L., Beck, K.L., Stumm, M.: Continuous deployment at Facebook and OANDA. In: Proceedings of the 38th International Conference on Software Engineering, ICSE, pp. 21–30 (2016)
16. Williams, L.: Agile software development methodologies and practices. Adv. Comput. **80**, 1–44 (2010)

ArchiMate as a Specification Language for Big Data Applications - DataBio Example

Andrey Sadovykh[1](✉), Alessandra Bagnato[2], Arne J. Berre[3], and Stale Walderhaug[3]

[1] Innopolis University, Innopolis, Russia
andrey.sadovykh@innopolis.ru
[2] Softeam, Paris, France
alessandra.bagnato@softeam.fr
[3] SINTEF, Oslo, Norway
{arne.j.berre,stale.walderhaug}@sintef.no

Abstract. In this paper we discuss our method on applying the ArchiMate modelling language for specification in the context of Big Data applications. The DataBio project [1] develops the pilot applications for bioeconomy industry by applying Big Data technologies. The project regroups 26 pilots from 17 different countries to be implemented and deployed with more than 40 components and services. The choice of ArchiMate [2] is motivated by the need to express the overall business context of each pilot in conjunction with the technical architecture for possible solutions from various perspectives. The ArchiMate bridges the gap between those perspectives and can serve as an input for the model-driven development of Big Data applications. The authors provide the essence of the method and illustrate it with an example.

Keywords: ArchiMate · DataBio · Specification · Big Data · Bioeconomy

1 Introduction

When it comes to the requirements many approaches exist such as story points, use cases or even formal specifications. We argue that in Big Data applications the technical requirements are strongly linked to the company strategy and should support the business goals. Filling the gap between company goals, Big Data applications and technical infrastructure is a tedious task. Enterprise Architecture approaches and ArchiMate modelling notation provide an interesting perspective, though they were not specifically applied to the Big Data domain. In this paper we intend to generalize our experience in modelling 26 Big Data applications with ArchiMate in DataBio project.

The DataBio project selected the Data-Driven Bioeconomy as data intensive target sector for the study. The project focuses on building Big Data application pilots to contribute to the production of the best possible raw materials from agriculture, forestry and fishery/aquaculture for the bioeconomy industry, in order to output food, energy and biomaterials, also considering various responsibility and sustainability issues [3]. More specifically, the project is handling massive flows of data collected through sensors

© Springer Nature Switzerland AG 2020
J.-M. Bruel et al. (Eds.): DEVOPS 2019, LNCS 12055, pp. 191–199, 2020.
https://doi.org/10.1007/978-3-030-39306-9_14

placed in the soil and air, as well as from aerial and satellite imagery. The DataBio [1] consortium includes 48 partners from 17 countries and over 100 associated organizations.

The project's mission is driven by the development, use and evaluation of the 26 new pilots covering agriculture (13), forestry (7) and fishery (6). The project is deploying over 90 state-of-the-art Big Data, Earth Observation and ICT technologies, linked together through the DataBio Platform. DataBio modelled the Big Data pilots from a number of perspectives i.e. technical and data, business motivation and processes, strategic. The technologies have been matched and combined with each other to form innovative complex solutions - data pipeline for each pilot. Currently the DataBio platform - a generic set of Big Data technology components and Big Data pipelines for all pilots are fully developed.

Given the scale, the project faced several challenges that are addressed in part by the authors with the approach described in this paper. These challenges include:

- Establishing communication between many business users who provided the pilots and technology components providers.
- Specifying the business goals, technical requirements, available data sets and thought data processing pipeline in a structured, linked manner with a possibility to trace to the technical architecture.

The use of Enterprise Architecture paradigm is advocated by many authors as an approach to reconcile business strategy, goals, organization with IT systems. In particular, [4] suggests the application of ArchiMate for modelling Enterprise Architectures following The Open Group Architecture Framework (TOGAF). This framework proposes several layered views that allow to structure the information for different stakeholders in an organization.

ArchiMate provides modelling concepts on each of TOGAF layers. Using ArchiMate as a specification tool in the DataBio project, each dataset/datastream is related explicitly to a set of pilot systems, stakeholders, components and/or pipelines. The ArchiMate motivation and strategy diagrams specify the goals, drivers and outcomes of each pilot system, indicating the relevance and use of the datasets/streams in business processes. In the following section we provide more details and give an example.

2   Applying ArchiMate to Modelling DataBio Pilot Systems

All pilots in DataBio are modelled in ArchiMate following the methodology outlined in [5] developed in part by the authors. In this paper we present the essence of the approach with an example.

In order to cover the most interesting aspects several ArchiMate views has been prioritized for each pilots specification. Views are specific diagrams that represent relations among certain concepts in a particular area. In the list below we provide the view name with the major concepts to be used in modelling DataBio pilots:

1. **Motivation** view with the major elements including *Goals*[1], *Stakeholders, Drivers, Assessment, Principle.*
2. **Strategy** view has outlined major *Resources, Capabilities* and *Course of actions.*
3. For **Business Processes** were summarized along with involved *Actors, Events, Interactions* and *Functions.*
4. **Data Structures** were modeled by borrowing *Business Object* and *Data Object* concepts
5. For the **Application Layers** we applied the Big Data Value Association (BDVA [6]) layered approach to represent the **Application** concepts such as *Components, Function, Collaboration* and *Service.* Those concepts contributed to map the pilot application structure in several BDVA-specific categories including Infrastructure, Data Management, Data Processing, Data Analytics, Visualisation and User Interface.

The ArchiMate motivation and strategy diagrams specify the goals, drivers and outcomes of each pilot system, indicating the relevance and use of the datasets/streams. Figure 1 shows a strategy diagram from the B2 fishery pilots where the goals and outcomes are realized through extensive data collection and processing.

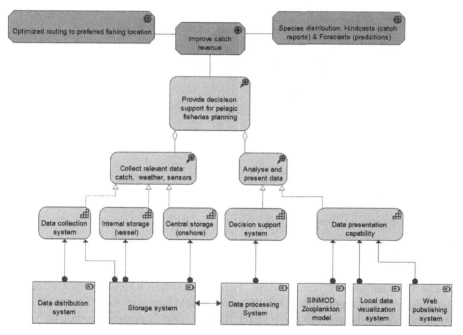

Fig. 1. ArchiMate strategy diagram showing how the pilot system will realize the defined goal.

As it is shown in Fig. 1 the major targeted *Goal* for that fishery pilot is to "improve catch revenue" related to major *Outcomes* such as "Optimized routing to preferred fishing location" and "Species distribution hindcasts and forecasts". Those goal and outcomes

---

[1] Note: hereafter, we will use *italic* in order to highlight the applied ArchiMate concepts.

are related to *Course of action* represented by "providing decision support for pelagic fisheries planning", which subsequently is divided into two more Courses of action. The *Courses of action* are *realized* by strategic *Capabilities* such as "Data collection system" and others. The *Capabilities* are supported by strategic *Resources* such as "SINMOD Zooplankton model".

Furthermore, ArchiMate is used to model pilot applications that realize outcomes. Figure 2 shows how the "Provide decision support for pelagic fisheries planning" (shown in Fig. 1) is supported by a set of *Business Processes* such as "Log catch details", *Business Objects* representing datasets such "Electronic catch report", *Stakeholders* such as "Vessel Master", *Actors* such as "Pelagic Vessel Skipper" and *Business Interactions* such as "Analyse catch", provided through *Business Interfaces* such as "Fuel consumption".

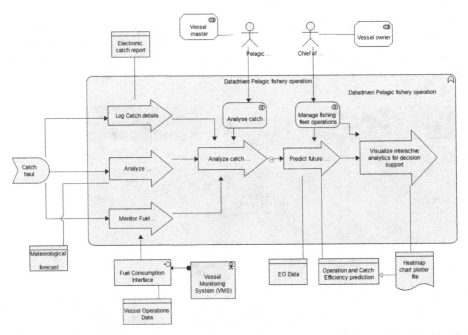

Fig. 2. ArchiMate business diagram showing the data processing, datasets and actors involved.

The information structure diagram (Fig. 3) identifies *Business Objects* such as "EO Data", "Vessel Operation Data", "Meteorological Forecast" and "Electronic catch reports" as required datasets/streams. Each *Business Object* dataset can then be broken down into *Data Objects* such as for example "Air pressure" realizing "Meteorological Forecast".

The above example is further described in details in [5]. In parallel, the technology partners specified their provided DataBio platform components with the ArchiMate Technical Application view concepts as detailed in [7].

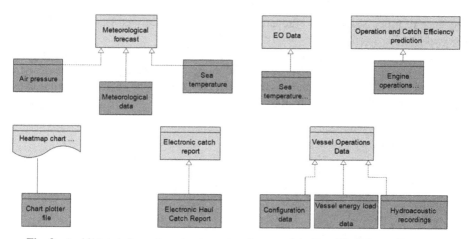

Fig. 3. ArchiMate information structure view for one of the DataBio fishery pilots (B2).

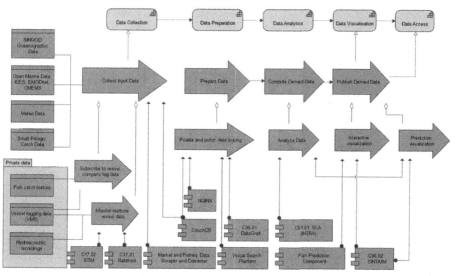

Fig. 4. The B2 fishery pilot lifecycle view showing how data is provided as input to processing steps.

At the later stages of the DataBio project, the pilot partners such as SINTEF developed their Big Data systems using both their data sets as well as components provided by technology partners. For coordinating the development activities and enable the sharing of data sets and technology components, it was required to provide a global view of pilot lifecycle. Figure 4 depicts the pipeline given by *Processes* such as "Collect input Data" as participating datasets represented by *Business Objects* such as "Small Pelagic Catch Data" and involved *Application Components* such as "Vespa Search Platform" or widely used "SINTIUM" for satellite data provision. The pipeline is emphasized by the sequence of processes such as "Prepare Data", "Compute Derived Data" and "Publish Derived Data".

To further specify the application architecture, a pipeline view is created for each pilot system as depicted in Fig. 5. The pipeline shows the *Application Components* such as "Vespa Search Platform" and "Fish Prediction Component" communicating over *Application Interface* such as "IF-REST-JSON".

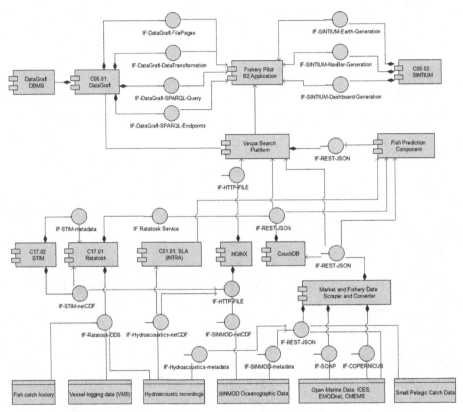

Fig. 5. The B2 fishery pilot pipeline view showing a logical view application components connection over interfaces.

For Big Data application components and data location may play a critical role. We proposed to apply a specific view to describe the location (Fig. 6). This helped to identify the major sites and need for specific telecommunication infrastructure for the data exchange.

This stage of the Big Data application specification is further developed in [8].

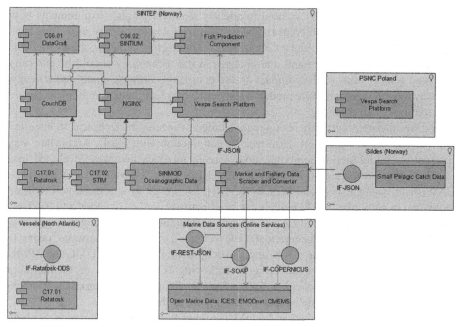

Fig. 6. The B2 fishery pilot location view specifying deployment of the application from location point.

3   Discussion, Related Works and Conclusions

The stakeholders of the project have appreciated the ability to describe their pilots from various perspectives. In particular the traceability integrated the Modelio ArchiMate modelling tool [9] was helpful in linking stakeholders, processes, requirements, data sets and technology pipelines. The technology providers could benefit from the automated derivation of requirements to the more detailed architectural level including UML. The data object concepts may map directly to UML classes. The ArchiMate model served to coordinate pilot and technology development activities. The method helped us at various stages of the project starting at the requirements specification in the very beginning giving means to identify the business goals for the pilot development as well as important constraints such as available data sets. In the middle of the project ArchiMate was helpful to centralize specification of over 40 technology components to identify compatibilities, overlaps and complementary services. Finally, at the pilot implementation ArchiMate provided sufficiently abstract and detailed modelling notation to represent mapping the needs by pilots and available technology components. Last but not least, the European Commission's Horizon 2020 projects are heavy on documentation deliverables. The ArchiMate model and tooling provided an important means for collaborative documenting of that complex project. The important information could be extracted to serve several reports. The tooling helped to represent that information in a consistent way, which is always a challenge when over 40 editors are involved.

In Big Data context it is essential to address rapidly changing requirements both business and technical. In this context dealing with specifications on the modelling level helps to quickly identify the impact of changes on the technical architecture - lifecycle and pipelines. On the other hand, the changes in the technology should be carefully monitored with regards to their impact on the company's business goals and strategy. That way having the ArchiMate model as a specification facilitates communication and helps to monitor all changes.

The ArchiMate is certainly not enough detailed to specify the technical architecture from the developer standpoint. However, in conjunction with UML, ArchiMate may represent an initial step to applying model-driven methods that was developed in a set of research projects such as SHAPE [10], REMICS [11], MODACLOUDS [12], JUNIPER [13], DICE [14] and MELODIC [15]. Moreover, as it is presented in those studies and in particular in [16] models can be effectively applied to Cloud and Big Data application with the goal to reduce coding and configuration by providing the right level of abstraction for automatic generation of the technical artifacts. Furthermore, rasing in abstraction, [17] indicated the way to apply in conjunction ArchiMate, UML and BPMN in the Enterprise Architecture modelling by following TOGAF. However, the literature is missing to provide concrete recipes for Big Data application modelling on the business level. In this context the current paper gives a glance at that domain.

We would like to conclude that ArchiMate allows to decrease the uncertainty about the purpose and structure of Big Data applications. The approach helped in coordinating efforts of many organizations involved in piloting DataBio and boosting the output of the project. Those results include Big Data technology components, data sets, pipelines and pilots for Bioeconomy [18] and are now publicly available.

Acknowledgments. This work is partially funded by the DataBio project grant No. 732064 under European Commission's Horizon 2020 research and innovative programme. In addition, this work was supported by the Russian Science Foundation grant No. 19-19-00623.

References

1. Databio. In: DATABIO Data-driven Bioeconomy. https://www.databio.eu/. Accessed 21 Nov 2019
2. ArchiMate® 3.1 Specification. http://pubs.opengroup.org/architecture/archimate3-doc/. Accessed 21 Nov 2019
3. DataBio European Commission's Horizon 2020 project. In: DATABIO Data-driven Bioeconomy. https://www.databio.eu/. Accessed 21 Nov 2019
4. TOGAF® Framework and ArchiMate® Modeling Language Harmonization: A Practitioner's Guide to Using the TOGAF® Framework and the ArchiMate® Language. https://publications.opengroup.org/w14c. Accessed 21 Nov 2019
5. DataBio: D3.1 Fishery Pilot Definition – v1.0. https://www.databio.eu/wp-content/uploads/2017/05/DataBio_D3.1_FisheryPilotDefinition_v1.0_2017_10_20_SINTEF_Ocean.pdf. Accessed 25 Nov 2019
6. BDVA. http://www.bdva.eu/. Accessed 25 Nov 2019
7. DataBio: D4.3 Data sets formats and models. https://www.databio.eu/wp-content/uploads/2017/05/DataBio_D4.3-Data-sets-formats-and-models_public-version.pdf. Accessed 21 Nov 2019

8. DataBio: D3.2 Fishery Pilots intermediate report. https://www.databio.eu/wp-content/uploads/2017/05/DataBio_D3.2-Fishery-Pilots-intermediate-report_v1.0_2018-12-28_AZTI1.pdf. Accessed 25 Nov 2019
9. Modelio BA - Archimate Enterprise Architect. In: Modeliosoft. https://www.modeliosoft.com/en/products/modelio-ba-archimate-enterprise-architect.html. Accessed 21 Nov 2019
10. Sadovykh, A., Desfray, P., Elvesaeter, B., et al.: Enterprise architecture modeling with SoaML using BMM and BPMN - MDA approach in practice. In: 2010 6th Central and Eastern European Software Engineering Conference (CEE-SECR) (2010)
11. Sadovykh, A., Hein, C., Morin, B., Mohagheghi, P., Berre, A.J.: REMICS- REuse and Migration of legacy applications to Interoperable Cloud Services. In: Abramowicz, W., Llorente, I.M., Surridge, M., Zisman, A., Vayssière, J. (eds.) ServiceWave 2011. LNCS, vol. 6994, pp. 315–316. Springer, Heidelberg (2011). https://doi.org/10.1007/978-3-642-24755-2_32
12. Nitto, E.D., Di Nitto, E., da Silva, M.A.A., et al.: Supporting the development and operation of multi-cloud applications: the MODAClouds approach. In: 2013 15th International Symposium on Symbolic and Numeric Algorithms for Scientific Computing (2013)
13. da Silva, M.A.A., Sadovykh, A., et al.: JUNIPER. In: Proceedings of the 10th Central and Eastern European Software Engineering Conference in Russia on CEE-SECR 2014 (2014)
14. Casale, G., Ardagna, D., Artac, M., et al.: DICE: quality-driven development of data-intensive cloud applications. In: 2015 IEEE/ACM 7th International Workshop on Modeling in Software Engineering (2015)
15. Horn, G., Skrzypek, P.: MELODIC: utility based cross cloud deployment optimisation. In: 2018 32nd International Conference on Advanced Information Networking and Applications Workshops (WAINA) (2018)
16. Bergmayr, A., Breitenbücher, U., Ferry, N., et al.: A systematic review of cloud modeling languages. ACM Comput. Surv. **51**, 1–38 (2018)
17. Desfray, P., Raymond, G.: TOGAF, Archimate, UML et BPMN - 3e éd. Dunod (2019)
18. DataBio Hub. http://www.databiohub.eu/. Accessed 21 Nov 2019

Fallacies and Pitfalls on the Road to DevOps: A Longitudinal Industrial Study

Alessandro Caprarelli[1], Elisabetta Di Nitto[1],
and Damian Andrew Tamburri[2(✉)]

[1] Politecnico di Milano, Milan, Italy
[2] TU/e - JADS, 's-Hertogenbosch, The Netherlands
d.a.tamburri@tue.nl

Abstract. DevOps has come into play to help companies in improving their product delivery. This paper offers an overview of the fallacies and pitfalls faced in this context by engineers and operators in an industrial case-study. We reveal a total of 8 key fallacies and pitfalls that span the organisational structure, technical structures, as well as software process and delivery mechanisms in the target case-study. Practitioners can use these challenges as references for diagnosing their own scenario while planning their own potential DevOps process migration strategy.

Keywords: Process migration · DevOps quality · Organizational and technical aspects

1 Introduction

DevOps is a methodology aiming at bridging the gap between Development (Dev) and Operations, emphasizing communication and collaboration, continuous integration, quality assurance and delivery with automated deployment [1]. It is based on a variety of practices, some of which very well-known and established such as Continuous Integration (CI) and Continuous Deployment (CD); as an overall movement, however, DevOps bases all its approaches in breaking down the barriers between the development and operations departments, stressing the point of a more collaborative culture. DevOps [2] has gained a wide popularity in the last decade thanks to some companies that have adopted it and received benefits from it. However, many companies are striving at adopting it, facing several key organisational, socio-technical, and technical challenges in process and product engineering due to their prior assets and production cycle.

This paper offers an overview of the fallacies and pitfalls faced by the engineers and operators involved in the migration to DevOps in a real-life industrial scenario. The analysis is based on a direct ethnographic observation [3] over a period of 9 months. We reveal a total of 8 key fallacies and pitfalls that span the organisational structure, technical structures, as well as software process and delivery mechanisms in the target case-study. For example, we reveal that testing, as part of the delivery activity that packages and prepares a product

© Springer Nature Switzerland AG 2020
J.-M. Bruel et al. (Eds.): DEVOPS 2019, LNCS 12055, pp. 200–210, 2020.
https://doi.org/10.1007/978-3-030-39306-9_15

for deployment, is often subject to latency times connected bottleneck effects [4] in the organizational structure. Similarly, manual pre-deployments are often needed for specific components or connectors in the infrastructure—these pre-deployments compromise the stability of the delivery pipeline and lead to time-waste.

The rest of this paper is organized as follows: Sect. 2 introduces the elements relevant to the presented case study, that is, Continuous Integration (CI), Continuous Deployment (CD) and DevOps; Sect. 3 presents our study and the challenges we have identified; Sect. 4 offers a preliminary idea of how to address the challenges and outlines a road map for further analysis aiming at assessing the impact of the proposed solution. Finally, Sect. 5 concludes the paper.

2   Background

2.1   Continuous Integration (CI)

CI is a software development methodology that requires developer to integrate their code more often in order to have faster feedback cycles and to reduce the overhead and workload of bigger and postponed integration.

The term was proposed by Booch et al. [5] already in 1991. He said "In this evolutionary approach there is no big bang integration" [5]. This practice has then gained momentum starting from around 2010 when open source software like Jenkins[1] and Travis-CI[2] had started to come out and made the life of developers easier.

Principles and Practices. Continuous integration puts a great emphasis on automation. Its core practice and enabler is the automation of the build process. On top of this, and second main point of *CI*, there is test automation. This is important for checking that the application is not broken whenever new commits are integrated into the main branch.

Another key practice of *CI* is to commit to the main code baseline daily or whenever an atomic development is completed [6]. Each commit should automatically trigger a build and test pipeline with the goal of assuring that no breaking code is merged into the main repository.

Benefits. One of the greatest benefits of *CI* is the reduced risks for developers when code integration is carried out. Bugs will always exist but thanks to frequent tests it is easier to find and remove them [6]. This faster error detection leads to higher productivity and more code quality [7]. Such faster error detection also increases the deployment frequencies thus reducing the time for feedback from end users [8].

---

[1] https://www.jenkins.com.
[2] https://www.travis-ci.com.

Typical Challenges. However, introducing *CI* practice is not pain-free. Organizations may face many challenges and problems in different areas, starting from the people to the technologies used, when they try to introduce more automation in the delivery pipeline. The most commonly found challenges from literature are:

- Smaller changes and commit often: this can be a paradigm shift for developers used to release big parts of code [8].
- Maintain a fast-running set of comprehensive automated unit tests: since developers should run tests often, those tests must be optimized and the tests suite should be easy to maintain and to enhance [6].
- Set-up and maintain the build and test system: this requires effort and work and it can become complex and costly. However, there are both proprietary and open-source software that can help with this [9].
- Dealing with large monolithic applications: normally legacy software is large and monolithic and it fits with difficulty in a fast-oriented *CI* pipeline [9].

The challenges include all the areas of a company. The process followed for delivering software may need some changes as well as the architecture of the components. Also, people need to be trained and others with a diverse skills set may need to be hired.

2.2   Continuous Delivery (CDE) and Continuous Deployment (CD)

Continuous Delivery, often abbreviated with *CDE*, is a software engineering approach that aims at building, testing, and releasing software with greater speed and frequency. The main idea behind *CDE* is keeping always the software in a deployable state. It can be seen as an extension of *CI* where the level of automation extends even to acceptance tests [10]. By doing so, almost all the possible parts of a deployment pipeline are extensively automated [11] except for the step that brings code from deployment to production. Automating also this latest step results in Continuous Deployment (*CD*).

Principles and Practices. As in *CI*, the core principle is the automation of repetitive tasks and should be based on the execution of tests in an environment that should be as similar as possible to the production one [12].

In addition to the tools related practices, *CD* requires also a change in people mentality and in the process. Big releases with a long and tense integration period are discouraged and people must collaborate more often in order to quickly solve the problems that may arise. The main code base should always be solid without failing tests.

Benefits. Similarly to *CI*, *CD* claims many benefits, mostly related to the heavy usage of automation practices. The main ones are:

- Reduced Deployment Risk: smaller changes are deployed at every push and therefore the possible problems and fixes should be smaller [11].

- Faster user feedback: once a fix or feature is ready it can be shipped to production and a feedback from end users can be received earlier [9,11].
- More reliable releases: at every push the build system runs a test suite and goes further only in case of successful tests. Also, since everything is automated, rollback in case of failures is almost painless [9].
- Less stress: the responsibility of a release is distributed among many actors of the delivery pipeline such as IT operations, testers, developers [13].

Typical Challenges. A key challenge for *CD* is the creation of substantial and durable test cases. More specifically, in connection to *CI*, tests must spread from code tests (unit tests) to end-to-end tests (*UI* tests). However, test suites showing high coverage percentages alone cannot ensure code quality, since intermittent, non-deterministic, or unknown bugs may still remain hidden [14]. To cope with these, approaches such as chaos tests are being developed.

2.3 Main Characteristics of DevOps

DevOps can be seen as an evolution of both CI and CD as it aims at covering the whole lifecycle of software, from its conception to its maintenance that can greatly benefit from the collaboration between Dev and Ops people. Thanks to this, DevOps is now one of the hottest topic in software engineering and has gained attention both by academic researches and industry practitioners [1,15,16].

Principles and Practices. As stated above, DevOps definitions cover many facets. The key principles are well summarized by the acronym CAMS, coined by Damon Edwards and John Willis at Devopsdays in Mountainview 2010 and later extended to CALMS [16–18]. The origin of this acronym can be traced mostly in gray literature, specifically in industry technical reports, industry journal and blog posts [16]. [16] and [17] both add to CALMS one more principle that is Quality Assurance. [19] agrees on the same principles, calling them enabler categories, and stresses the collaborative culture point. Therefore, the key principles behind a successful DevOps adoption are:

- **Culture** of collaboration between all the people involved in the development and operations team.
- **Automation**, usually linked with deployment automation and test automation, infrastructure provisioning and management, monitoring and recovery automation [19].
- **Lean**, that is, focus on incremental improvements and splitting the work into small batches, which are then released frequently.
- **Measurement** of the right information to give insight on the performances of the processes and to support the decision-making process [16].
- **Quality Assurance** as an integral part of the DevOps process.
- **Sharing** and learning among the people.

These principles have been instantiated in a number of practices needed for a successful DevOps adoption [20]. These practices are grouped in the three macro areas people, process, technology [21] that drive successful organization transformation plans.

DevOps is historically seen as the one that evolved from CI and CD. When an organization wants to improve its software development process, it often starts with adding more CI practices that are the foundation for higher software quality and more frequent releases. Then it increments the automation reaching a more mature state (CDE) in which the software can be deliverable at any time, until the point in which software can be automatically pushed to production without worrying (CD). Figure 1 shows this evolution toward the complete automation of the testing and deployment pipeline.

DevOps, however, is more than automation as it focuses also on cultural and human aspects highlighting the roles and importance of people and emphasizing the responsiveness of the process.

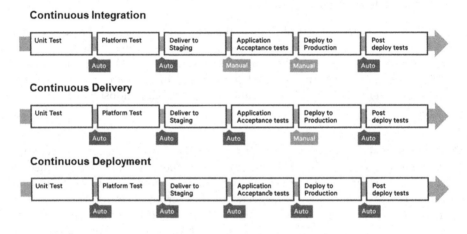

Fig. 1. CI, CD and DevOps.

Benefits. Organizing the software lifecycle around DevOps has the potential to produce several benefits. It enables more collaboration between development and operations, the two departments that are opposed by nature, it allows the whole team to achieve a better understanding of the system in terms of both its design characteristics and its properties at runtime (resilience, availability, performance, robustness...), it increases the frequency of releases and deployment (PuppetLabs states that deploys can increment up to 200x [13]), it results in an improvement of system reliability thanks to a deeper understanding of the system by all the people involved.

Typical Challenges. Even though many researches still say that there is little about DevOps in literature, enough works already list a considerable number of challenges faced by organizations during a DevOps adoption. First of all, DevOps adoption requires an in-depth revision of the processes and the structure of the involved organization. Typically, it affects departments, Dev and Ops, that are traditionally separated. The siloed approach does not help in this case and must be broken down. Development and operation department should be collaborating and working together rather than relate to each other on a service basis.

Another big challenge is the lack of awareness in DevOps and in its implications and potential. The greater opportunity to share information between Dev and Ops, implies also the need for retraining or hiring new people with a wide range of skills on both development and operation.

Even the toolset being adopted in the software lifecycle requires a DevOps transformation. In fact, a CI/CD pipeline, that is fundamental in DevOps, implies the set-up and maintenance of new tools and services. In addition, automated build and test processes may require automation also in infrastructure management and alignment of data between the development, testing and operational environments.

3   Migrating to DevOps: A Longitudinal Study

Stemming from the aforementioned background, we have analysed the case of a company that was in the process of starting a migration toward DevOps. The purpose was to properly elaborate on the most critical organisational, socio-technical, and technical challenges to be faced during the migration, such that researchers and practitioners can focus their efforts around the most dire and urgent/impactful issues. We adopted a longitudinal study methodological approach, that is research design that involves repeated observations of the same variables (e.g., practitioners in our target organization) over long periods of time (i.e., uses longitudinal data) [22].

3.1   Research Question and Method

This study addresses a single key Research Question (RQ):

What challenges have emerged during the DevOps adoption process?

The method employed for answering the aforementioned RQ was software process [23] ethnography [3], where the lead author researched and studied the available documentation, as well as observed the daily activities of the teams involved, noting down incrementally in a fully-catalogued and coded lab journal [24] any technical, social, or organisational detail concerning the process in question. Finally, the researcher in question applied theme coding [25] and taxonomy analysis [26] over the dependencies and documentation of all the available tools and code in order to draft an overview of the delivery process. In addition to this self-study, a round of semi-structured interviews to the 18 developers involved in the study was carried out as control and triangulation data in order to verify the correctness of the assumptions and findings elaborated via ethnographic research. Moreover, the interviews served for understanding better the real problems and for collecting possible ideas and solutions.

3.2 Case-Study Context

The studied organization is part of a big multinational operating in many sectors from databases to cloud products, from Infrastructure-as-a-Service (*IaaS*) to Software-as-a-Service (*SaaS*). The unit considered in the study is the consulting unit of the company and focuses on selling and setting up Enterprise Resource Planning (*ERP*) and Customer-Relationship Management (*CRM*) for medium and big enterprises. In particular, the team that has been involved in the research study works as a system integrator, with the goal of integrating the several systems involved in this context. This practice is also known as Enterprise Application Integration and its main goals are:

- Data integration: maintain the data consistency in the multiple systems.
- Vendor Independence: business rules are implemented in the integration layer in order to avoid strict dependencies with the final applications.

The case under study features $1 + 5$ projects, one sub-project for common and reusable components that shape the core architecture of the project – this is referred to as *SP-C* – and five sub-projects, each of them addressing different business areas of the main project – these are referred as *SP*-x (x from 1 to 5).

The two types of sub-projects have different team compositions, organization and goals. Our study has focused on all the aforementioned projects over the duration of our longitudinal observational study.

3.3 Fallacies and Pitfalls Found

As previously outlined, the fallacies and pitfalls reported in this section stem from the thematic coding of available longitudinal data. The coding itself was analysed through card-sorting [27]. The challenges reported below emerged from said card-sorting exercise. For the scope of this section, the labels {IC, FC, TST, DEL, OPS, INT} identify roles of the 40+ people involved in the development and operations of products maintained in our industrial case.

1. **Testing Latency.** Integration Consultants *IC* and Functional Consultants *FC* wait for a long time before a release from development is deployed to the *TST* environment for final testing. This is due to the insufficient number of resources in the Delivery (DEL) and Operations (OPS) team. In Fig. 2 the problem is graphically explained and defined as the "Papillon effect". The Delivery and Operations team results to be a bottleneck for the delivery process as it is composed only of two people that have to serve at least 20 DEVs and a similar number of OPS.

Fig. 2. Papillon effect, an overview.

2. **Technical Re-skilling.** The automation tools used for build and deploy requires technical skills (linux, bash, network, DBs, cloud instances configuration..) that not everybody owns. This prevents the possibility to open its usage to *IC* and *FC* because this would require an intense training for them.

3. **Ops Time-Waste.** The workload of the people in Delivery and Operations team is extremely high. They spend an incredible amount of their time in repeating the same instructions for deploying new components, because nobody else is able to do it, while they should focus on more important tasks such as controlling the health of the system and assuring high quality of the deliverables. This is related to problems 1 and 2 where *IC* and *FC* wait for *DEL* and *OPS*. Furthermore, the aforementioned conditions altogether reflect conditions known as *community smells* which were themselves previously seen in literature [28–30].

4. **Staging Isolation.** Developers do not use the automation tools for builds and deploys to INT environment. This environment should be used for integration tests, possibly automated tests, with the objective of early detecting problems in the release process or the deployment itself.

5. **Manual Pre-deployment.** Some components are being deployed manually, pushing the artifacts to the right environment. This is prone to human error (wrong version chosen, artifact placed and executed in wrong environment or wrong location...) and time-consuming for the people in charge of deploying new releases. Also, the components that are deployed manually are not tracked in the Registry tool, therefore, no information on their deployments exist.

6. **Build-Times Invisibility.** No information on build time is stored in the aforementioned Registry tool; this does not allow to improve the tool itself or the rest of the pipeline based on the telemetry about the tool performances.

7. **Build Unaccountability.** The access to the build server is shared among all the people, therefore there is no control on who has started previous builds and deploys.

8. **Test Lintering.** TESTERS (*IC, FC*) requested to have an automated system for doing simple integration tests at every release in order to save time and

early detect issues such as missing configuration, wrong naming conventions and others blocking problems.

4   Road Map

According to interviews and final focus groups with the project stakeholders and teams, the solution we identified and started to implement concerns the creation of an automated infrastructure to support the work of the DEV&OPS team. We will then be able to elaborate further on the challenges illustrated previously.

On the one hand, from a more qualitative perspective related to the aforementioned challenges, we should try to enact content [31], root-cause [32], as well as SWOT analyses [33] in a data-driven fashion (e.g., using predictive or preemptive analytics in the scope of large-scale DevOps pipelines) to further elaborate on each challenge and individually determine the dimensions along which every challenge is born, evolved, and eventually reduced or solved.

On the other hand, from a more quantitative perspective, we should cross data collected before and after the introduction of new capabilities designed to address the aforementioned challenges. This research should bear the target of understanding whether the introduced changes had improved (or made worse) the delivery process performances as well as the software organizational structure around that process.

The general purpose of both research streams should be to provide practices and patterns that elaborate further on the identified challenges as well as automated ways to measurably quantify and manage the impact of each individual challenge. One final research line should concentrate on embedding both aforementioned research streams within state of the art and state of practice tools currently used in DevOps pipelines.

5   Conclusions and Future Work

This paper offers a preliminary outline of the issues and fallacies connected to the typical software process scenarios that companies typically try to address by adopting DevOps practices. The work in this paper harnessed an ethnomethodological longitudinal approach to study a real-life industrial case of migration to DevOps. The scenario in question presented a bounty of issues and challenges useful for practitioners to assess their own scenario with respect to a similar case.

In terms of our own future work, we aim at investigating whether the tools we implemented and deployed as part of the case-study DevOps pipeline actually brought about an improvement of (1) the metrics typically used to appraise the performances of the pipeline as well as (2) any perceivable improvement of the software quality. The former can be addressed by analysing the metrics previously used in the studied software process for the management appraisal of that process—being an integral participant of the target case organisation, we do have access to those metrics and plan to analyse them quantitatively along the cases we studied in the context of this paper. The latter can be addressed by studying the number of issues opened and the number of tests failing. Finally, on the longer term, we aim at replicating the study on other organizations in order to assess the validity of the challenges we have identified.

References

1. Jabbari, R., Ali, N., Petersen, K., Tanveer, B.: What is DevOps?: A systematic mapping study on definitions and practices, p. 1, May 2016
2. Bass, L., Weber, I., Zhu, L.: DevOps: A Software Architect's Perspective. SEI Series in Software Engineering. Addison-Wesley, New York (2015)
3. Hammersley, M., Atkinson, P.: Ethnography. Routledge, London (2003)
4. Palomba, F., Tamburri, D.A., Serebrenik, A., Zaidman, A., Fontana, F.A., Oliveto, R.: How do community smells influence code smells? In: Proceedings of the 40th International Conference on Software Engineering: Companion Proceeedings, pp. 240–241. ACM (2018)
5. Booch, G.: Object Oriented Design: With Applications. The Benjamin/Cummings Series in Ada and Software Engineering. Benjamin/Cummings Pub., San Francisco (1991)
6. Fowler, M., Foemmel, M.: Continuous integration (2005). http://www.martinfowler.com/articles/continuousintegration.html
7. Infosys: getting started with continuous integration in software development (2017)
8. Duvall, P., Matyas, S., Duvall, P., Glover, A.: Continuous Integration: Improving Software Quality and Reducing Risk. A Martin Fowler signature book. Addison-Wesley, Boston (2007)
9. Chen, L.: Continuous delivery: huge benefits, but challenges too. IEEE Softw. **32**, 50–54 (2015)
10. Ries: Continuous deployment in 5 easy steps (2009)
11. Fowler, M., Foemmel, M.: Continuous delivery (2013)
12. Thoughtworks: Continuous integration (2018)
13. PuppetLabs: Top benefits of continuous delivery: an overview (2014)
14. Luo, Q., Hariri, F., Eloussi, L., Marinov, D.: An empirical analysis of flaky tests. In: Proceedings of the 22nd ACM SIGSOFT International Symposium on Foundations of Software Engineering, FSE 2014, pp. 643–653. ACM, New York (2014)
15. Dyck, A., Penners, R., Lichter, H.: Towards definitions for release engineering and DevOps. In: 2015 IEEE/ACM 3rd International Workshop on Release Engineering, p. 3, May 2015
16. França, B.B., Jeronimo Junior, H., Travassos, G.: Characterizing DevOps by hearing multiple voices, September 2016
17. Erich, F., Amrit, C., Daneva, M.: A mapping study on cooperation between information system development and operations. In: Jedlitschka, A., Kuvaja, P., Kuhrmann, M., Männistö, T., Münch, J., Raatikainen, M. (eds.) PROFES 2014. LNCS, vol. 8892, pp. 277–280. Springer, Cham (2014). https://doi.org/10.1007/978-3-319-13835-0_21
18. Erich, F., Amrit, C., Daneva, M.: A qualitative study of DevOps usage in practice. J. Softw. Evol. Process. **29**, e1885 (2017)
19. Luz, W.P., Pinto, G., Bonifácio, R.: Building a collaborative culture. In: Proceedings of the 12th ACM/IEEE International Symposium on Empirical Software Engineering and Measurement - ESEM 2018 (2018)

20. Freeman, E.: DevOps For Dummies. Wiley, Hoboken (2019)
21. Leavitt, H., March, J.: Applied Organizational Change in Industry: Structural, Technological and Humanistic Approaches. Carnegie Institute of Technology, Graduate School of Industrial Administration (1962)
22. Hund, H., Gerth, S., Loßnitzer, D., Fegeler, C.: Longitudinal data driven study design. In: Lovis, C., Séroussi, B., Hasman, A., Pape-Haugaard, L., Saka, O., Andersen, S.K. (eds.) MIE. Studies in Health Technology and Informatics, vol. 205, pp. 373–377. IOS Press (2014)
23. Fuggetta, A., Nitto, E.D.: Software process. In: Herbsleb, J.D., Dwyer, M.B. (eds.) FOSE, pp. 1–12. ACM (2014)
24. Hsieh, H.F., Shannon, S.E.: Three approaches to qualitative content analysis. Qual. Health Res. **15**(9), 1277–1288 (2005)
25. Clark, A.Y., Li, Y., Jiang, Y.: Using natural language processing and qualitative thematic coding to explore math learning and critical thinking. In: ICBDE, pp. 38–43. ACM (2018)
26. Carrion, B., Onorati, T., Díaz, P., Triga, V.: A taxonomy generation tool for semantic visual analysis of large corpus of documents. Multimed. Tools Appl. **78**, 32919–32937 (2019)
27. Lewis, K.M., Hepburn, P.: Open card sorting and factor analysis: a usability case study. Electron. Libr. **28**(3), 401–416 (2010)
28. Tamburri, D.A., Kazman, R., Fahimi, H.: The architect's role in community shepherding. IEEE Softw. **33**(6), 70–79 (2016)
29. Palomba, F., Tamburri, D.A.A., Arcelli Fontana, F., Oliveto, R., Zaidman, A., Serebrenik, A.: Beyond technical aspects: how do community smells influence the intensity of code smells? IEEE Trans. Softw. Eng., 1 (2018)
30. Tamburri, D.A., Kazman, R., van den Heuvel, W.J.: Splicing community and software architecture smells in agile teams: an industrial study. In: Bui, T. (ed.) HICSS, ScholarSpace/AIS Electronic Library (AISeL), pp. 1–11 (2019)
31. Krippendorff, K.: Content Analysis: An Introduction to Its Methodology, 2nd edn. Sage Publications, Thousand Oaks (2004)
32. Josefsson, T.: Root-cause analysis through machine learning in the cloud. Master's thesis (2017)
33. Khurana, A.: Understanding and using SWOT analysis. Technical report, About, Inc. (2004). http://businessmajors.about.com/cs/casestudyhelp/a/SWOT.htm

Author Index

Printed in the United States
By Bookmasters